THE CASE FOR AFFIRMATIVE ACTION
IN UNIVERSITY ADMISSIONS

THE CASE FOR AFFIRMATIVE ACTION
IN UNIVERSITY ADMISSIONS

Bob Laird

Bay Tree Publishing
BERKELEY, CALIFORNIA

Central Islip Public Library
33 Hawthorne Avenue
Central Islip, NY 11722

3 1800 00216 4057

© 2005 Bob Laird
Foreword © 2005 Jesse L. Jackson
All rights reserved.

Published by Bay Tree Publishing
721 Creston Road, Berkeley, CA 94708

Printed in the United States of America

Cover design by Twin Engine Studio, LLC
Page composition/typography
by BookMatters, Berkeley
Copyedited by Jim Norrena

LIBRARY OF CONGRESS
CATALOGING-IN-PUBLICATION DATA

Laird, Bob, 1939-
The case for affirmative action in university admissions /
by Bob Laird ; foreword by Jesse Jackson.
    p.   cm.
ISBN 0-9720021-4-6
1. Discrimination in higher education—United States.
2. Affirmative action programs in education—United
States. 3. Universities and colleges—United States—
Admission. I. Title.
LC212.42.L35 2005
379.2'6—dc22   2004026322

To the memory of Joe Allen

For Casey, Sam, and Karen

CONTENTS

. . . and the expensive delicate ship that must have seen
Something amazing, a boy falling out of the sky,
Had somewhere to get to and sailed calmly on.

— W. H. AUDEN, "MUSÉE DES BEAUX ARTS"

FOREWORD

"I have a dream," Dr. Martin Luther King intoned, "that one day . . ."
Every child in America learns about this dream in school. We're reminded of it each year when we celebrate Dr. King's birthday and com-
memorate the March on Washington. The abiding question, of course,
is how do we achieve that dream?

There are some who would declare that we've already achieved a "level
playing field." Because upholding segregation is against the law, they
argue, the dream of a color-blind society in which all can be judged by
the content of their character and not the color of their skin has already
been achieved.

That was not Dr. King's view; he understood and tried to teach us
about the lasting scars of race in this society. It started with two hundred and fifty years of slavery, wherein Africans were brought to this
society, sold as property, and their families were torn asunder—association, speech, liberty, property, and even religion taken from them. It
took a civil war to bring that to an end.

Then after a brief moment there followed 100 years of legal
apartheid—segregation that's both separate and unequal. The promise
of forty acres and a mule for freed slaves was never met. Law locked

out African Americans. Separate schools, racially exclusive housing, neighborhoods, public transport, and accommodations; and the doors closed to the better schools, the best clubs, and the elite firms. Legally this only ended less than fifty years ago. When I was a child, my first civil rights "protest" was the simple act of trying to use the public library that was closed to African Americans.

It took a civil rights movement with the sacrifice of many lives and the heroism of many ordinary people to end legal apartheid in this country. Dr. King led that effort and exulted in its success, but he knew that it was not enough.

Dr. King taught that we were living in a country that was separate and unequal and that African Americans were living on an island of despair in a sea of affluence. He marched on Washington to ask for America to redeem the check that had bounced, open the doors of opportunity, and repair the accumulated centuries of injustice that had locked so many into poverty and shattered so many dreams.

What was the remedy for 250 years of slavery and 100 years of legal apartheid? Some argued for reparations. We paid reparations to the descendants of the Japanese Americans shamefully deprived of their property and placed in camps during World War II. We support the efforts of Jewish families (and others) to collect reparations from those who waged genocide on them under the Nazi regime. Where are the reparations for slavery that robbed African Americans of the fruits of their labor for over two centuries?

The conservative answer—championed by Richard Nixon—was affirmative action. Require affirmative action to open locked doors—to gain admission to colleges, jobs, mortgages, and business loans, et cetera. This would not remedy past harms, but would at least create opportunity for future generations.

However, affirmative action immediately generated negative reaction—and nowhere so fiercely than in college admissions, particularly to elite universities. It is easy to understand why that is so. Those admissions are limited in number. They are viewed as immensely important—opening the doors to life's successes. If affirmative action benefits minorities, then members of the majority will be "discriminated against." The intensity of the assault on affirmative action—beginning formally with a case concerning admission to an elite medical school—is not surprising.

In this compassionate and learned study, Bob Laird strips away the myths, lies, and hypocrisies that have surrounded the debate on affirmative action in college admissions and forces us to deal with the basic questions and realities. Laird, who as director of admissions to the University of California, Berkeley during the assault on affirmative action, was navigating a key embattled ship in the midst of these storms. By combining a passion for justice with a detailed and hardnosed look at reality, he lays out the choices we are making.

Laird argues that we have to choose between two ideals: a society that is fully integrated and one that is color-blind. If we are to achieve Dr. King's dream of a society in which everyone is judged by the content of their character, then we must first achieve integration—and that requires taking affirmative actions to knock down doors and open opportunities.

Laird's argument is particularly true in admission to colleges, and even more so in elite colleges where the furor about affirmative action has been the greatest. Accomplished white students, often with grade point averages over 4.0 (given honors-course bonus points) and particularly high test scores, are denied admission to UC Berkeley or the University of Michigan or other elite schools. (This incidentally is also true of African American students with 4.0 plus grade averages but that gets little attention.) African American, Latino, and Native American students, often with lower test scores, are given admission. Not surprisingly, outrage and lawsuits ensue.

Laird shows that the university admissions process is an art form, not a ranking of test scores and grades. Universities seek to build classes that reflect a rich mix of attributes: the intellectually curious, those who have overcome adversity, athletes, musicians and dancers and artists, math and science maestros. Wealthy legacies often gain a leg up because no university is blind to ensuring financial support.

For elite public schools like UC Berkeley, Laird argues it is particularly important that this mix of attributes includes racial diversity—that efforts be made to have the incoming class reflect the diversity of the society at large. Under affirmative action, no student would be admitted who was unqualified to succeed at the school, but efforts would be made to ensure diversity, even if that meant turning away students with higher test scores.

The resulting outrage ignores how mild a remedy this is to the scars of racism in this society. Today America is growing once more toward separate and unequal. The great middle class that was the triumph of America after World War II—and the expression of the American dream—was closed by segregation and racism to African Americans, Latinos, and Native Americans. Now the laws have changed, but so too has the middle class, which is disappearing as America enters a new Gilded Age, increasingly divided between the affluent few and an ever more hard-pressed declining many. For minorities this is something of a cruel joke—similar to the removal of laws locking them out, the opportunity beyond the door was reduced.

This decline of middle-income opportunity hits minorities directly. They live increasingly in racially segregated neighborhoods that are poorer and less safe. Their children navigate mean streets to go to schools that are overcrowded and under-repaired; their classes are the largest, and their teachers often the least experienced and with the worst pay. Their textbooks and equipment are outdated; their curricula are more limited, and their access to more competitive courses and more sophisticated opportunities minimal.

The best of those children overcome enormous pressures to achieve. Yet then they must compete to get into elite schools that face ever more applications for limited spaces. Had these children grown up on the other side of town, with their drive and intelligence, they might well have done honors work, scored higher on tests, and so forth. Minority children have shown that they can jump extraordinary hurdles with weights on their feet, but they haven't jumped as high as those students who were trained from birth and given springs for their shoes.

Laird argues that the society has a stake in reaching out and nurturing these success stories because we have a stake in building an integrated society. To do that, we have to open access to the best schools, for the best schools provide access to the best law schools, grad schools, businesses, et cetera.

Moving toward equal access seems to be a matter of fairness. Yet consider the simple matter of legacies: "legacy admissions" are the benefits given to the children of wealthy alumni (provided our current president with an admission to Yale). One can understand university admission officers being sensitive to the wealth of various applicants as part of securing the university's future. Of course African Americans had their ability to accumulate wealth stripped away from them for 250 years under slavery, and drastically limited by segregation and racial exclusion. African Americans are pretty much locked out of legacy-admission categories.

Dr. King never had any doubt about the need to be aware of race and to take affirmative steps to remedy racism in order to move toward a color-blind society. Affirmative action, for Dr. King, was imperative, but not sufficient.

Here is the other reality that this impassioned study exposes: opportunity is being constricted for everyone. States are cutting back on support for higher education (and, for that matter, not providing even the basics for pre- and early K-12 education). College slots are not keeping up with the explosion of high school students. More tellingly, college grants are not covering the cost of college. A recent study concluded that even after grants and loans most states are failing to make four-year public universities affordable for most families in that state.

This closing of middle-class opportunity is mirrored in the decline of decent jobs with good benefits, reduced job security, and the growth of debt and personal bankruptcy.

Laird suggests that we've moved from seeing college as a public good and educating the next generation as something that we all have a stake in to viewing it as a private, individual benefit and therefore something for which the individual should pay. Similarly, we've moved from recognizing health care as a right in which we all have a stake to regarding it as an individual problem that we should take care of ourselves. We're moving from a society of shared opportunity and shared security to one in which you are on your own.

Yet when opportunity declines generally in the society, racial and economic divides grow harsher. The Civil Rights movement and affirmative action developed in the great post-World War II prosperity, when America was growing together and the middle class was expanding. The argument that minorities should have a seat at a growing table was compelling. The reaction to affirmative action comes as America is growing apart, and the middle class is under pressure. In these conditions it is relatively easy to use politics of racial division to distract people from society's failure.

At the same time, it is challenging for people of good will to get a sense of what can be done and what should be done. Here this fine study is invaluable; Laird shows how affirmative action works, why it works, and why we all have a stake in defending it.

However, for this to happen those arguing for diversity and equal opportunity have to become as passionate as those who are pushing division and selfishness. Wendall Phillips, the great abolitionist, once gave a powerful oration railing against slavery. A colleague asked him later, "Wendall, why are you so on fire?" "I'm on fire," he said, "because we have great mountains of ice before us to melt." Bob Laird is a sober analyst with a passionate cause because he understands up close just how high are the mountains of ice that we must melt.

—Jesse L. Jackson

ACKNOWLEDGMENTS

Portions of this book appeared in somewhat different form in *Choosing Students: Higher Education Admissions Tools for the 21st Century* (Lawrence Erlbaum Associates), *National CrossTalk*, *San Francisco Chronicle*, *The Chronicle of Higher Education*, and *The Sacramento Bee*.

I am particularly grateful to the Reverend Jesse Jackson for writing the Foreword, Bob Borosage and Butch Wing from Rev. Jackson's staff, Nicholas Lemann, Dolores Huerta, Eva Paterson, Lori de Leon, Ed Apodaca, and Gene Royale.

Thank you to Bill Villa for his friendship, ideas, and support; all of the people with whom I worked at UC Berkeley—and who worked so hard—in 103, 110, and 37 Sproul Hall; Gregg Thomson, Tom Cesa, and Ken Wahl in the Office of Student Research; Marie Felde, Janet Gilmore, and Shirley Wong in the Office of Public Affairs; Maureen Morley and Nancy Purcille in the Office of the Academic Senate; Jesus Mena; Anita Madrid; Libby Sayre, Margy Wilkinson, and Albert Lucero; Barbara Stratton in the University of California Office of the President; Anne Shaw in the Office of the University of California Board of Regents; Jack Blackburn, Bill Kolb, Nancy McDuff, Rick Shaw, Ted Spenser, Bruce Walker, and Tim Washburn, all outstanding directors or deans of admission; Ken Weiss of the *Los Angeles Times*; Matthew Howard of *The New York Review of Books*; Bill Trombley; and Pam Burdman.

Finally, thank you to David Cole for convincing me to write this particular book, for his willingness to pursue publishing it, and for his instrumental editorial suggestions; Jim Norrena for excellent copy-editing and valuable suggestions; Paul Rabinow for good writing and sound publishing advice; Ellie Patterson, Linda Gallego, and Howard Yank for being good readers; Michael Perna for being a good reader—and a good attorney; Sam Laird and Casey Laird for their patience and support during this project; and Karen Marie Rice, the best editor and advisor.

INTRODUCTION

On June 23, 2003, the United States Supreme Court ruled on two cases that challenged the use of race and ethnicity in admissions policies at the University of Michigan. The two cases, *Gratz v. Bollinger* and *Grutter v. Bollinger*, marked the first time in twenty-five years that the Court had reviewed the uses of affirmative action in college and university admissions. Both cases involved complaints of white applicants who accused the University of Michigan of having discriminated against them on the basis of race through preferences the university had given to African American, Latino, and Native American applicants. *Gratz* focused on the freshman admissions process at the university while *Grutter* challenged the admissions policies of the Law School. The stakes were very high, and the Court, by a 5 to 4 vote in *Grutter*, upheld the consideration of race and ethnicity. The majority opinion in this case, written by Justice Sandra Day O'Connor, was a powerful victory for supporters of affirmative action—but the struggle over this issue will continue, the stakes will remain quite high, and the Court could easily reverse its position in the next few years.

The first affirmative action program in university admissions began in 1966 at Harvard Law School, as Derek Bok and William Bowen have noted in *The Shape of the River—Long-Term Consequences of Considering Race in College and University Admissions*. The debate over the consideration of race in university admissions began almost immediately thereafter. At the undergraduate level, the national struggle over affirmative action in university admissions began—in at least one important way—in 1973. That was the year when UC Berkeley first denied admission to freshman applicants who met the published minimum requirements to be eligible for the University of California system. Over the next three decades, the role of affirmative action in selective university admissions became one of the most heated issues in America, culminating in the nasty turbulence of the 1990s that led directly to the Supreme Court decisions in 2003.

For a number of reasons, California has been the principal battleground for this issue. The first important legal case on the use of affirmative action in university admissions, decided by the U.S. Supreme Court in 1978, was *Regents of the University of California v. Bakke*, a lawsuit filed by an unsuccessful white applicant to the medical school at UC Davis. Beginning in the late 1980s and extending through the late 1990s, UC Berkeley was the primary national target of opponents of affirmative action. In July 1995, the UC Board of Regents became the first university governing board in the nation to end the consideration of race and ethnicity in admissions. In November 1996, California voters passed Proposition 209, the first state law to ban the consideration of race and ethnicity in the operation of public education, including university admissions. And since the passage of Proposition 209, California has become a cautionary tale for the rest of the country—an example of what can happen when affirmative action in university admissions is eliminated before the conditions that created the need for it in the first place have been resolved.

After California voters passed Proposition 209 in November 1996, the focus of the national struggle over affirmative action shifted, first to Texas, then to Washington and Florida, then to Georgia, and then to Michigan. But even with the passage of Proposition 209, the issue of race in university admissions has remained a heated subject in California.

In March 1994, I was appointed director of undergraduate admission and relations with schools at the University of California, Berkeley. I had already served nine months as interim director, so from July 1993 until my retirement November 16, 1999, I held what Nicholas Lemann, author of *The Big Test* and current dean of the Graduate School of Journalism at Columbia University, has described as the most difficult admissions job in the country.

My first job with the University of California in 1977 was to visit high schools and community colleges all over California to explain the mysteries of the University of California to counselors, students, and parents. (Even in those early days, a lot of students—and their parents—believed that the UC system—and in particular, UC Berkeley—was the absolute key to their futures.) I got a remarkable education in geography and sociology. For one thing, I learned how rural nearly all of California is. Traveling to places like Brawley, Julian, Oxnard, Dinuba, Leggett, Crescent City, Cloverdale, and South Fork was a constant series of lessons in the vast scale of California. For another, I learned over and over again how uneven economic circumstances are for people in the world's fifth largest economy and, by visiting high schools in inner-city Oakland, San Francisco, Los Angeles, and San Diego, how similar the forces are in California that sharply limit the lives of both inner-city and rural kids.

I also saw how important the University of California was to the hopes and dreams of Californians. As UC Berkeley and UCLA became more and more selective in their admissions, I became deeply interested in and then passionate about who got to attend the university and, in a broader view, what should be the role of the flagship public university campus in a state with the extraordinary racial, ethnic, economic, and geographic richness and complexity of California. This passion wasn't simply about Berkeley's numbers but about what the education of all students at Berkeley and other elite institutions should include—and about the future of California and the rest of the United States.

Because California has been one of the focal points of the struggle over affirmative action and because I worked at UC Berkeley for many years, I cite many examples from the state and from my experience at Berkeley in this book. But of course the issue of affirmative action in university admissions isn't just a matter for California, it's also one of the most important issues we face as a nation. In my experience, it truly does matter—in terms of access to the strongest graduate and professional programs and opportunities with the most influential public and private sector organizations and companies—where a person has gone to college and what his or her experiences have been there. Because there is such a clear connection between the most selective public and private colleges on the one hand, and the most elite segments of American society on the other, it is crucial that the most selective public and private colleges also be fully integrated. I also believe that the long-term outcome in the national battle over racial integration will be fundamental in determining whether America ever does live up to its professed values and, even more basic, in determining whether we survive as a society.

In *The Case for Affirmative Action in University Admissions,* I argue the importance of affirmative action for all of us and describe the national battle over affirmative action, part of our country's long, painful struggle with the issues of race and a fair society. The book also focuses on California's attempts—some modestly successful, others not so at all—to deal with the elimination of race and ethnicity in university admissions, challenges that every state may face if the Supreme Court reverses its recent position on the issue.

Even with the clear decision in *Grutter v. Bollinger,* the battle over affirmative action will continue to be fought at the national and state levels. It is vitally important that Americans understand how high the stakes are in this battle, how important affirmative action is to the country, and how fragile is the thread by which affirmative action hangs.

I WHY IT MATTERS

They want what we've got, and we're not going to give it to them.

— PRESIDENT LYNDON JOHNSON, referring to the rest of the world, in a speech to U.S. troops at Camp Stanley, Korea, November 1, 1966. (Quoted by John Gerassi in *The New York Review of Books*)

THE HEART OF THE MATTER

The national debate over affirmative action in college and university admissions has raged for almost forty years, and certainly intensified after the 1978 United States Supreme Court decision in *Regents of the University of California v. Bakke.* In that case, the Court ruled that the medical school at the University of California at Davis had illegally set aside seats that were reserved for minority applicants. More important, however, the Court ruled, in an opinion written by Justice Lewis Powell reflecting a 5 to 4 vote, that race could be considered as a plus factor in the admissions consideration of individual applicants.

The core issue in the debate over race in university admissions in the United States appears as a conflict between two democratic ideals: a fully integrated society on the one hand and a color-blind society on the other. Neither of these ideals by itself has fully existed in our history, let alone co-existed with the other. How we resolve this conflict will determine to a significant extent how close we come as a society to achieving the professed ideals of America. Color-blind, it should be noted, means a society in which no one is penalized legally or socially on the basis of race or ethnicity. It does not mean some sort of melting pot in which bubbles a bland, homogenized paste, but a society that acknowledges, values, and celebrates differences, a society in which most people understand and appreciate the richness of diversity.

In this book, I argue that affirmative action, imperfect as it may be, is one of the few mechanisms that move us toward the goal of a fully integrated, color-blind society. To eliminate affirmative action before we repair the basic economic inequities in our society—so many of which are tied to race—makes it almost certain that we will never achieve that goal of a fair society. Rather than eliminate affirmative action now, we need first to eliminate the inequities that have led to the need for it. When we no longer need affirmative action, we can let it go.

Throughout this book, the term *affirmative action* applies to African Americans, Latinos, and Native Americans. In some parts of the country, however, Asian Americans are also included in university affirmative action programs. Although the term Chicano is used in California and a few other states as a specific term for people of Mexican descent, the term Latino is used throughout this book to describe people of Mexican descent as well as those from Central and South America.

There are certainly demagogues and principled people of good will on both sides of the affirmative action conflict, and pursuing either a color-blind society or a fully integrated society at the expense of the other will inevitably carry with it a social cost. Part of the debate over affirmative action is a disagreement over what these social costs will be and an inability to agree on the impacts that they will have on our society.

We also have to ask ourselves if a person can truly be considered educated and prepared to be a leader or an active citizen—not just in California or Texas or Florida or New York but in any of our states— if he or she has not experienced, explored, and sometimes struggled with the most difficult and unresolved issues in our society: race, ethnicity, economic inequality, and the quest for a fair society. Put another way, how can a state like California resolve the tension between the fall 2004 freshman class at UC Berkeley, the state's flagship public university, that was expected to be 12.9 percent African American, Latino, and Native American compared to the state's June 2004 public high school graduates who were projected to be 44.1 percent African American, Latino, and Native American?

THE KEY PUBLIC POLICY QUESTIONS
FOR THE COUNTRY

For the United States, these are the public policy questions:

1. What are the fundamental responsibilities of the entire country, but especially of those states like Texas, New York, Florida, New Mexico, Arizona, and California with their extraordinarily complex populations?

2. How do we distribute fairly and to the greatest benefit for the country and the individual states an increasingly scarce public commodity—admission to the most prestigious and most selective public and private universities?

3. What should constitute the education of students graduating from the most prestigious and most selective public—and independent—colleges and universities in the country at the beginning of the twenty-first century?

The goals of affirmative action are to enrich the education of all students, to help integrate all levels of American society—especially the most elite levels—and to help build a fair and equitable society in which affirmative action will no longer be necessary. No university should admit a student who does not have, in the considered judgment of admissions professionals and of faculty, a reasonable chance to graduate. No supporter of affirmative action argues that the policy should last forever. The goal is to get to a point as rapidly as possible where affirmative action is no longer necessary.

Access to the most elite positions in American society is determined to a significant extent by where a person has gone to college. So when critics of affirmative action say, "It doesn't matter whether students of color go to Yale rather than Bridgewater State or to UC Berkeley rather than UC Riverside or Cal State Northridge," supporters of affirmative action disagree strenuously. It matters a lot, first because the education of all students at Yale or Berkeley will be enriched by racial and ethnic diversity in the classroom and in the residence halls (the results of UC Berkeley's Senior Survey of graduating students, for example, confirms this view) and, second, because access to prestigious graduate and professional schools, internships in Sacramento or Washington, D.C., and job interviews with the most influential private companies or public-sector organizations are not evenly distributed across the spectrum of American colleges and universities.

Although it may be less true than it was twenty years ago, the faculty at the most elite graduate schools are tightly connected to each other, often as mentor-mentee or as co-authors on publications or as former colleagues within the same department. They are connected to each other by e-mail and their co-publications, and they talk with each other regularly by telephone and at conferences. Their letters of recommendation to each other on behalf of their undergraduates applying to graduate school carry tremendous weight, and, in many cases, are powerfully reinforced by a personal telephone call or e-mail on behalf of a promising student. If top corporations or public-sector organizations want to interview prospective employees but are only willing to visit twenty colleges or universities, which twenty are they almost certain to choose? It isn't that a student can't get admitted to Harvard Law School or the Stanford Medical School from Cal State University Los Angeles; it's just that it's many times more difficult to do so than it is from UC Berkeley or UCLA.

THE UNRESOLVED DILEMMA OF RACE IN AMERICA

Americans hold dearly to our traditional mythology, including the myth of the melting pot, but our history of race has, not surprisingly, left us with a continuing legacy of racism and, at some level, a sense of national shame. The overt expressions of this racism are easy to identify, and it is easy for most whites to feel morally superior, even self-righteous, in response. The subtle strains of racism in whites are much more difficult to identify and deal with, and they often co-exist with, at the same time and sometimes in the same person, a sense of shame over our history of racism. This past and present shame combines in some kind of odd way to make many, perhaps most, white Americans particularly irritable when faced with discussions of race in America. Most white Americans have almost no meaningful contact with African Americans or Latinos. And the further away from the lives of African Americans and Latinos one is, the easier it is to perceive the overworked metaphor of the playing field as level. There are also people of privilege who see society in strictly Darwinian or class-struggle terms and who are simply determined to maintain and expand their own level of advantage. They see the world of privilege as a zero-sum game: if your share increases, my share decreases. Because race and class are closely correlated in this country, these people have a selfish interest in keeping people of color from prospering.

In the last few years, substantial attention has been focused on the differences in SAT I scores by race and ethnicity. More recently, research has focused on the differences in SAT I scores by race and ethnicity within the same range of family incomes. These differences have been cited as evidence that the SAT I is racially or culturally biased. In 1997, the College Board formed the National Task Force on Minority High Achievement. The Task Force was co-chaired by Eugene Cota-Robles, professor of biology emeritus at UC Santa Cruz, and Edmund W. Gordon, professor of psychology emeritus at Yale University, and also included Bruce Alberts, president of the National Academy of Sciences; Henry Louis Gates Jr., of Harvard; Freeman Hrabowski III, president of the University of Maryland-Baltimore County; Lee Raymond, CEO of Exxon; Professor Claude Steele of Stanford; and a number of other distinguished scholars and policy-makers.

In October 1999, the Task Force released *Reaching the Top*, its first report that documented the fact that the so-called achievement gap within the same family-income bands isn't confined only to SAT I scores; it extends to almost every other academic measure as well. This finding means that the questions raised by the Office for Civil Rights in "The Use of Tests When Making High-Stakes Decisions for Students: A Resource Guide for Educators and Policy-makers" apply much more broadly across the spectrum of academic measures rather than to only standardized tests, such as the SAT I. Admissions officers in California weren't surprised by this conclusion because they had seen Proposition 209, which banned consideration of race and ethnicity in 1996, have its most devastating effect on middle-income African American and Latino students.

Acknowledging an achievement gap by race and ethnicity within the same income bands is extremely important for the national conversation about race and opportunity, and it raises rather complicated questions that the report was able to answer only partially. *Reaching the Top* offers several reasons for the achievement gap, but the authors do not fully account for it. Scott Miller, who was the executive director of the Task Force, has said that almost all of the research on the causes of achievement differences by race has focused on differences in family income levels and that there simply isn't much research on the causes of achievement differences by race within similar family income bands.

There are, however, two areas of research that may go a long way toward explaining this gap. The first is Claude Steele's research on "stereotype threat." Steele has documented that particularly capable African American students will perform significantly below their capabilities on standardized tests if they perceive that they are being tested on a quality or characteristic—intelligence, for example, or college aptitude—that forms part of a negative stereotype of African Americans. When such a test is presented to these students as unimportant or as merely a research exercise, however, their performance rises dramatically. Roxanna Harlow, an assistant professor of sociology at McDaniel College, whose work on the different experiences of white and African American professors within the same university was described in the February 27, 2004, electronic issue of *The Chronicle of Higher Education*, reported similar findings. According to Professor Harlow, "white professors operate in a social space where whiteness is crediting and privileged, but is invisible and thus taken for granted; African-American professors function in a space where blackness is discrediting and devalued." If these subtle burdens of racism can be fully documented in other studies, it will add a very important dimension to the debate over affirmative action.

A second area of research focuses on differences in academic achievement compared to family wealth or net assets rather than simply to family income. William Darity Jr., in the December 1, 2000, issue of *The Chronicle of Higher Education*, refers to important work in this area by Melvin Oliver and Thomas Shapiro in *Black Wealth, White Wealth* and by Dalton Conley, who concludes that "the difference in wealth among racial groups is one of the most powerful factors explaining racial differences in performance on standardized tests." Simply measuring annual family income masks how long a family has been middle income, to take one example, and therefore ignores what assets a family may—or may not—have amassed over time, including what some observers have called "cultural capital" but what is really political/social acumen and connections. The December 18, 2003, electronic issue of *The Chronicle of Higher Education* notes that Amy Orr, an assistant professor of sociology at Linfield College, has come to similar conclusions. In the fall 2003 issue of *Sociology of Education*, Professor Orr writes, "While blacks have come closer to parity with whites in income, education, and occupation, the substantial racial differences in wealth continue to affect educational and social opportunities."

In an article in the October 18, 2004, *San Francisco Chronicle*, the Associated Press reported, "The enormous wealth gap between white families and blacks and Hispanics grew larger after the most recent recession, a private analysis of government data finds." The article then noted, "After accounting for inflation, net worth for white households increased 17 percent between 1996 and 2002, from $75,482 to $88,651. Net worth rose for Hispanic homes by 14 percent to about $7,900. It decreased for blacks by 16 percent, to roughly $6,000." This area of research may help counteract a common objection of whites to extending some consideration of race and ethnicity to middle-income students. That objection, a kind of inversion of another popular racist stereotype, the Welfare Queen, focuses on the apocryphal black neurosurgeon's daughter.

Because there is a documented achievement gap by race within the same family income bands, with African American and Latino students performing less well than whites and Asian Americans, and if emerging research suggests explanations—stereotype threat and differences in wealth by race—that would be quite difficult to assess in a college or university admissions process, we have a particularly difficult dilemma: either continue to use those academic measures—the SAT I, for example—in selective college admissions despite what appears to be a disparate impact on underrepresented minority students or take race into account when evaluating the academic achievement of students, including middle-income students, in selective admissions.

It should be noted that both critics and supporters of affirmative action disagree over the appropriateness of the term "underrepresented minority students," arguing that comparing the admission or enrollment of African American, Latino, and Native American students to their percentages in a state's overall population or to their percentages among the most recent cohort of a state's high school graduates may be interpreted as the use of illegal quotas. Nevertheless, it is useful to have such a comparison point both as a stand-alone measure and, perhaps, as a general overall goal. The most reasonable comparison is to use as the base the percentage of a particular group in the most recent cohort of state high school graduates. That is how the term "underrepresented" is used throughout this book.

In addition to the melting pot myth, many white Americans also cling to the level-playing-field myth, a part of which asserts that we have made steady progress in racial equality in this country. This belief allows us to say, "Things used to be bad for racial minorities, but now things are much better . . . maybe even good. So what's the problem? Get over it." In *The Unsteady March*, Philip Klinkner and Rogers Smith demonstrate that progress toward racial equality is highly uneven and that there have been only three periods in the last 150 years in which significant progress has been made. In the last chapter ("Shall We Overcome?"), they point out that the fundamental conditions that have been present during periods of advancing racial equality have receded. In addition, they identify eleven characteristics of contemporary America, including calls for government to be color-blind and a resurgence of "scientific" racism, that have also been present during periods, particularly the late nineteenth century, when the country has lost ground in the struggle for racial equality or attempted to stifle that progress entirely. Klinkner, in a brief interview with Peter Monaghan in the November 19, 1999, issue of *The Chronicle of Higher Education*, also noted that the myth of steady progress is profoundly comforting to whites, enabling them to abdicate personal responsibility for this issue and to believe that the ideals of America are in fact reality, a belief in which many people have a deep personal and emotional investment. It's pretty easy to embrace a kind of sentimental, benevolent, but highly theoretical liberalism living in Westchester County, Evanston, or Palos Verdes Estates.

THE SINGLE MOST IMPORTANT QUESTION WE HAVE TO ANSWER

Many—perhaps most—of us would agree that our national goal is a fully integrated, color-blind society, and most of us would probably agree that we aren't there yet. Some of us, including Jonathon Kozol in *Savage Inequalities*, would argue that we're not even close. The single most important question we all have to answer, then, is this: If we can't achieve both simultaneously, is it more important to have a color-blind society or a just society that is racially integrated? In her June 2003 majority opinion in *Grutter*, Justice Sandra Day O'Connor declared emphatically that a racially integrated society is the more important imperative.

The pretentious title of University of California Regent Ward

Connerly's recent book *Creating Equal* notwithstanding, if we move to a color-blind society before we achieve a racially integrated society—as California has done under Connerly and former Governor Pete Wilson's leadership—we essentially guarantee that we will never achieve that integrated society. It is clear that it will take centuries to achieve such an integrated society, especially at the most elite levels, if we do nothing forceful to make that change happen. Both opponents and some supporters of affirmative action have suggested replacing the consideration of race and ethnicity with consideration of surrogate factors for race, such as low family income or preferences for students from specific high schools or specific zip codes in order to achieve racially integrated colleges and universities. Yet these surrogates either do not achieve the desired outcome, often because of complex demographics in many parts of the country, or they depend on highly undesirable conditions, such as segregated school systems within a particular state, in order to be effective. (Chapters 8 and 9 examine four of these surrogates in detail.)

The entire quest for surrogates is foolish from the start. In the first place, the more closely a surrogate criterion approximates race, the more likely it is to be rejected as a violation of the law in those states—currently California, Florida, and Washington—where affirmative action has been eliminated in public universities when such practices are inevitably challenged in the courts. If the Supreme Court ever eliminates affirmative action, this surrogate dilemma will apply to the entire country. Second, and more important, there is something fundamentally absurd in saying that we value racial integration but we can't consider race to achieve it. The frantic scurrying for surrogates seems especially foolish when we know that there is a direct policy response—affirmative action—that has been demonstrated to work. Finally we also have to acknowledge that social science research demonstrates that race compounds economic disadvantage, and that poor African American, Latino, and Native American families are therefore much less likely to escape from poverty than poor white families.

Creating a color-blind society before we have created an equal society is completely backward. To take one example, California has now created a color-blind society that will perpetuate and even accelerate the current national divisions of wealth along racial lines, in which twenty percent of the people in the country control eighty percent of the wealth, as Molly Ivins points out with insistent regularity. In September 2000, UC San Francisco and the Field Institute released the results of a study that, according to Janet Wells in the *San Francisco Chronicle*, found "Latinos and African Americans—who make up one-third of California's workforce—are far more likely to have poverty-level incomes, lose their jobs, and have poor health and less education than their white and Asian counterparts in the workforce. . . ." Wells quotes Laura Trupin, a researcher in the study, who says, "There are a lot of indications that we're moving towards a more polarized society, and the divide continues to be defined by race and ethnicity, even in the year 2000." Chapter 10 examines this division in detail.

This polarization was reflected in the fall 2001 freshman class at UC Berkeley. The median family annual income was $70,000. Twenty-five percent of the students, however, came from families with annual incomes of $30,000 or less (mostly African American, Asian American, and Latino students) while another twenty-five percent came from families with annual incomes of $120,000 or more. Moreover, twenty-seven percent of the freshmen reported that they expect to contribute money to their parents to help pay bills or provide for other family members, a fact that will clearly affect persistence and graduation rates for those students. Some of these students with full financial aid packages had higher incomes than their parents.

It should also be pointed out that the number of low-income students at Berkeley is highly unusual among selective colleges and universities across the country. According to Tom Mortenson, a senior scholar at the Center for the Study of Opportunity in Higher Education, Berkeley ranks second in the number of undergraduate students eligible for Pell Grants, one of the key indicators of low-income status—and the top six selective universities in the enrollment of low-income students are all University of California campuses. Across the rest of the country, low-income students are mostly excluded from such institutions.

In *The Winner-Take-All Society*, Robert Frank and Philip Cook point out that these financial divisions are magnified by the growing tendency in our economy to reward extravagantly the few truly outstanding performers in a particular field at the severe expense of almost everyone else in that field. The signs of our burgeoning lust to be rich are easy to find: according to Nielsen Media Research, the second most-watched television program in America during the week of November 6–12, 2000, was "Who Wants to Be a Millionaire," shown on Sunday evening, and the third most-watched program that week was "Who Wants to Be a Millionaire," broadcast on Wednesday evening. The *San Francisco Chronicle* on August 21, 2001, carried a story by David Bonetti on the decision of David Ross, the director of the San Francisco Museum of Modern Art, to resign his $393,000-a-year position at the museum to go to work for Eyestorm, a commercial website that offers artworks for sale. "I decided to just go make some money," said Ross. "I have to think about myself a bit." And there was Dinesh D'Souza, long-time opponent of affirmative action, popping up in the November 10, 2000, issue of *The Chronicle of Higher Education* to urge leftist university faculty to relax into their recent six-figure incomes because this new affluence will free them to accomplish more good works. "It's time for academe to get over its psychological hang-up about wealth," writes D'Souza, "and discover the virtue of prosperity."

We have to choose between a color-blind society that is sharply unequal along color lines—and which will become even more unequal—or continued movement toward a racially integrated society that depends upon the judicious use of racial preferences, individual by individual, until the causes of that racial inequality have been eliminated.

THE TENSION BETWEEN SELFISHNESS AND SELFLESSNESS

The United States has a remarkably powerful economic system that is driven by self-interest. When self-interest pushes into selfishness and greed and when it is combined with a widespread sense of high anxiety or even fear that many of us feel about our own prospects and those of our children over the next twenty years, we have a real struggle within our national character that goes all the way back to the founding of this country.

We are clearly in a period when the balance between these two qualities is shifting rather quickly and quite massively from what has been at least some degree of enlightened self-interest and concern for the greater good to a much heavier interest on selfishness and self-interest, the continuous enriching of what *Newsweek*, in a cover story as far back as July 1995, called "the overclass." It's the ascendancy of a nineteenth-century Darwinian view of society at the expense of something more compassionate and humane that acknowledges the responsibility of all of us for all of us. The needle has moved all the way over to the red line on the selfishness side of the gauge.

In the August 1998 issue of the "Postsecondary Education Opportunity" newsletter, publisher Tom Mortenson carefully documented our national shift toward what he called "a public selfishness" in public policy making over the last twenty years. The gap between rich and poor in this country is widening rather than narrowing. In California the gap is not only widening but more people are becoming poor. UCLA Professor Allen Scott describes this distribution of income as an "hourglass economy." In reality, however, the bottom of the hourglass is much larger than the top and that what we actually have is a pear economy. According to a Federal Reserve report released in August 2000, the average California family saw its real income decline during the 1990s and lost ground compared to families in other states.

In California and many other states, we are creating not just a permanent underclass but an increasingly large underclass, and that underclass includes huge numbers of people who are described by the phrase "working poor"—that is, people who are often working long hours, often at more than one job but who are still living below the poverty line. The *Newsweek* cover story referred to just above described this phenomenon most accurately ten years ago.

The proliferation of private schools, the push for vouchers, and certainly the explosion in home schooling are examples of a conscious and deliberate movement away from a balance where shared social values are taught in the public schools and moral training is taught at home, with these two value sets existing in some kind of blend even though there may occasionally be some tension between them. More people seem increasingly determined to live only on their terms, to be saying, "I want things entirely *my* way and I am withdrawing from important parts of the community to be sure that I get things my way." "My values" rather than a mix of "my values and our values."

The United States Congress has directly contributed to this shift in many ways over the last twenty years. One of its policies that has most directly affected equal access to college is its financial aid policy. The massive shift from grant money to loans to support poor students in college has redefined college education from a public good beneficial to the greater society, and therefore supported by the greater society, to an individual good which benefits solely the individual and for which the individual must bear the primary financial burden. This policy is something like that attitude of people who vote against school bonds because they don't have kids or because their kids are out of school. It's a pretty narrow focus. And maybe it's more than just myopia; maybe it's deliberately selfish. Stephen Metcalf in an article from the January 28, 2002, issue of *The Nation* says:

> Why the infatuation with testing? For its most conservative enthusiasts, testing makes sense as a lone solution to school failure because, they insist, adequate resources are already in place, and only the threat of exposure and censure is necessary for schools to succeed. Moreover, among those who style themselves "compassionate conservatives," education has become a sentimental and, all things considered, cheap way to talk about equalizing opportunity without committing to substantial income distribution.

Another indication of this trend toward selfishness is the establishment of full and comprehensive college advising services by for-profit, national companies, such as Kaplan, the Princeton Review, and Achieva. These companies make it more likely that affluent families will increase their advantages in the competition for places at selective colleges and universities, especially as less-affluent schools continue to have overworked counselors or no counselors at all. And school test scores now appear instantly on national real estate websites as part of the real estate marketing effort across the country. When California released its Academic Performance Index (API) scores in fall 2000, real estate prices around the state reacted immediately, climbing sharply in those areas where schools' APIs were high and suffering in areas where they were not.

Colleges and universities have contributed shamefully to this trend as well by embracing Early Decision admissions policies, by shifting to non-need–based financial aid, and by adopting the policy of financial aid leveraging. A college that employs financial aid leveraging takes money from students with financial need and gives it to students with less or, more commonly, no financial need at all in order to get those students to choose that particular college. As part of this practice, which was pioneered by the Noel-Levitz consulting firm, these colleges often probe individual families' financial and credit histories in order to estimate family financial strength and therefore to predict with a fair degree of precision how much scholarship money it will take to make that student decide to come to that institution—a repugnant practice. Often times the largest of these leveraging awards go to students with the highest test scores in order to improve the standing of an institution in the national rankings, such as those of *U.S. News*. Early Decision admission policies, non-need–based financial aid, and financial aid leveraging all reflect the selfishness of the institutions that embrace these practices at the expense of the greater good—and, in the case of financial aid policy, at the expense of low-income students in general from whom potential dollars are diverted to those with less or no financial need. These practices contribute directly to the widening gap between rich and poor in the United States, as Robert Reich, Secretary of Labor under President Clinton, has demonstrated in an important essay, called "How Selective Colleges Heighten Inequality" in the September 15, 2000, issue of *The Chronicle of Higher Education*.

In *The Lexus and the Olive Tree*, Thomas Friedman has identified and described the forces of globalization that are transforming the world, including secondary and higher education. The most telling part of the book is the chapter near the end, called "If You Want to Speak to a Human Being, Press 1," in which Friedman warns all of us that, under globalization, the extraordinary shift taking place from the collective good or the greater good to an egoistic emphasis on the individual at the expense of what used to be called the social compact—me instead of we—may be too unfair to too many of the world's people. There is a real danger that the ruthlessly impersonal, Darwinian forces of globalization may obliterate our sense of social conscience, which, in this country, we have always had to struggle to maintain. Friedman uses the same metaphor repeatedly: the globalization train has already left the station and is way down the track—and no one is driving.

It may be that the Reagan years legitimized greed. It may be that people got really scared when the economy collapsed in the late 1980s and again in 2001–02. It may be that many young men and women believe that they don't have a realistic chance to live at the economic level of their parents. And it is certainly true that, in California and many other places, states abandoned public policy planning for higher education for twenty years. This abdication of public responsibility has contributed directly to the extraordinary competition at many flagship public universities and has fueled the fear that the factors just cited, and others, have created: someone else is getting what should be mine. Ultimately, however, it doesn't matter what forces have caused us to reach this point. What matters is what, if anything, we do about it.

Marian Wright Edelman, head of The Children's Defense Fund, reminds us all constantly how many children in the United States live in poverty. Figures released by the Census Bureau in September 2000 showed that 16.9 percent of American children live at or below the poverty line. In California, according to the Public Policy Institute of California, the figure is twenty-five percent. For a family of four, the federal poverty level is an income of $18,400. That is something more severe than just poverty—it's cruelty.

Affirmative action is especially important because the terms "poverty" and "low-income" have become antiseptic, almost neutral. They gloss over and desensitize most of us to the true levels of pain, deprivation, hardship, cruelty, neglect, violence, homelessness, mental illness, hunger, malnutrition, sexual violence, gang membership—including parents who are gang members—illness, shame, and fear that characterize the lives of so many children and adults in this country. It is a sobering experience to read freshman applications to public universities in California and many other states. The combination of pain and multiple hardship in many of these students' lives makes the concept "low-income" seem like some sort of vacation, and the level of determination and grit that many of these students have repeatedly demonstrated in order to just get to the point where they can apply to a public university is staggering. And these are the survivors. There are hundreds of thousands of children who have already been defeated, and, in many cases, destroyed, by their circumstances and who will never come close to applying to colleges and universities, let alone have a chance for any sort of healthful, fulfilling lives.

Edelman speaks passionately and eloquently about what should be our sense of shame. We need to take up her cry and remind ourselves constantly how obscene it is that the richest country in the history of the world treats so many of its people—so many of its children—so callously. We should be ashamed that we have to be reminded by Edelman that every child is sacred and that every one of us is responsible for every child. Until we get to that point, until we really push back against this notion that what's mine is mine and what's yours is mine if I can get it, we're headed toward a future of not just gross inequity but quite possibly social collapse.

We have to make the public conversation broader and more complex—a difficult thing to do in the land of the sound byte. We have to remind ourselves that the essence of the American Dream isn't just to get enormously rich, that the core of the Dream, the true promise of America, is to create a society in which everyone truly has a fair chance to pursue his or her own dreams. We need to remind ourselves that merit isn't reducible to a number—that it isn't a grade-point average or an SAT score but rather everything that a person has achieved measured against every set of challenges and opportunities that person has faced.

There is a fundamental question whether we can survive as a society with the widening gap between rich and poor, with a rapidly growing underclass, and with the perception of many people: "What's the point in trying?" The idea that we don't all have a fundamental stake in our public schools is remarkably naive and narrow. "I don't have kids," or "Our kids are grown," or "We're all right—our kids are in private school" all reflect a shift away from the common good to the selfish.

Cruz Bustamente, the Lieutenant Governor of California, used to point out that in California it took sixty-seven percent of the voters to approve a new school but only fifty-one percent to approve a new prison. Although California voters recently reduced that new-school majority requirement to fifty-five percent, prisons remain the true growth industry in California—and the contemporary counterpart to prison is a gated community. Near the end of October 1999, the *Los Angeles Times* carried an amazing article about a community in the Coachella Valley between Palm Springs and Indio called Indian Wells. The article pointed out that seventy percent of the people in Indian Wells live in gated communities—and that those people think that those gates are a solution to something. Even the remote Bitterroot Valley in rural Montana has a new-gated community developed by Charles Schwab for the super-rich. In the case of California, the state has gone, in just a few years, from the Golden State to the Gilded State to, now with our prison empire and barred communities, the Gated State. Yet the idea that we will just build more prisons and more gated communities and still survive as a society is folly.

If there are no surrogates for race and if Congress and state legislatures are not truly serious about ending poverty and rebuilding the public schools in economically depressed areas, then we're in a difficult spot. Some historians still refer to "the American experiment," the bold and extraordinary attempt to build a democratic society that truly provided ample and equal opportunity for all its citizens. We have put this experiment at great risk. Affirmative action is the single most-effective policy that moves us toward the goal of a fully integrated, color-blind society.

Here are the last three lines of W. H. Auden's "Musée des Beaux Arts":

> . . . and the expensive delicate ship that must have seen
> Something amazing, a boy falling out of the sky,
> Had somewhere to get to and sailed calmly on.

To end affirmative action is to make a pragmatic—and, quite possibly, self-destructive—error of immense proportion in social and economic policy. If those of us who are prospering nicely under our current social and economic structure sail calmly on in our expensive delicate ship, we will also have made a terrible moral error.

THE MOST IMPORTANT AFFIRMATIVE ACTION CASES TO BE DECIDED SINCE 1978

In June 2003, the United States Supreme Court decided two cases, *Gratz v. Bollinger* and *Grutter v. Bollinger,* that challenged the use of race and ethnicity in admissions policies at the University of Michigan. Those decisions marked the first time that the Court had reviewed the uses of affirmative action in college and university admissions since the *Bakke* case in 1978, in which the Court had ruled 5 to 4 that race could be considered as a plus in admissions decisions. In the 1990s, however, federal courts decided a number of cases that conflicted directly with *Bakke.* The two University of Michigan cases were therefore extremely important to the standing of affirmative action in university admissions.

By a 6 to 3 in *Gratz,* the Court found unconstitutional the undergraduate admission policy at the University of Michigan, primarily on the grounds that the practice of awarding a fixed number of points in the freshman admissions process to every member of a racial or ethnic group was a de facto quota and therefore illegal. By a 5 to 4 in *Grutter,* however, the Court found that the consideration of race and ethnicity by the University of Michigan Law School was a compelling interest of the university and was permissible because the Law School conducted an individual review of each applicant and considered race or ethnicity among a range of other qualities and factors in making its admissions decisions. "Here, the Law School engages in a highly individualized, holistic review of each applicant's file," wrote Justice Sandra Day O'Connor in her majority opinion, "giving serious consideration to all the ways an applicant might contribute to a diverse educational environment."

Justice O'Connor's majority opinion in *Grutter v. Bollinger* strongly supported affirmative action in university admissions and comes remarkably close to being a national policy statement on the importance of accessibility and opportunity for all members of American society—this despite a divided 5 to 4 vote on the decision and a Bush administration hostile to affirmative action. "Effective participation by members of all racial and ethnic groups in the civic life of our Nation is essential," wrote O'Connor, "if the dream of one Nation, indivisible, is to be realized."

Toward this end, the O'Connor opinion declared that racial and ethnic diversity is a compelling interest of colleges and universities and that such institutions are justified in considering race and ethnicity in their admissions decisions in order to build a critical mass of underrepresented minority students within their student bodies. The Court noted that the university's definition included many other criteria in addition to race and ethnicity and agreed with the university's argument that a diverse student body, reflecting a wide range of experiences and viewpoints, is essential for the education of all of its students. In the opinion of the five-justice majority in *Grutter*, the goal of a fair, fully integrated society clearly trumps, at least temporarily, Title VI of the Civil Rights Act of 1964, which prohibits racial discrimination by any public or private institution that receives federal funds, and the Equal Protection Clause of the Constitution. In addition, the *Grutter* decision cleared a number of conflicting federal court rulings and established uniform law for the entire country—with the notable exceptions of public colleges and universities in California, Florida, and Washington.

The Supreme Court decision in *Grutter* meant that the consideration of race and ethnicity in university admissions was now legally permitted (but not required) at both public and private colleges and universities in all but three states, where voters—or in the case of Florida, Governor Jeb Bush—have banned such practice in public universities. That is a painful irony for admissions officers in Washington, Florida, and—most particularly—California, the most racially and ethnically diverse state in the Union.

There are also as yet unanswered questions related to the two University of Michigan decisions.

- Can a college or university consider race in the awarding of scholarships?
- Can outreach programs specifically target students by race?
- Can colleges and universities consider race in hiring faculty?

The *Grutter* decision precipitated intense legal and political maneuvering in the three states that have eliminated affirmative action. In January 2004, for example, Washington Governor Gary Locke announced that he intended to ask state legislators to modify Initiative 200 (the 1998 measure that banned the consideration of race in that state) so that public universities may return to considering race and ethnicity as they did prior to 1998 in order to be in alignment with the Supreme Court's decision in *Grutter*. By early February 2004, however, Peter Schmidt, writing in the electronic version of *The Chronicle of Higher Education*, reported that both houses of the Washington legislature had let the governor's measure die in committee without ever coming to a vote. What will happen in California and Florida remains an important question—that is, if anything will happen at all.

A STINGING DEFEAT

While it is clear that the struggle has continued over what universities and their states should do following the Court's decision in *Grutter v. Bollinger*, it is also clear that *Grutter* was a pronounced defeat for the individuals and organizations opposed to affirmative action, such as the Center for Individual Rights (CIR) and Ward Connerly, the former

University of California Regent who heads the American Civil Rights Institute in Sacramento. CIR in particular had spent years identifying plaintiffs, framing cases, and choosing what it thought would be quite favorable federal court jurisdictions, including the two Michigan cases. After the Supreme Court announced its decisions on June 23, 2003, Connerly, Curt Levey of CIR, and others provided much initial huffing and puffing. In mid-July 2003, Connerly made a splashy appearance in Michigan to announce a similar initiative campaign to Proposition 209. The most strained response among opponents of affirmative action, however, came from CIR President Terence Pell who, according to Peter Schmidt in *The Chronicle of Higher Education*, claimed, "Today's ruling is a mixed decision that signals the beginning of the end of race-based preferences in America."

DIFFICULT CHOICES

While the *Grutter* decision clearly permits the consideration of race and ethnicity in college admissions, it also carries with it specific requirements that may create difficult choices for the leaders of colleges and universities across the country, specifically large, selective public universities that have made bulk admissions decisions on large numbers of applicants through the use of formulas or indices and that have not read applications individually. On behalf of the citizens they represent and serve, these institutions must answer carefully the following questions:

- What are the goals of our admission policy and how do those goals relate to the mission statement of our institution?
- What criteria should we consider in our admissions process in order to best achieve those goals?
- How can we most effectively and most fairly assess these criteria among our applicants?
- How can we evaluate the effectiveness of our policy and process over time to be sure that the criteria and tools we are using are achieving our goals to the maximum extent possible?

Admissions policy-makers must consider, among other criteria, how to evaluate and weigh courses completed, grades in those courses, test scores, intellectual curiosity and accomplishment, extraordinary talent, leadership, service to others, motivation, tenacity, and demonstrated achievement in the face of hardship.

These are complex issues, and they are sometimes made more difficult because colleges and universities frequently have unexamined assumptions embedded in their admissions policies—for example, the specific intent of such policies. Some policy-makers believe the purpose should be solely to reward achievement in high school. Others believe that such achievement should be measured carefully against the opportunities and challenges faced by each individual applicant. Still others believe that the purpose should be to select students who have the best chance of success or who will contribute the most to the intellectual and community life of the institution. The last chapter of this book makes a series of specific recommendations on this topic and others for admissions policy-makers.

The central criterion under *Grutter* is that any institution that wishes to consider race and ethnicity in its admissions process must conduct a full review of each individual applicant and compare each applicant against all other applicants as it makes its admission decisions. Justice O'Connor writes, "What is more, the Law School actually gives substantial weight to diversity factors besides race. The Law School frequently accepts nonminority applicants with grades and test scores lower than underrepresented minority applicants (and other nonminority applicants) who are rejected. . . . This shows that the Law School seriously weighs many other diversity factors besides race that can make a real and dispositive difference for nonminority applicants as well." O'Connor's observation recognizes that a careful, thoughtful concept of diversity includes many factors other than race and ethnicity. This complex definition of diversity and the type of comprehensive individual review process she describes have long been the practice at most private colleges and universities (although there are exceptions) but have generally not been used by large, selective public universities.

Many large universities, some private, most public, that receive many thousands of applications use formulas—often a combination of grade-point average and test scores—to sort their students and, in many cases, to make actual admissions decisions. Going from a process in which few or no applications are actually read in full to a process in which every applicant is given a comprehensive review means adding lots of readers, building a technological capacity to track and record individual and collective admissions decisions, and developing the capacity to evaluate the consistency and reliability of individual readers.

A comprehensive review process requires thinking about applicants in more complex, subtle, nuanced ways, and some—perhaps, many—universities may not be conceptually equipped to approach admissions in this way. The University of Virginia and UC Berkeley are the models for public universities, reading every single one of their freshman applicants and using no formulas or clumsy point totals.

It is admittedly a complicated undertaking to go from a mechanical, formula-driven admissions process to a comprehensive review process that requires skilled professional judgment on the part of all admissions readers, but it is a transformation that in recent years has been successfully undertaken in part or in full by the University of Florida at Gainesville, the University of Texas at Austin, and, following Berkeley's lead, other campuses in the UC system (although some UC campuses still rely on a basic academic formula and then add points for other qualities or experiences gleaned from the application). While a campus might still use some sort of point system in parts of its process, the *Gratz* opinion explicitly outlaws assigning points on the basis of race or ethnicity to an entire group of applicants, arguing that such a practice, without an individual review of each applicant, amounts to a de facto quota.

On August 28, 2003, the University of Michigan became the first college or university to announce its freshman admission policy and process crafted under the *Grutter* and *Gratz* decisions. The campus has modified its admissions process to include a review of each individual applicant and to eliminate the point assignments that the Supreme Court found unacceptable in *Gratz v. Bollinger*, the second University of Michigan case decided by the Court in June 2003. The university has shown its intent to comply fully with the Supreme Court decisions and to consider race and ethnicity to the full extent permitted by them.

Depending on an institution's application volume and the kind of individual review process it adopts, moving to such a process will cost a significant amount of money. When the admissions office at UC Berkeley moved to such a process for fall 1998, it required an additional $200,000, mostly for increased staff and more advanced technological capabilities. The University of Michigan calculates that its new process will cost the campus between $1.5 million and $2 million in its first year. In return for such expense, an institution gains not only the ability to consider race and ethnicity in its process but also a process that makes better informed and, almost certainly, fairer decisions about each individual applicant—fairer because each applicant will have been reviewed as a distinct individual based on all of the information included in the application, rather than as a one-dimensional set of summary numbers. According to Peter Schmidt in the July 4, 2003, issue of *The Chronicle of Higher Education*, Christopher Edley, currently dean of the Boalt Hall School of Law at UC Berkeley, pointed out that "institutions must be prepared to bear the expense to do it right."

At a national meeting in Washington, D.C., just a few weeks after the University of Michigan decisions, a number of university presidents argued that they simply couldn't afford to operate such an expensive process. The O'Connor opinion emphasizes, however, that an institution that considers race and ethnicity in its admissions process may not avoid a comprehensive review of applicants by pleading that such a process would impose an administrative burden or excessive costs on that institution.

The we-can't-afford-it argument, of course, isn't true at all—even in the states that have had the most severe budget cuts. Regardless of difficult budget times, many colleges and universities have increased their funding to admissions offices. That money, however, has gone to marketing, outreach, and recruitment—rather than to increasing the professional admissions reading staff—as part of the intense competition for students among institutions. Colleges have resources, even in strenuous budget times. What those presidents were really saying is that they don't want to take money from faculty research or faculty and staff salary increases or expansion of the physical plant and redirect it to a more careful and thorough admissions process. It's a question of where to put those resources—and faculty interests traditionally dominate administrative interests. It will be interesting, however, to see how many presidents hold to this position over time. It may prove difficult politically in many places to say "We're not willing to pay the financial price to give more African American, Latino, and Native American students an opportunity at our university."

While the University of Michigan quickly announced its intention to comply with the Supreme Court's guidelines, Robert M. Gates, the president of Texas A&M University, declared in December 2003 that his university would not reinstate the consideration of race and ethnicity. According to Michael Arnone in *The Chronicle of Higher Education*, Gates said, "Students at Texas A&M should be admitted as individuals, on personal merit, and on no other basis." The following month, however, Peter Schmidt, writing in *The Chronicle of Higher Education*, reported a study by the *Houston Chronicle* that concluded more than 300 white freshmen applicants had been admitted to A&M because of their legacy status, "an amount roughly equal to the total number of black applicants admitted to Texas A&M." Under criticism for this policy, Gates announced that A&M would discontinue its practice of giving preference to legacies—that is, applicants who are related to alumni. Supporters of affirmative action have long pointed out that legacy consideration was simply a form of affirmative action for the wealthy.

It will be particularly important to watch the progress of Gates's policies since the state's other flagship university, UT Austin, is moving expediently to reincorporate race and ethnicity into its admissions criteria. The likelihood is that the undergraduate student body at Texas A&M will continue to be overwhelmingly white while UT Austin increasingly will reflect the racial and ethnic diversity of the state.

Since *Grutter*, faculty admissions committees, presidents and chancellors, and boards of trustees and regents at many public and private universities have struggled to articulate their position on the use of race and ethnicity in admissions and to formulate admissions policies that reflect those deliberations. And many public universities have worked to reconcile the ability to consider race and ethnicity against the sharp increase in costs and labor that an individual review process would entail if they had not had such a process in the past. It is certainly clear from the O'Connor opinion, however, that the price of considering race and ethnicity is a process that considers each applicant individually and fully.

HANGING BY A THREAD

In her majority opinion, Justice O'Connor writes, "We expect that 25 years from now, the use of racial preferences will no longer be necessary to further the interest approved today." Opponents of affirmative action have taken this sentence to mean that affirmative action must end in twenty-five years. Proponents interpret this sentence as a pious hope on O'Connor's part. Despite repeated claims by opponents, however, no serious supporter of affirmative action sees it as some kind of permanent entitlement.

It also seems clear from ballot initiatives in California and Washington and from opinion polls that the country is pretty evenly divided on the issue of affirmative action. California's Proposition 209, deceptively titled "The California Civil Rights Initiative," passed in 1996 by a margin of fifty-four to forty-six percent. In California and many other states, a shift by, say, ten percent of the voters or a handful of legislators could change a particular outcome on this issue. Even the Supreme Court's vote upholding the consideration of race in *Grutter* was remarkably close—5 to 4.

As elated as the supporters of affirmative action were by the O'Connor opinion in *Grutter*, most observers also recognized how short-lived that decision might prove to be. Over the next few years, there will certainly be challenges to admissions policies that consider race and ethnicity in compliance with the O'Connor opinion. Indeed, Justice Antonin Scalia in effect laid out a map for such challenges in his dissenting opinion in *Grutter*:

> Some future lawsuits will presumably focus on whether the discriminatory scheme in questions contains enough evaluation of the applicant "as an individual," and sufficiently avoids "separate admissions tracks," to fall under *Grutter* rather than *Gratz*. Some will focus on whether a university has gone beyond the bounds of a "good faith effort" and has so zealously pursued its "critical mass" as to make it an unconstitutional *de facto* quota system, rather than merely "a permissible goal." Other lawsuits may focus on whether, in the particular setting at issue, any educational benefits flow from racial diversity.

Those challenges, however, will be difficult to mount and the cases are likely to be quite difficult to prove, particularly because of the deference the Court has shown to colleges and universities in the *Grutter* and *Gratz* decisions and because of the leeway that the Court has given higher education institutions to define critical mass and to develop admissions processes based on individual review. At the same time, there are still many federal judges, specifically in the appellate courts, who are hostile to affirmative action and eager to rule against it. In addition, there are the still unanswered questions regarding the consideration of race in awarding scholarships, in choosing students to participate in outreach programs, and in hiring faculty.

The greatest vulnerability of the O'Connor opinion, however, is created by the thin 5-to-4 vote margin in that decision and by the relatively advanced age of two of those five justices who comprised the majority: John Paul Stevens was eighty-three years old at the time of the *Grutter* and *Gratz* decisions, and Justice O'Connor was seventy-three. Rumors of their imminent retirements have circulated for sometime. If one or both of them were to be replaced by justices hostile to affirmative action, it is most likely that both *Bakke* and *Grutter* would be overturned the first time a suit challenging affirmative action were to reach the Court.

In addition to being subject to the power of the courts, affirmative action is also deeply influenced by senior administrators in the federal government. The president has the constitutional power to appoint federal judges and senior federal administrators, and this power to appoint carries great influence. George W. Bush, for example, appointed outspoken opponents of affirmative action to key positions in his Cabinet and in the federal courts. The most crucial Cabinet positions are those of Attorney General and Secretary of Education. Just below Cabinet level, the Assistant Secretary of Education for Civil Rights is also crucial. Within the federal court system, the most crucial positions are appellate judgeships and, of course, those on the United States Supreme Court.

Supporters of affirmative action were dismayed when John Ashcroft was confirmed as Attorney General of the United States. Much more crucial, however, was Bush's nomination of Gerald A. Reynolds in late June 2001 to serve as Assistant Secretary of Education for Civil Rights in the U.S. Department of Education, where he would head the Office for Civil Rights. Reynolds is a thoughtful, articulate African American who ran the Center for New Black Leadership, which opposes affirmative action. The Assistant Secretary for Civil Rights has had more influence over the national affirmative action policy debate during the past fourteen years than any other federal official, except possibly the president and, as of June 23, 2003, Justice Sandra Day O'Connor.

Reynolds' nomination was held up for many months in the Senate Health, Education, Labor, and Pensions Committee, which Senator Edward Kennedy chaired. With no resolution to Reynolds' confirmation by the time Congress recessed for two weeks in March 2002, Bush appointed Reynolds to the position, using what is called a "recess appointment." That meant that Reynolds could officially serve as Assistant Secretary for Civil Rights but only for a limited time without Senate confirmation. More than a year and a half later, Reynolds resigned his position, most likely to avoid the Senate confirmation process, and accepted an appointment as deputy associate attorney general at the Justice Department, where he would most likely specialize in civil rights cases. The satisfaction of supporters of affirmative action at Reynolds' resignation was tempered somewhat by the influence of the position he would be assuming at the Justice Department.

Bush put together a formidable team of top federal officials who oppose affirmative action. His strategy of appointing African Americans who oppose affirmative action to lead the struggle against it, including Reynolds; Secretary of Education Roderick Page; Brian W. Jones, who was confirmed in September 2001 as general counsel for the Department of Education; and Solicitor General Theodore B. Olson, the top lawyer for the Justice Department, is undeniably powerful and, as former University of California Regent Ward Connerly demonstrated in California, can be highly effective.

The irony of George W. Bush, who has benefited from preferential treatment his entire life, working so determinedly to dismantle affirmative action is pronounced. The "Doonesbury" comic strip that ran on July 2, 2000, had a telling press conference with then-Governor George W. Bush, represented by cartoonist Garry Trudeau as an empty cowboy hat. Mark Slackmeyer, one of Trudeau's enduring characters, asks a rather pointed question:

"Sir," says Slackmeyer, "most people know you went to Harvard and Yale, two of the most selective universities in America. Given your dismal grades, how is it you were ever admitted to those two schools?"

"Well," says the Hat, "you'd have to ask the admissions folks, but I'd say they saw some . . . some whiff of potential! Just like the National Guard folks who let me skip the waiting list, and the family friends who bankrolled my businesses, and the bankers who got me the ball club!"

"To follow up, sir," says Slackmeyer, "do you still oppose affirmative action?"

"What do you mean, follow up?" he asks.

3 DUELING FEDERAL JUDGES AND THE ENSUING CONFUSION

The *Grutter* and *Gratz* decisions were not only fundamentally important statements by the Supreme Court on the importance of racial equality and full participation in all levels of American society, they also cleared an enormous amount of legal and policy chaos over affirmative action in university admissions that had accumulated since the mid-1990s through quite aggressive rulings on both sides of the issue by federal judges in several federal courts. It was in part this confusing and contradictory state of legal affairs that led the Supreme Court finally to take up the two University of Michigan cases. There is little doubt that there will be legal challenges to admissions policies crafted under *Grutter*, and it is quite possible that this creeping confusion may reappear, specifically as a result of conflicting federal court-of-appeals decisions. If it does reappear, it will be damaging not just to affirmative action as a specific policy but also to the broader goal of coherent and consistent public policies in general.

Conflicting court decisions were just part of what led to such confusion; the decisions by voters in California and Washington to end affirmative action in public universities and the executive decree Governor Jeb Bush issued to do the same thing in Florida have also contributed. And these measures were unaffected by the Supreme Court's decision in *Grutter*, which permits the consideration of race and ethnicity in university admissions but does not require it.

LEGAL GEOGRAPHY

Prior to the two University of Michigan Supreme Court decisions in June 2003, one of the truly great challenges of contemporary geography was to draw a map of the legal status of affirmative action in the United States. A person needed such a map to understand the subject, but the map had to be updated almost every week. Here is where things stood prior to *Grutter* and *Gratz:*

California. Proposition 209, passed in November 1996, made it illegal to discriminate against or grant "preferential treatment to any individual or group on the basis of race, sex, color, ethnicity, or national origin, in the operation of public employment, public education, or public contracting." That, of course, included consideration of such items in undergraduate or graduate admission to public colleges in the state. Private colleges in California, however, were free to continue to consider race and ethnicity in admissions should they choose to do so and were still bound by the *Bakke* decision (and now by *Grutter* and *Gratz*) of the U.S. Supreme Court. Some private universities in the state, most notably the University of Southern California, have greatly benefited from the restrictions that Proposition 209 has placed on public universities. These institutions have recruited, admitted, and ultimately enrolled African American, Latino, and Native American students who have been shut out of the University of California system or who have not applied to the UC system because, as a result of UC Regents' actions and/or Proposition 209, they have felt unwelcome.

Although, as an initiative, Proposition 209 required only a simple majority to pass, the backers of Proposition 209 shrewdly framed it as an amendment to the California Constitution. It is now Article 1, Section 31 of that document and, as such, would require in the future a two-thirds majority of either the state legislature or the state's voters to change or eliminate it.

Ward Connerly, the UC Regent who led the campaign for Proposition 209, and others have claimed that there are more underrepresented minority freshmen now than in fall 1997, the last year of affirmative action. That is numerically accurate but ignores the fact that UC campuses have enrolled about 10,000 more students overall. The important measures are the comparative proportions of each class. Even more crucial, these aggregate statistics mask a huge redistribution of African American, Latino, and Native American students away from the Berkeley and Los Angeles campuses and to UC Riverside, the least selective UC campus, and to UC Irvine.

At Berkeley, the most competitive of the UC campuses during this period, African American students declined from 6.1 percent of the undergraduate student body in fall 1997 to 3.9 percent in fall 2001. Over that same period, Chicano (as distinct from Latino, in this instance) undergraduate students declined from 9.4 percent to 6.9 percent, and Native American undergraduates dropped from 1.2 percent of all undergraduates in fall 1997 to .6 percent in fall 2001. In the aggregate, underrepresented minority students went from 16.7 percent of the undergraduate student body in fall 1997 to 11.4 percent in fall 2001.

In an effort to mitigate the losses in minority enrollments that resulted from the end of affirmative action, the University of California adopted a Top Four-Percent plan in March 1999. This policy deemed UC-eligible the top four percent of the seniors graduating from each high school in the state and took effect fall 2001. Chapter 8 closely examines the effects of this policy and at those of similar plans adopted in Texas and Florida.

Washington. In November 1998, voters in Washington passed Initiative 200. Worded almost exactly like Proposition 209, I-200 eliminated the consideration of race, ethnicity, and gender in public university admissions. As in California, private universities could continue to consider race, ethnicity, and gender in admissions decisions should they choose to do so and were bound by the *Bakke* decision of the U.S. Supreme Court. (Sandwiched between California and Washington, Oregon's public universities are unencumbered by measures such as Proposition 209 and I-200.)

In the fall 1998 enrolled freshman class at UW, the last class admitted before I-200 took effect, there were 373 African American, Hispanic/Latino (the term used by UW), and Native American students. They comprised 8.9 percent of the class. For fall 1999, students from these racial and ethnic backgrounds declined to 255, or 5.7 percent of the enrolled class. In raw numbers, that is a one-year decline of 31.6 percent. Yet as UW President Richard McCormick pointed out in a January 20, 2000, speech to the Association of American Colleges and Universities, the fall 1999 freshman class was larger than that of fall 1998 so the proportional loss was even greater than that 31.6 percent figure. That is, given the size of the fall 1999 class, the university would have expected to have enrolled about 400 African American, Latino, and Native American students absent I-200. Measured against this standard, the decline in raw numbers was 36.3 percent.

Texas. In March 1996, the Fifth Circuit Court of Appeals issued an opinion in a case called *Hopwood v. Texas*, in which a white applicant denied admission to the University of Texas Law School sued the university arguing reverse discrimination. The *Hopwood* decision ended affirmative action in both public and private college and university admissions in the Fifth Circuit, which includes Texas, Louisiana, and Mississippi. Because colleges and universities in Louisiana and Mississippi were under a federal desegregation order, however, the *Hopwood* ruling applied only to public and private colleges and universities in Texas.

The plaintiffs in the *Hopwood* case in Texas had been solicited by the Center for Individual Rights (CIR), a conservative public interest law firm in Washington, D.C. Michael Greve, at the time executive director of CIR, said publicly that the Center deliberately looked for a case in the Fifth Circuit because the federal appellate judges in that Circuit were the most conservative and the most hostile to affirmative action of any circuit in the country. CIR wasn't particularly concerned with which side won the initial decision (in fact, the university won the initial case); what was important was that the loser appeal to the Fifth Circuit. The decision in such an appeal, in turn, would then almost certainly be appealed to the U.S. Supreme Court. Indeed, the central purpose of the *Hopwood* suit was to force the Supreme Court to review *Bakke* and, in the hopes of CIR, overturn that decision.

The *Hopwood* decision went well beyond overturning the admissions process at the law school of the University of Texas at Austin. It explicitly stated that the *Bakke* decision of the U.S. Supreme Court was no longer governing law, in effect overturning the Supreme Court. Most legal observers thought that the U.S. Supreme Court would have to agree to review *Hopwood*, if for no other reason than to reestablish its hegemony over the Fifth Circuit. Most astonishingly, the Supreme Court refused to take the case. There followed a series of legal maneuvers over the next several years with the Supreme Court in late June 2001 again declining to hear the case. Finally, on November 27, 2001, the University of Texas formally abandoned the *Hopwood* case.

As part of its effort to compensate for the loss of affirmative action under *Hopwood*, the state of Texas adopted a Top Ten-Percent plan in 1997 (it took effect for fall 1998). Nevertheless, as Michael Arnone noted in the June 25, 2004, issue of *The Chronicle of Higher Education*, minority freshman enrollment at Texas A&M at College Station dropped from 18.8 percent in fall 1995 to 12.6 percent in fall 2003. Although the Top Ten-Percent policy has significant drawbacks, UT Austin, however, did benefit from it, seeing its minority freshman enrollment actually increase from 17.5 percent in fall 1995 to 20.6 percent in fall 2003.

Florida. In 1999, Ward Connerly took his Proposition 209 campaign to Florida and began an initiative campaign to qualify a measure similar to 209 for the November 2000 ballot. Governor Jeb Bush, George W. Bush's younger brother, moved to head off Connerly's campaign by proposing that the state end the practice of considering race in public university admissions and replace that practice with a guarantee that the top twenty percent of the graduates of each high school in the state be guaranteed a place at one of the ten public universities in Florida. Bush called this policy One Florida but also referred to it as "The Talented Twenty Program." It seemed clear that Republican strategists believed that having a Connerly measure on the November ballot would damage the presidential chances of the Republican nominee George W. Bush. Jeb Bush denied any such connection to One Florida.

Governor Bush ended the consideration of race and ethnicity in public university admissions by executive decree. He then put great political pressure on the University Board of Trustees to approve One Florida. The Board approved the policy but, because of a sit-in in the governor's office, did not do so until February 2000. That same month, the Florida chapter of the National Association for the Advancement of Colored People (NAACP) challenged One Florida in court. In mid-July 2000, an administrative law judge ruled against the NAACP, and the policy took effect for the fall semester, which was to begin just a few weeks later. Immediately after the implementation of One Florida, the enrollment of African American freshmen at the Flagship University of Florida in Gainesville began to drop sharply.

Affirmative action in Florida's public universities was therefore ended not by initiative as in California and Washington, nor by legal decision as in Texas, but by gubernatorial fiat—in much the same way that Pete Wilson in California pushed Special Policy 1 (SP-1), the measure that ended affirmative action in University of California admissions even before Proposition 209 was voted on, through the UC Regents in July 1995. Private colleges and universities in Florida remain free to consider race and ethnicity as part of their admissions criteria should they choose to do so.

Georgia. Under the leadership of President Michael Adams, the University of Georgia at Athens had developed aggressive affirmative action admissions policies in the 1990s. These policies were challenged in several different lawsuits, and in the late 1990s and in July 2000, U.S.

District Judge B. Avant Edenfield ruled against the University of Georgia in two different cases. In the first case, Edenfield ruled in favor of plaintiff Kirby Tracy and against the admissions process that was in effect at the University of Georgia from 1990 through 1995. Edenfield went out of his way to attack the process, even though it was no longer in effect at the time of his ruling. In the second case, called *Johnson/Bogrow v. Board of Regents*, Edenfield ruled in July 2000 that the university's consideration of race in its fall 1999 freshman admissions process was unconstitutional, flatly rejecting the university's argument that racial diversity and integration were compelling reasons to justify the consideration of race in the university's admissions process. Edenfield found the University of Georgia process to be in compliance with *Bakke* but, as did the justices in the Fifth Circuit decision in *Hopwood*, ruled that *Bakke* was no longer sound law.

In August 2000, the university decided to appeal this decision to the Eleventh Circuit and to suspend its consideration of race in subsequent years while the appeal was pending. Edenfield's decision, therefore, in effect ended affirmative action in University of Georgia admissions, until the resolution of the appeal. A year later, on August 28, 2001, a three-judge panel of the U.S. Court of Appeals for the Eleventh Circuit also ruled against the university, creating a precedent for that Circuit, which includes Alabama, Florida, and Georgia. During this time period, the university had settled two other reverse discrimination lawsuits with fourteen plaintiffs who had sued the university over their fall 2000 denial of admission, in order to minimize confusion with the appeal of *Johnson/Bogrow*.

Early on in these legal battles, President Adams had vowed publicly to take the case all the way to the U.S. Supreme Court in order to resolve the conflicting opinions and laws governing the use of race in university admissions and to clarify the legal status of affirmative action. Adams has been a strong defender of affirmative action and he has been supported by Stephen Portch, the chancellor of the University System of Georgia, and by Chair of the Board of Regents Glenn White. In November, however, just a few weeks after the appellate court ruling, Adams said that the university would not appeal that decision to the

U.S. Supreme Court. Three weeks later, on November 29, 2001, Adams announced that the university would eliminate the use of race in its fall 2002 freshman admissions process.

Adams clearly struggled over whether or not to take the case to the U.S. Supreme Court. On the one hand, if the university were not to appeal, affirmative action at the University of Georgia would be dead, and Adams would be criticized as a less-than-ardent supporter of affirmative action after all. On the other, if the university appealed the case and lost, the Supreme Court would have an opportunity to overturn *Bakke* and eliminate affirmative action across the entire country. Many legal observers and supporters of affirmative action admired Adams' courage and determination to take the case all the way to the U.S. Supreme Court. At the same time, many of these same people thought that pushing to the Supreme Court was a bad idea because of the clumsiness of the freshman admissions process the university was trying to defend and the likelihood that the university would lose.

Over time, a consensus emerged among supporters of affirmative action that the best cases to take to the Supreme Court were the cases pending against the law school and the freshman admissions process at the University of Michigan, *Grutter v. Bollinger* and *Gratz v. Bollinger*, rather than *Johnson/Bogrow* from Georgia or *Hopwood* from Texas. Lots of people worked feverishly to convince Adams that affirmative action across the country would be much better served by the university letting the appellate decision stand. That, of course, would have been facile for people outside the state of Georgia to say, but, with the outcome of *Grutter*, it is clear that he made an astute decision under the most difficult circumstances.

Washington (again). When the Supreme Court refused to hear *Hopwood* in late 1996, Greve and other staff at the Center for Individual Rights were extremely disappointed. CIR then solicited lawsuits against the flagship public universities in two other states, Washington and Michigan, in which CIR attorneys felt there was some legal vulnerability in university admission practices and where a majority of the federal judges was clearly hostile to affirmative action.

At the University of Washington, a white applicant who was denied admission to the law school filed suit in March 1997, supported by the Center for Individual Rights. In that case, *Smith v. University of Washington Law School*, attorneys for the plaintiff argued that the school employed different admissions standards for white and minority applicants. This case moved back and forth between Federal District Court and the Ninth Circuit Court of Appeals. On December 4, 2000, a three-judge panel of appellate judges ruled that diversity, as Sara Hebel wrote in *The Chronicle of Higher Education*, "can be an adequate justification for public colleges to use race as a factor in deciding whom to admit." The decision explicitly reaffirmed *Bakke* as governing law in such matters and, in what seemed to be a message deliberately aimed at the Fifth Circuit Court and at Judge Edenfield in Georgia, pointedly refused to overturn *Bakke*. Writing for the panel, Judge Ferdinand Fernandez, described by Bob Egelko in the *San Francisco Chronicle* as "one of the court's most conservative judges," wrote, "We, therefore, leave it to the Supreme Court to declare that the *Bakke* rationale regarding university admissions policies has become moribund, if it has. We will not." On May 29, 2001, the U.S. Supreme Court declined to review Smith, letting stand the appellate court's decision that race could be considered in college and university admissions. Coupled with its refusal to review *Hopwood*, this action meant that the Supreme Court had let stand two diametrically opposed federal appeals court decisions.

Despite that appellate court ruling, the University of Washington was still subject to Initiative 200 and thus unable to use race in its admissions decision. The decision was important, however, because it reaffirmed *Bakke* throughout the Ninth Circuit, which includes Alaska, Arizona, Hawaii, Idaho, Montana, Nevada, and Oregon, plus Washington and California, where I-200 and Proposition 209 already banned public colleges and universities from considering race, but private colleges and universities were not.

Michigan. In Michigan, conservative state legislators helped the Center for Individual Rights by running ads asking for white students who believed that the University of Michigan at Ann Arbor had discriminated against them. CIR ended up supporting plaintiffs in two lawsuits against the university, one at the freshman level, called *Gratz v. Bollinger* (originally called *Gratz and Hamacher v. Bollinger*), and a second at the graduate level against the law school, called *Grutter v. Bollinger*. (These, of course, are the two cases on which the Supreme Court ultimately ruled June 23, 2003.) In an unusual move, General Motors filed briefs in both lawsuits in late July 2000 defending the university's use of affirmative action as necessary to build a diverse work force. According to Peter Schmidt in the November 24, 2000, edition of *The Chronicle of Higher Education*, twenty Fortune 500 companies filed a similar brief on behalf of the university in October 2000.

On November 17, 2000, Judge Patrick Duggan heard arguments from attorneys on the two sides in *Gratz v. Bollinger*, each urging an immediate decision in their favor rather than letting the suit go to trial. The Associated Press, in an article that appeared in the November 18, 2000, *San Francisco Chronicle*, quoted Duggan as saying, "Without question we all know this case is going to a higher court after I hear it." On December 13, 2000, Judge Duggan, who, according to Jody Wilgoren in *The New York Times*, was appointed by Ronald Reagan, issued a ruling in the case, finding that the university was justified in considering race in its admissions process because of the educational benefits of diversity. In making this ruling, Duggan found the process used by the university from 1995 to 1998 to be unconstitutional according to the standards of *Bakke*. He found, however, that the process adopted in 1999 to be narrowly tailored and permissible within the bounds of *Bakke*.

This decision was a major victory for the University of Michigan and for the supporters of affirmative action across the country. It reflected careful political work done by the university in building corporate support for its case and in relying on and then expanding the contemporary research base that underscores the value of diversity in higher education.

Less than four months later, however, U.S. District Judge Bernard

Friedman issued a decision in *Grutter v. Bollinger*, the lawsuit against the University of Michigan Law School. Friedman ruled that the law school's admission policy was unconstitutional and he rejected the university's argument that racial diversity is a compelling state interest that justifies the consideration of race in the admissions process. That decision left the university with a set of diametrically opposed rulings. These rulings—support for the freshman admission policy and rejection of the law school policy—would turn out to be exactly the opposite of the U.S. Supreme Court decisions in those cases.

After a set of appeals in both cases and a series of legal maneuvers, the Sixth Circuit Court of Appeals agreed to hear and consider both cases at the same time and to do so *en banc,* meaning that all nine judges of the Sixth Circuit would hear the cases, rather than the usual three-judge panel. The initial *en banc* hearing took place in Cincinnati in early December 2001. This unusual step consolidated the overall appeals process because the next step after a review by a three-judge panel would be to request an *en banc* hearing. On May 14, 2002, the Sixth Circuit ruled in favor of the University of Michigan Law School in *Grutter v. Bollinger*, in a bitterly disputed 5-to-4 decision. The court also said that it would rule on *Gratz v. Bollinger* at some later date. The *Grutter* decision meant that two federal appeals courts, the Sixth and the Ninth, had now ruled in favor of affirmative action and that two, the Fifth and the Eleventh, had ruled against it.

The decisions in *Smith v. University of Washington Law School, Gratz v. Bollinger,* and *Grutter v. Bollinger* were tremendous boosts for supporters of affirmative action, and they helped offset the momentum that opponents of affirmative action had received from the *Hopwood* decision and from Judge Edenfield and, later, from Judge Friedman.

Pennsylvania. For a brief period, Pennsylvania also seemed to be considering eliminating the use of race in university admissions. In April 2000, Jeffrey Selingo reported in *The Chronicle of Higher Education* that the Pennsylvania state-university system would consider adopting a policy that would "automatically admit the top fifteen percent of graduates from every public high school in the state." The policy under discussion would apply to fourteen state institutions but not to four institutions that are described as "state-related institutions": Lincoln University, Pennsylvania State University, Temple University, and the University of Pittsburgh. A spokesperson for the system emphasized that the fifteen-percent plan would not replace affirmative action. In the November 3, 2000, edition of *The Chronicle of Higher Education*, Selingo reported that the state-university system had dropped its plan to admit the top fifteen percent of each high school graduating class in the state. According to Selingo, "Officials decided to abandon the fifteen-percent plan because of negative publicity surrounding similar plans in Florida and Texas, and after the U.S. Commission on Civil Rights condemned such plans as a replacement for affirmative action." Instead, the state-university system in Pennsylvania "may guarantee admission to students who score high on a statewide standardized test and take a college preparatory curriculum."

Everywhere else. For all the public and private colleges and universities in states other than those named above, for all the public and private colleges and universities in Georgia except the University of Georgia at Athens, and for the private colleges in California, Washington, and Florida, *Bakke* continued to be governing law, pending the outcomes of *Gratz v. Bollinger* and *Grutter v. Bollinger* in Michigan. Sara Hebel, in the November 24, 2000, issue of *The Chronicle of Higher Education,* provided an excellent summary of the lawsuits working their way through courts in Georgia, Texas, Michigan, and Washington, called "Courting a Place in Legal History." In discussing the Supreme Court's refusal to review *Smith v. University of Washington,* Ben Gose in *The Chronicle of Higher Education* quoted attorney Martin Michaelson: "It's been a very long time since [the justices] looked at the *Bakke* question. They'll probably take another look at affirmative action in college admissions in the next few years, but I would not predict which case they'll take."

The extraordinary range of conflicting judicial decisions on affirmative action created a nightmare for admissions policy-makers, not just in the states directly affected by the individual court decisions but in other states as well where policy-makers tried to figure out what policies might survive legal challenge within their own federal district. That uncertainty was magnified by the realization that so much depended on which judge or group of judges within a particular federal district happened to be appointed to a particular case. This was a time of remarkable confusion, and a contemporary map of the status of affirmative action made a standard Mercator map projection seem unified and symmetrical. And, of course, there was the 800-pound gorilla waiting in the wings: the U.S. Supreme Court.

WHERE WAS THE SUPREME COURT?

As noted, the *Hopwood* decision went well beyond overturning the admissions process at the University of Texas at Austin Law School, in essence overturning *Bakke*. Then, Judge Edenfield in Georgia sided with the Fifth Circuit in also discrediting *Bakke*. At the same time, Judge Duggan in the University of Michigan case, the Ninth Circuit Court of Appeals in the University of Washington case, and the Sixth Circuit Court in *Grutter v. Bollinger* all upheld *Bakke*. With the federal appeals courts divided at 2 to 2, the polarization among federal court judges and, more important, three-judge panels of federal appellate courts, plus the Sixth Circuit Court's 5-to-4 split in its *en banc* ruling in *Grutter* seemed to put enormous pressure on the U.S. Supreme Court to accept a relevant case and revisit the court's 1978 decision in *Bakke*. Justice Ruth Bader Ginsburg, as Ben Gose pointed out in the July 6, 2001, issue of *The Chronicle of Higher Education*, said in a statement, which she issued when the Supreme Court first refused to review *Hopwood*, that the court would wait for a program "genuinely in controversy." That seemed to many observers a truly bizarre comment because it was difficult to imagine a case more genuine in controversy than *Hopwood*, and the Court's refusal to review that case set off a period of deep legal confusion.

Some observers speculated, however, that the Justices were waiting for a national consensus on the issue of affirmative action to evolve rather than adjudicating the issue for the entire country. This "follow, don't lead" strategy seemed in some ways to enable the Court to directly avoid its responsibilities. Given the deep and abiding divisions over race in this country, however, it also seemed naïve to think that some sort of clear consensus might emerge anytime soon. It may also have been that the Justices realized how divided they were on the issue and that they—naïvely, as it turned out—hoped to avoid polarizing the court.

Several Court observers believed that the Justices would split four votes to four votes with Sandra Day O'Connor the swing vote, a situation very similar to that in 1978 when the court, ruling on *Bakke*, split four to four, with Justice Lewis Powell casting the swing vote in the two separate parts of that decision. In *Grutter*, this analysis proved accurate. At the same time however, other commentators looked at the Court's vote in adjudicating the U.S. presidential election in December 2000 and concluded that O'Connor might not be a swing vote at all. This point of view held that the justices would almost certainly vote along political lines as they clearly did in the presidential election.

By early 2000, however, almost all of the other contending lawsuits had fallen away in one manner or another, leaving the principal focus—and speculation—on *Gratz v. Bollinger* and *Grutter v. Bollinger*. Finally, in December 2002, the Supreme Court announced that it would review *Grutter v. Bollinger* and that, at the same time, it would also review *Gratz v. Bollinger*, even though the Sixth Circuit had not yet issued its decision on this case.

More than perhaps any other area of the law, affirmative action has triggered judicial opinions that seem to have been powerfully affected by the personal views of the judges in question: Thelton Henderson, the Chief Judge of the Ninth Federal Court in San Francisco who suspended Proposition 209 in December 1996 for what seemed to be remarkably thin reasons; Judges Kleinfeld, O'Scannlain, and Levy, the three-judge motions panel of the Ninth Circuit Court of Appeals which overturned Henderson's injunction in harsh, highly critical language;

Judge Jerry E. Smith, writing also for Judges Weiner and DeMoss of the Fifth Circuit Court of Appeals in the opinion in *Hopwood v. Texas* that scathingly criticized both affirmative action and the *Bakke* opinion; and Judge B. Avant Edenfield in Georgia, who blasted the University of Georgia's admissions policies. The behavior of these judges and the tone of some of their opinions recall the semi-famous quote about statesmanship: "Diplomacy consists of doing what you want and citing history afterwards." Here, on both sides of the affirmative action issue, what we have often seems to be this: "Jurisprudence consists of doing what you want and citing legal precedent afterward—or citing nothing at all if you don't feel like it."

It is vitally important that we learn from what has happened to minority enrollments at flagship public universities in the states or federal court jurisdictions in which the consideration of race and ethnicity in university admissions was eliminated. In particular, the huge declines in the enrollment of African American, Latino, and Native American freshmen in the flagship public universities of California, Florida, and at Texas A&M should be cause for serious concern, particularly given the extraordinary racial and ethnic diversity among their overall state populations.

It is also important to remember the chaos and uncertainty that resulted from the very aggressive decisions by some federal judges. It is certain that there will continue to be legal challenges to affirmative action as it has been permitted under *Grutter*. As these new cases come forward, one has to hope that federal courts will see themselves bound by the parameters set out in *Grutter* and *Gratz* and that they will avoid the temptation to lapse into a kind of balkanized legal geography where affirmative action law is determined federal circuit by federal circuit by federal circuit.

4 PROBLEMS WITH EARLY AFFIRMATIVE ACTION POLICIES

As colleges and universities consider which course of action to take following the *Grutter* and *Gratz* Supreme Court decisions, they would do well to rely on the body of expert legal knowledge and advice that has been created since those decisions, and to avoid the damaging errors made by institutions in the first two decades of affirmative action in admissions. A most useful tool in avoiding these kinds of errors is *Preserving Diversity in Higher Education: A Manual on Admissions Policies and Procedures After the University of Michigan Decisions*, a comprehensive analysis published in 2004 by three San Francisco law firms (Bingham McCutchen LLP, Morrison & Foerster LLP, and Heller Ehrman White & McAuliffe LLP). Another helpful source is *Diversity in Higher Education: A Strategic Planning and Policy Manual Regarding Federal Law in Admissions, Financial Aid, and Outreach*, written by Arthur L. Coleman and Scott R. Palmer of Nixon Peabody LLP, and published by the College Board.

One reason why the struggle over affirmative action in university admissions has been so bitter is that in the 1970s and 1980s many public universities adopted admissions policies that were clumsy or much too broad. Part of the explanation for this ineptness is that many of these public universities in a remarkably short time went from being unselective—that is, able to admit all of their qualified applicants—to being selective—that is, having to choose among qualified applicants and therefore denying admission to students who could clearly succeed if given an opportunity to enroll.

In addition, many public and private institutions adopted affirmative action polices or processes that were not carefully crafted in light of the *Bakke* decision. One explanation for this lack of care was the overwhelming sense of urgency felt by some colleges and universities to sharply increase the numbers of African American, Latino, and Native American students they enrolled. In their sense of urgency and haste, some colleges and universities simply forgot about *Bakke*. Another part of the explanation is that there was no body of expert legal knowledge and advice, such as the compliance manuals listed above, for institutions that wished to engage in aggressive affirmative action in admissions. Even when an institution wished to pay careful attention to the legality of its admissions policies, it was not easy to do so. As a result, colleges and universities often modified their often crude affirmative action admissions polices in response to equally crude criticism of those policies, criticism that came from public commentators, the Office for Civil Rights (OCR) in the U.S. Department of Education, or law suits. There was often the feeling of staying one step ahead of the sheriff.

Affirmative action in university admissions is, of course, most important for institutions that receive more applications from qualified students than they can admit—that is, selective colleges and universities. One reason why many of the early affirmative action admissions policies were somewhat crudely formulated is that most of the colleges and universities that adopted those policies—specifically public universities—did not start out as selective. In many cases, they became selective before their policy-makers had been able to think through the implications of that new status.

California—UC Berkeley in particular—makes an interesting case study. UC Berkeley did not become selective until the 1970s. Although its academic reputation had soared prior to World War II and particularly after the war, the campus had been able to admit every freshman applicant who met the published minimum eligibility requirements. Under the Master Plan for Higher Education in California, the University of California's minimum admission requirements (courses, grades, and test scores) were designed to identify the top 12.5 percent of the students graduating from California high schools. In the mid-1960s, the UC system opened new campuses at Santa Cruz, San Diego, and Irvine in order to keep up with rising demand for places in the system. Through the fall 1972 freshman admission cycle, any California resident who qualified within the top 12.5 percent of the state's high school graduates and who applied to UC Berkeley was admitted. In fall 1973, Berkeley, for the first time, turned away some freshman applicants who were UC-eligible.

UC Berkeley's international reputation and prestige and its history of liberal policies and actions meant that 1973 became an important marker in the struggle over affirmative action in university admissions. As long as there appeared to be enough admission places to go around at Berkeley and other highly sought-after colleges and universities, most people simply didn't concern themselves with the role of race in admissions. And, in fact, there was little need up to this point for the University of California to take race into account at the undergraduate level except in programs such as Admission by Exception (which admitted a small portion of students—including athletes—who were not UC-eligible) and the Educational Opportunity Program (which focused on students from low-income families whose parents had not attended college).

In the span of just fifteen years, however, Berkeley went from admitting all eligible freshman applicants to being a highly selective university (defined as one which admits fewer than fifty percent of its applicants)—and not just a highly selective university but also a highly selective *public* university. This shift was accelerated by a 1986 change in UC system-wide policy that permitted an applicant for the first time to apply to as many UC campuses as he or she wished, rather than to just a single campus, as had been the case for many years. UC Berkeley went from 11,000 freshman applicants for fall 1985 to more than 19,000 freshman applicants for fall 1986. By fall 2002, the campus had received 36,414 freshman applications and was able to admit only about 8,500 students—23.3 percent of its freshman applicants.

The degree of selectivity was also powerfully affected in 1984 when the UC Regents, on the recommendation of the Board of Admissions and Relations with Schools—or BOARS, the system-wide faculty admissions committee—enacted an honors grade-point policy. This policy awarded students an extra grade point for each honors-level course taken in the last two years of high school (now the last three years) in the calculation of their grade-point averages for UC. An "A" in such a class, for example, was now worth five grade points, rather than the usual four, a "B" was worth four, and a "C" worth three. That meant that, at least mathematically, it was now possible for a student to have a GPA of 5.0.

Two things immediately happened. The number of students in California high schools taking Advanced Placement courses, the most common type of honors-level class, began to increase rapidly. That was the intent of the policy. The other thing that happened, however, was that the number of applicants to UC with GPAs of 4.0 and above also began to shoot up. By fall 1998, for example, 13,700 freshman applicants to UC Berkeley out of a total of 30,042—45.6 percent—had GPAs of 4.0 and above. By fall 2002, the number had grown to more than 17,500 out of a total of 36,414 freshman applicants—or forty-eight percent. For fall 2002, Berkeley admitted just under 8,500 students. That meant that Berkeley had more than twice as many freshman applicants with GPAs of 4.0 and above than it could admit.

Because of the honors grade-point policy, most of those students with GPAs of 4.0 and above did not have straight A's, yet a curious thing happens to many students when they hit that 4.0 mark. They—and, more often, their parents—begin to think of themselves as "perfect," and their sense of entitlement expands exponentially. Denying thousands and thousands of freshman applicants with GPAs of 4.0 and above, as Berkeley has done for many years, creates political and public relations problems of enormous magnitude for the campus.

Although the United States had long had a small number of highly selective private universities, the highly selective public university was a new phenomenon and carried with it unanticipated problems and challenges.

THE LIABILITIES OF BEING A HIGHLY SELECTIVE
PUBLIC UNIVERSITY

Some of the differences between both selective private and public institutions are evident. People who pay taxes to support a public university system over the years believe, often quite reasonably, that their children are entitled to places there. Denying out-of-state residents is a relatively low-risk activity for public universities, but they deny tax-paying state residents at their peril. The freshman applicant pools of the University of Virginia or the University of North Carolina at Chapel Hill, both public universities, contain a large proportion of out-of-state students. At Berkeley, however, the composition of the freshman applicant pool is about ninety percent California residents, and at UCLA, the figure is even higher.

The state-resident dilemma is compounded by the fact that parents who graduated from Berkeley when it was admitting all eligible applicants have a particularly difficult time understanding that the campus has become so selective, and that among the large number of freshman applicants it turns away will be some exceptional students—perhaps even their sons or daughters. Put another way, most people expect to be denied by Stanford or Harvard, but these same people are often outraged when Berkeley or UCLA turns them down. That view of the elite private universities is a bit like a paraphrase of an old Groucho Marx line: "How could I respect a university that would admit someone like me?" This humility, however, seldom extends to the highly selective publics.

The scrutiny of highly selective public universities is another important difference. Private universities have long been able to screen their admissions processes and sensitive data from public review. Public universities, however, are often bound by public records acts or so-called sunshine laws that make every part of their operations, except confidential personnel actions—open to the public. This exposure has contributed significantly to the fact that the attacks on affirmative action have centered almost entirely on public universities. Critics have access to information and data that they usually cannot obtain on selective private universities.

In addition, the public universities are still significantly dependent on their state legislatures for their operating budgets. This dependence means that legislators are often extremely interested in admissions issues, not just on the public policy level but on the level of the individual applicant because many of the tax-paying parents of denied applicants do not hesitate to contact them in the heat of their anger and disappointment.

Although public universities receive some portion of their financial support from their legislatures, that support had been declining sharply over the past twenty years. That decline, in turn, has caused public universities to build huge private fund-raising machines to compensate for the loss of public money. Increasingly, potential large donors want not just a "naming opportunity" on a new building or fountain in return for their millions but an "admissions opportunity," that is, preferential consideration for a son or daughter, niece or nephew, or neighbor in the freshman admissions process. Private universities, of course, have long given such preference with little or no public criticism. Such preference from public universities, however, not only angers a great many people but also raises important public policy questions.

ADMISSIONS AS A CLERICAL TASK

Like many other public universities subsequently, UC Berkeley in 1973 found itself in a noticeably awkward situation when it first received more qualified applicants than it could admit. With no experience of its own to draw upon, the campus had to decide on what basis to choose some qualified applicants over others. Although responsibility for admission standards has been delegated by the UC Board of Regents to university faculty (not everyone in the university's senior administration agrees on this point), the faculty up until 1973 mostly had to concentrate on making recommendations to the Board of Regents on minimum eligibility. One result of this situation was that faculty admissions committees on individual campuses were often relatively passive or inactive.

The truth is that, until fall 1973, an admissions officer at Berkeley was, in fact, a clerk whose job was to compare an applicant's transcript to the UC-eligibility requirements and determine whether or not that applicant had satisfied them. Depending on the determinants, the clerk either admitted or denied the student.

In many cases, this evaluation was a difficult task. Many years earlier, the university had made a bold and admirable policy decision to publish as widely as possible exactly what it would take to qualify for the University of California. Every student in California, in theory, could look at the list of required college-prep courses needed (called at the time the "a through f pattern" because the courses were listed in outline form) and the grades needed in those courses (roughly a B average) and know exactly where he or she stood. Very quickly, however, the complexity of the universe caught up with the idealism of the faculty, and thick binders, called "Working Rules," were developed ("What if I made a D grade in the first semester of Algebra 1 but an A in the second semester—Can I get credit for the first semester?"). This unintended complexity caused many of these admission evaluators to become guardians of an arcane lore and to feel like nineteenth-century scriveners or, perhaps more accurately, medieval Irish monks preserving the legacy of western civilization. The complexity also created nightmares for high school counselors, nightmares that still persist in California high school guidance offices today—at least in those high schools that still have counselors.

A BASIC DILEMMA:
OPERATING EFFICIENCY AND COST CONTAINMENT
VERSUS GREATER FAIRNESS TO ALL APPLICANTS

Selective private universities often celebrate the fact that they read all of their applicants individually and carefully. Most of them probably do so—although at least a few of them use formulas or indexes to sort and make preliminary judgments. Selective public universities, on the other hand, have often relied on such formulas and indexes or on simple—or in some cases, simplistic—numeric measures to sort their applicants and to partially (or entirely) make admission decisions. This practice has in part been the result of thousands more applicants to flagship public universities than to small elite liberal arts colleges. It's one thing to read 2,300 applications from January to the end of March, but quite another to read 18,000 or—in the case of Berkeley for fall 2002—36,414. In part, the reliance on numbers by the large publics also reflects the impersonal nature of many of these institutions, which were famous until just a few years ago for their proud, twisted Darwinian gardening metaphor: "We weed out half our freshman class!"

More than anything, however, the large public universities' reliance on indexes and formulas is the result of the tension between the imperative of operational/budget efficiency and the goal of treating every applicant fairly and as an individual. In the large research universities, there are many, many competitors for budget dollars and, in most of these institutions, admissions is pretty far down the list of institutional priorities (Berkeley has been a distinct exception). No one argues that his or her institutions should be unfair to applicants, only that the university doesn't have the resources—that is, the money and the will—to read each applicant individually and fully. It is interesting to note, however, that this attitude has a way of shifting as an institution becomes more exposed to legal challenges and/or as the consideration of race and ethnicity is eliminated from the admissions process, either by the passage of a law (as in Proposition 209 in California or Initiative 200 in Washington); by a court case (as in the *Hopwood* decision in Texas); or by executive pressure (as was the case in Florida).

Courts have never accepted the argument of burdensome workload as a justification for illegal practices or as an argument why a different process cannot be undertaken. Justice O'Connor makes this point emphatically in her majority opinion in *Grutter*. Nevertheless, not nearly enough attention has been paid to the operational imperatives that are forced on admissions offices by senior administrators and budget officers. It is quite difficult in most large universities to get the attention of the president or chancellor and to convince that person that the need for good practices and the legal risks surrounding admission are important enough to take a significant portion of that institution's budget. In fact, there is already in many colleges and universities a significant degree of admissions-envy—even, in some cases, rancor—because of the media attention currently devoted to college admissions and to the modest budget increases to admissions offices that have in some cases accompanied that attention.

A CLUMSY TRANSFORMATION

When Berkeley began to receive more UC-eligible applicants than it could admit, the director of admissions and records (the "records" part was the Office of the Registrar) was Robert Bailey, whose background was not in selective admissions but in records management, an area in which he was highly respected. As the campus began to turn away eligible freshman applicants, Bailey, working with a docile faculty admissions committee, developed an admissions process that relied heavily on a test-score formula to admit most of the freshman class without having to read actual transcripts. Bailey then ranked all of the remaining applicants in descending order by grade-point average. He then counted down that ranking to the point where, in combination with the test-score eligible admits, he would fill ninety percent of his admission target and then draw a cut-off line. The remaining ten percent of the spaces he held in reserve for students admitted through special programs, including affirmative action (at that time, African American, Chicano, Filipino, Latino, and Native American students). It's still disconcerting to think that an institution of Berkeley's stature used such a clumsy, unsound method for admitting its freshmen not so long ago.

The distinction between Chicano and Latino has contributed to the confusion that sometimes affects affirmative action discussions. For both political and policy reasons, UC Berkeley and the other campuses in the UC system have, since the 1960s, distinguished between Mexican

Americans ("Chicanos") and other peoples originating in Central and South America ("Latinos"). This distinction became particularly important at Berkeley in the early 1990s when the faculty admissions committee voted to end affirmative action preferences for Latinos but to preserve them for Chicanos. The *Los Angeles Times*, on the other hand, uses the term "Latino" to describe both Mexican Americans and peoples originating in Central American and South America. As noted in Chapter 1, that is also the practice that this book follows. The term "Hispanic" is used only when that is the term used by a specific source to which the text refers—for example, the Demographic Research Unit of the California State Department of Finance.

THE EARLY 1980S: IRA MICHAEL HEYMAN AND THE DIVERSITY IMPERATIVE

In 1980, Ira Michael Heyman was named chancellor of UC Berkeley. At about the same time, demographers had begun to track huge racial and ethnic shifts in the population of California. Their conclusion was stark, even if grossly overstated at the time: colleges and universities, particularly in California, would have to make up for the anticipated losses of white students by enrolling many, many more minority students—or perish.

Prior to Heyman's inauguration, Berkeley had been working steadily, though perhaps somewhat unimaginatively, to recruit African American, Chicano, Filipino, Latino, and Native American students (Asian American students other than Filipinos even then made up a sizeable portion of the undergraduate student body). Heyman, however, made it clear that racial and ethnic diversity at Berkeley would be one of his highest priorities.

Heyman, for both pragmatic and moral reasons, was determined to increase the enrollment of African American, Chicano, Filipino, Latino, and Native American students at Berkeley. The most significant step he took was to create the Task Force on Minority Recruitment, which soon added "Enrollment" and then "Retention" to its name. The Task

Force, co-chaired by Assistant Vice Chancellor B. Thomas (Bud) Travers and Special Assistant to the Vice Chancellor for Undergraduate Affairs Francisco Hernandez, brought together staff from across the campus who had anything to do with student recruitment and enrollment. There was a sense of high moral purpose to the group and people worked diligently. The Task Force re-examined every aspect of student recruitment and admission and adopted pretty much anything that could be changed to benefit underrepresented minority students. One of the first and most sweeping changes was a decision that every UC-eligible African American, Chicano, Filipino, Latino, and Native American student would be guaranteed admission to Berkeley if he or she applied to the campus.

Even though the United States Supreme Court had issued its *Bakke* decision just three years before the Task Force was formed, no one on the Task Force ever referred to *Bakke* or asked if a particular step being contemplated was consistent with Justice Powell's opinion that race could be a plus among applicants who were similarly qualified, which was the central finding of that decision. Berkeley, like many other colleges and universities across the country, just pretty much forgot about *Bakke* in its sense of urgency to solve a complex and critically important problem. At Berkeley, this amnesia lasted until the late 1980s (the campus, for example, ended guaranteed admission for UC-eligible underrepresented minority students for the fall 1990 admission cycle). In other places, it lasted much longer.

ONE COST OF POORLY THOUGHT-OUT ADMISSIONS POLICIES: THE ASIAN AMERICAN ADMISSION CONTROVERSY

As a direct result of Berkeley's inexperience in thinking about and crafting a careful, balanced freshman admission policy, especially one that took into account all of the effects of an aggressive affirmative action effort, the campus in 1984 stumbled into what became known as the Asian American admission controversy. From that year until 1989, the campus learned painful lessons about the danger of arrogance and political ineptitude, about the newly emerging political clout and savvy of Asian Americans, and about the intensity of feeling and determination that could be summoned by racial and ethnic groups that had experienced firsthand and repeatedly the ugly history of racism in this country.

The increase in underrepresented minority freshman applicants who were guaranteed admission if they were UC-eligible, and the increase in overall freshman applications began to put substantially heavy pressure on the Admissions Office, which was not accustomed to the harsh phone calls from the angry parents of denied applicants and the other kinds of pressures that are a fact of life for selective institutions. Bailey, the director of the Office of Admissions and Records, cast about for a way to ease some of that pressure and hit upon what turned out to be a disastrous solution: ending guaranteed admissions to all students who qualified for EOP—the Educational Opportunity Program. EOP targeted low-income, first-generation college-going applicants and included students from all races and ethnicities. Bailey decided that for fall 1984 the campus should end that guarantee for all EOP students who were not African American, Chicano, Filipino, Latino, and Native American—that is, for low-income white and Asian American students other than Filipinos. Because there were many more poor Asian American applicants than poor white applicants within the EOP pool, this decision had a disparate and profound effect on Asian Americans. Not anticipating the disparate effect of this decision was a major error.

At the same time, the Office of Planning and Analysis, which set enrollment targets as part of its responsibility for managing overall enrollment, decided that Berkeley should enroll a smaller freshman class in fall 1984. The combination of fewer low-income Asian Americans admitted through EOP (largely immigrants) and fewer total places in the fall freshman class meant that if one compared the raw number of fall 1993 Asian American freshmen against the raw number for fall 1984, one found a drop of twenty-four percent. That comparison, however, is statistically questionable because it does not acknowledge the smaller enrollment of fall 1984. A more accurate comparison—percentage of each year's class—shows that Asian American enrollment declined from 26.7

percent of the fall 1983 class to 23.5 percent of the fall 1984. That drop of 3.2 percentage points should still have been cause for scrutiny, but it was the twenty-four percent figure that Asian American advocates cited over and over, suggesting how quickly the debate became political.

Almost immediately, Asian American community groups and civic leaders formed the Asian American Task Force on University Admissions, and, in a noteworthy strategic move, named Judges Ken Kawaichi and Lillian Sing as co-chairs. The Task Force, particularly member Henry Der, pressed the university greatly, and university administrators made a major blunder: in their arrogance, they didn't take the Task Force seriously, and they thought they could stonewall. That attitude began a harsh political lesson for Berkeley that lasted five years.

Once Berkeley revealed its arrogance, the Task Force put into effect an extraordinary set of political and media connections that resulted, among other things, in a full-scale investigation into freshman admissions at Berkeley by the Auditor General of the State of California. In addition, investigations instigated by the Task Force uncovered a 1983 report by a campus staff member that claimed some administrators and staff felt there were too many Asians at Berkeley and then, after a long and ugly argument between the Task Force members and campus administrators, located a copy of another memo that established a minimum SAT verbal score of 400 for resident alien freshman applicants without Academic Senate approval. This minimum-score policy had been rescinded after just a single day, however, and no applicant was ever affected by it. The SAT memo was found and produced by Pamela Lee Burnett, a Chinese American woman who at that time served as assistant director of admissions.

Both the 1983 report and the SAT memo were repugnant, but all of the investigations concluded without any widespread, conclusive evidence being uncovered that demonstrated that the university had deliberately attempted to discriminate against Asian American applicants in its freshman admissions process.

On March 1, 1989, Chancellor Heyman and Judges Kawaichi and Sing held a joint press conference during which Heyman apologized to the Task Force and other Asian Americans, not for a pattern of intentional racial discrimination, but for insensitivity in responding to the concerns of the Task Force. Although State Senator Art Torres held a splashy public hearing two weeks later on the issue, it was this press conference—after five years of struggle—that finally ended the so-called "Asian American admission controversy."

It was striking how much damage an institution could sustain in an investigation that took five years and ended with an almost neutral statement about "insensitivity to your concerns"—an investigation that, at least from one point of view, was actually about a three-percentage–point drop in the Asian American portion of the fall 1984 freshman class. Although the results of this investigation were inconclusive, the burden of the investigation was massive and very punitive—a huge workload increase, a pervasive disruption of normal work cycles, and a high degree of tension. And UC Berkeley outreach and admissions officers are even today asked over and over again by Asian American students and parents: "Do you still discriminate against Asians?"

One of the most immediate effects of the controversy was that Heyman removed Assistant Vice Chancellor Travers and appointed Patrick S. Hayashi, who had served as special assistant to Heyman, to be associate vice chancellor for admissions and enrollment. Hayashi had held a variety of jobs at Berkeley with no clear career trajectory until Heyman had tapped him to serve as special assistant, but he knew nearly all of the members of the coalition aligned against the university in the Asian American admission controversy (he had been born in a Japanese American relocation camp during World War II), and he was an impressive political strategist.

A second effect of the Asian American admission controversy was a skilled political effort by Heyman, Vice Chancellor Roderick Park, and Hayashi to reshape the Academic Senate Admissions Committee and to have this committee produce a formal written document on freshman admission policy at Berkeley. This decision was not fueled solely by the Asian American admission controversy. That controversy had also increased sharply the public and media attention focused on affirmative action as well. It was clear that Berkeley needed (for policy, political, and perhaps legal reasons) a comprehensive philosophical policy statement from the faculty that could be used to govern freshman admission at Berkeley for some time to come.

Professor Jerry Karabel, a respected sociologist who had written extensively on social stratification, affirmative action, and the interconnections of race and economic class in the United States, became chair of the Admissions Committee. Karabel was a fervent supporter of affirmative action—as were the other members of his committee, including the two student members. As chair, Karabel blended the committee members into a single voice and pretty much single-handedly wrote what became *Freshman Admissions at Berkeley: A Policy for the 1990s and Beyond,* quickly shortened to *The Karabel Report.* For the first time, the Admissions Committee set out a series of principles—ten of them—to govern freshman admission at Berkeley:

1. As an institution of international renown and as one of the nation's leading research universities, Berkeley has an obligation to admit students with exceptionally distinguished academic records.

2. As a taxpayer-supported public university, Berkeley must strive to serve all of California's people.

3. Berkeley should actively seek diversity—socio-economic, cultural, ethnic, racial, and geographic—in its student body.

4. Berkeley will absolutely not tolerate quotas or ceilings on the admissions or enrollment of any racial, ethnic, religious, or gender groups.

5. In its admissions criteria, Berkeley will recognize outstanding accomplishment in a variety of spheres, including (but not limited to) art, athletics, debating, drama, and music.

6. While continuing to grant preference to California residents, Berkeley will continue to admit out-of-state students.

7. Berkeley should accept only those students who have reasonable chance of persisting to graduation.

8. The admissions process should include a human element and must not be based on grades and test scores alone.

9. In constructing and altering Berkeley's admission practices, the faculty should insist upon at least a co-equal role with the administration.

10. The admissions criteria and practices of the College of Letters and
    Science as well as those of the professional schools should continue
    to be described in detail and to be made fully available to the public.

In addition, the Report also increased the percentage of students
admitted by Academic Index Score (AIS) from forty to fifty percent;
established flexible target admission ranges for a number of different
groups, including underrepresented minority students; and ended the
practice of guaranteeing admission to every UC-eligible African
American, Chicano, Latino, and Native American student who applied
on time (preference for Filipino applicants had been phased out beginning in the mid-1980s). The Academic Index Score was calculated by
multiplying an applicant's GPA by 1000 and adding the applicant's scores
from the SAT I with three required SAT II tests. (SAT II tests are one-
hour tests in specific academic subjects with a score range of 200 to 800
and are required by many highly selective colleges and universities.) The
maximum Academic Index Score was 8,000 (4,000 possible points on
the GPA portion because the GPA was capped at 4.0 and 4,000 possible points on the test segment).

When *The Karabel Report* was issued on May 19, 1989, the campus
sent copies to everyone it could think of, including major newspapers
and periodicals. *The Washington Post* actually wrote an editorial in praise
of the report, and Andrew Hacker reviewed it in the October 12, 1989,
issue of *The New York Review of Books*—pretty heady attention for a
statement on university freshman admission policy. The reaction to *The
Karabel Report* underscored the increased attention that college admissions was beginning to receive, and the Report placed freshman admission policy at Berkeley on a new—and solid—foundation, bearing the
clear imprimatur of the faculty.

THE ECONOMY GOES DOWN, APPLICATIONS GO UP, AND FEAR REARS ITS UGLY PUBLIC HEAD

Although the Asian American admission controversy was a primary reason why Heyman, Park, and Hayashi wanted more control over under-

graduate admission at Berkeley, it wasn't the only reason. The public debate over affirmative action in general—and criticism of Berkeley's practices in particular—was rapidly increasing as well.

Although Berkeley, and other campuses, had engaged in aggressive affirmative action practices since at least 1980, almost no one ever publicly challenged those policies at high school events such as college information nights until 1988. It was an odd thing, actually. It seemed as if there were a tacit public agreement not to attack affirmative action, but in reality it was probably not so much an agreement as it was palpable social pressure that kept people who disagreed with affirmative action from saying so in public.

That proscription began to change sometime during 1988. For the first time, people would stand up during the question period at high school college nights and say that they opposed affirmative action in university admissions. In those days, it took a lot of courage to do that. Over a fairly short period of time, those statements became stronger and then often quite angry. These viewpoints were paralleled—and perhaps influenced by—articles that appeared in print in 1988. *The Karabel Report*, for example, noted that the fall 1988 issue of *Public Interest* carried a long piece on affirmative action at Berkeley by John Bunzel, who was one of the earliest and most persistent critics of that policy. The Report also pointed out that Donald Werner wrote "College Admissions: Shaky Ethics" for *The New York Times* in June of that year and that James Gibney published "The Berkeley Squeeze" in the April 11, 1988, issue of *The New Republic*.

Sizeable forces contributed to this change in the public conversation, but much of it happened because the California economy plunged into a deep decline at the same time that freshman applications to Berkeley and UCLA were continuing to climb steeply. More applications meant more UC-eligible students denied admission, and the denial of admission in a depressed economy was widely perceived to be badly damaging to a person's life chances. Almost overnight, one saw and heard fear in the faces and voices of students and their parents. Affluent students began saying—and writing in their applications essays—that they were afraid that they wouldn't be able to attain the same standard of living that their parents had enjoyed. In some ways, knowing how many truly poor families there were in California, it was challenging for admissions officers to feel sympathetic, but the fear among applicants and their parents was quite real. It's a fear that is still most present today among high school students and their parents and that largely fuels the high level of anxiety that continues to surround admission to the fifteen or twenty most selective colleges and universities in the country.

And once people began to speak publicly against affirmative action, their criticisms touched a lot of other feelings and attitudes in people. The fear that someone else is getting something that I'm not, coupled with affirmative action and the history of race in the United States, quickly led to acrimony and rancor in both the public and private conversations on college admissions.

THE RIGHT RACE

Among other things, the Asian American Task Force on University Admissions had criticized the university for having almost no Asian Americans in its senior administrative positions. After his appointment as associate vice chancellor for admissions and enrollment, Patrick Hayashi would often joke in his public speeches, "I just happened to be in the right race at the right time." The line would almost always draw a laugh. Over time, however, the line became less funny to Hayashi, and he stopped using it.

That line seemed to be a much broader description of our society and, more than anything, seemed to describe the essence of white experience in American history. And, after just twenty years or so of affirmative action, the counterattack on it had clearly begun.

5 ATTACKING THOSE EARLY POLICIES

The early affirmative action polices described in the preceding chapter in turn gave rise to early attacks on those policies, some of them quite virulent and many quite clumsy in their own right. From the late 1980s to about 1993, the emerging struggle against affirmative action had several different stages, although there are overlapping edges. In almost all of these campaigns and attacks, the target was UC Berkeley.

Throughout the long public argument over affirmative action, one of the nagging questions that would periodically recur to admissions officers at Berkeley was, "Why Berkeley? How did Berkeley become the focus of the national debate over affirmative action in undergraduate admissions?" The response to such a question is more involved than merely Berkeley's national and international reputation for academic excellence, and it's also an interesting question to try to answer.

The most obvious part of the answer is that Berkeley had been one of the most persistent and most aggressive campuses in the country in its pursuit of racial and ethnic integration. Berkeley had the first Upward Bound program—a federally funded outreach program for low-income, high school students—in the country in 1964 and the first Educational Opportunity Program in 1965. EOP gave low-income and minority students additional consideration in the admissions process and then provided them with financial, academic, and personal support once they had enrolled at Berkeley.

When the campus intensified its drive for undergraduate affirmative action in the early 1980s under Chancellor Ira Michael Heyman, it did so publicly and vocally. Heyman was a compelling public speaker on the subject, and he never ducked the issue. In fact, he sought opportunities to make the case for why Berkeley must do what he believed it should do. And when Berkeley began to succeed in this effort, he let the world know that fact, in part because he was proud of this success and also because he wanted to ease the pressure from constituencies that had been jamming Berkeley for not having done more sooner.

The fact that Berkeley is a public university also contributed to the campus becoming a target of criticism and polemics because anyone can get the policy documents and admission data under California's Public Records Act. The five-year graduation rate for African American students who entered Berkeley in 1980 and 1981—twenty-seven percent—probably never would have surfaced at a private university, instead of replicating itself for almost two decades in the media. And certainly, mostly as result of inexperience, some of Berkeley's early efforts were heavy-handed and clumsy—for example, the guaranteed admission of any UC-eligible African American, Chicano, Latino, or Native American freshman applicant to the College of Letters and Science—and this clumsiness understandably angered some observers.

Affirmative action, however, was certainly not the first undertaking at Berkeley to inflame political and social conservatives. The campus has an established and often wild history of active involvement in liberal/radical causes, including, of course, the Free Speech Movement in 1964, vigorous and occasionally violent opposition to the Vietnam War, riots over the university's attempt to build on People's Park in 1969, disruptive and violent protests against the invasion of Cambodia in 1970, a huge student strike for a third-world college in 1971, and strong opposition to the university's investments in companies doing business in South Africa during the period of anti-apartheid demonstrations in the mid-1980s. Even before the 1960s, Berkeley students protested vigorously against the appearance of the House Un-American Activities Committee in San Francisco in the early 1950s, and many faculty had opposed the imposition of an anti-communist Loyalty Oath in 1949–50.

In a strange irony, the university also contributed mightily to the rise of Ronald Reagan in California. Reagan made great political gains, first by firing Clark Kerr from his position as president of the University of California (inspiring Kerr's famous line that he was leaving the presidency as he had entered it: "fired with enthusiasm") and then by coming down strongly on student demonstrators. During some of his early campaigns, Reagan sounded a lot like George Wallace when Wallace would rail against "pointy-head intellectuals." It's easy to forget how much so many people, patriotic supporters of the war in Vietnam or not, truly hated UC Berkeley for its student demonstrators and its riots during the 1960s and early 70s.

That bitterness toward the Berkeley campus certainly persists. The October 29, 2001, segment of the political comic strip "Mallard Fillmore," carried in *The Denver Post* and probably scores of other papers across the country, showed Mallard crouched behind a large rock, looking a bit like Geraldo Rivera and holding a microphone. He looks at the reader and says, "This is Mallard Fillmore reporting from behind enemy lines . . . few hundred yards from where hard-line zealots . . . pump young recruits full of hatred for western culture . . . here on the campus of the University of California at Berkeley." The last panel has in the distance a sketch of the Campanile, the campus bell tower.

Another part of the explanation of UC Berkeley as target is that many people who live outside the city of Berkeley confuse the city with the university—and the farther away that they are, the more confusion there usually is. It is certainly true that the city has some rough edges, especially Telegraph Avenue and neighboring People's Park, both of which are situated next to the campus. It's also easy to make fun of the city: the People's Republic of Berkeley, *Berserkeley*, the Home of the Conspiracy Theory, the Only City with a Foreign Policy. Even the California Cheese Board recently ran an ad that read: "The only thing Berkeley has never protested—It's the Cheese." In the early 1990s, the Berkeley

City Council officially changed the name of the holiday Columbus Day to Indigenous Peoples Day. Berkeley is a city where massive ideological wars are waged and truly unsolicited advice is imparted on the bumpers of cars.

PAYING MORE ATTENTION

The attacks on affirmative action varied immensely in their strategies and their sophistication, but the shared goal of all of them was to end affirmative action in university admissions. More than anything, however, they put growing pressure on admissions policy-makers at Berkeley and, to a lesser extent at the time, other institutions. That was a good thing in that it focused Berkeley's attention on the laws governing affirmative action and pushed the campus to examine its policies and practices more carefully in order to build in as much legal protection as possible.

One of the effects of the Asian American admission controversy, described in the preceding chapter, and the first attacks on affirmative action was that Berkeley administrators and faculty began to pay much more careful attention to the legal framework that underpinned affirmative action, especially the *Bakke* opinion from 1978. As the pressure increased, Berkeley made several important policy changes. The first two of these—the careful restructuring of the faculty admissions committee in 1988 and the creation of *The Karabel Report* in 1989, were described near the end of last chapter. The third policy change occurred in the fall 1990 freshman admission cycle when Associate Vice Chancellor Hayashi skillfully engineered faculty consent to end the policy of guaranteeing admission to Berkeley to any African American, Latino, or Native American applicant who met the published UC-system minimum admission requirements.

Under *The Karabel Report*, this change was scheduled to occur fall 1991, but Hayashi's political intuition told him that it should happen as soon as possible. Although managing this policy change with the faculty admissions committee was complicated, Hayashi's instinct turned out to be correct, and the change helped the campus in the full compliance review subsequently conducted by the Office for Civil Rights. It seems virtually certain that had the same Supreme Court that issued the *Gratz* and *Grutter* rulings reviewed this policy, the policy would have been struck down.

As the public struggle over affirmative action continued into the mid-1990s, admissions policy-makers at Berkeley realized that one of its long-term goals should be the adoption of a freshman admission policy in which there would be no formulas or indexes used as sorters and in which every single application would be read fully and carefully by at least two readers. In part, the campus wanted to move in this direction to create a fairer, more educationally sound policy and process, particularly as it became increasingly clear that the policy/process in place at that time was putting more and more emphasis on test scores. In addition, however, administrators and faculty believed that such a policy would give the campus the greatest degree of flexibility in the event that the UC Board of Regents voted to end affirmative action in admissions, a move that began to seem increasingly probable. Hayashi and other Berkeley administrators proposed such a policy to the faculty admissions committee in 1995. The process took two years, and the new policy took effect for the fall 1998 freshman admission cycle.

Because it was the target for most of the early challenges to affirmative action and because it had begun to think more carefully about the policy and legal issues, Berkeley became the de facto leader among colleges and universities nationally on this issue, especially among selective public universities. This leadership role also came about because Berkeley initiated a series of conversations among such institutions. In 1991, Hayashi invited the directors and deans of admission at the most selective public universities in the country to breakfast before one of the sessions of the College Board National Forum in San Francisco. Hayashi and André Bell, who was then the director of undergraduate admission at Berkeley, laid out the issues related to affirmative action that they saw confronting selective publics and asked, "What are you all doing?" There was a long silence before Jack Blackburn, the highly respected dean of admission at the University of Virginia, said, "We're all watching to see what you do."

EARLY RUMBLINGS

The first thrust was through the media, often in little-known publications, beginning with people like John Bunzel and, on a minor scale, Arthur Hu, a self-styled auditor of UC Berkeley admissions who wrote a column called "Hu's On First" for the publication *Asian Week*. As noted near the end of the previous chapter, Bunzel, Donald Werner, and James Gibney had all written about Berkeley in 1988, but, while their articles had increased the pressure on Berkeley, that pressure had been modest and somewhat unsustained. The truth is that not many folks wait with elevated pulse by their mailboxes for the arrival of *Public Interest* every three months.

ATTACK THROUGH GOVERNMENT AGENCY:
THE OFFICE FOR CIVIL RIGHTS

In *The Big Test*, Nicholas Lemann points out opponents of affirmative action made three different attempts to get first President Reagan and then President Bush to abolish affirmative action by executive order. When these efforts failed, opponents turned to a different strategy. This second stage of attack came through formal complaints to federal agencies such as the OCR in the U.S. Department of Education. As part of this effort, OCR opened investigations at UCLA in 1989 (involving graduate admission) and at UC Berkeley (two, in fact, against Berkeley—one involving freshman admission in 1989 and one involving Boalt Hall in 1990) that led to full compliance reviews by OCR attorneys. These complaints were initially seen by opponents of affirmative action as the most expedient way to end affirmative action quickly. Once the complaints were made public, conservative politicians, such as Congressman Dana Rohrabacher (R., California), pushed hard on the Department of Education to find against Berkeley and to do so quickly. Much of Rohrabacher's pressuring came from his chief of staff Gary Curran, who had worked in OCR before joining Rohrabacher's office.

As part of the research for his weekly column, Arthur Hu had asked for and received major portions of Berkeley's freshman admission database. Because Berkeley is a public university, those databases are considered part of the public record and are obtainable under California's Public Records Act. After two or three years of ineffectively carping away at Berkeley through his modest newspaper column, Hu raised the stakes considerably in July 1989 by filing a formal complaint with OCR, claiming that Berkeley had deliberately discriminated against Asian Americans in its fall 1989 freshman admissions process. When he reexamined the data, however, Hu, only mildly embarrassed, concluded that Berkeley had not in fact discriminated against Asian Americans but had done so against white applicants. He therefore amended his complaint to OCR.

OCR accepted the complaint and assigned it to its San Francisco Regional Office. As the OCR investigation unfolded, it became clear that there was significantly strong tension between the central OCR headquarters in Washington, D. C., and the San Francisco office. The Washington office had been powerfully reshaped by Reagan appointees and had a strong conservative focus. The Assistant Secretary of Education for Civil Rights—the head of OCR—was Michael Williams. At the same time, some of the regional offices of OCR—especially the San Francisco office—were staffed by many attorneys who had worked for OCR for years and who had originally joined the staff of OCR to fight for minority access and rights. These attorneys often now found themselves pursuing allegations of discrimination against whites and investigating the institutions that were doing the most to advance the social values that had brought many of them to OCR in the first place.

Although Hu himself was only a mildly irritating gadfly, the complaint he filed became most significant for Berkeley. OCR quickly expanded its initial investigation into a full compliance review, which meant that OCR would look at every aspect of the freshman admissions process at Berkeley. Next, OCR added the fall 1990 admission cycle to the fall 1989 cycle included in the original investigation.

By the time the review was completed in March 1996, the review had lasted six and a half years and covered fall 1989 through fall 1995. The only good news in all of this was that OCR focused entirely on the College of Letters and Science, ignoring the other four colleges that were separate parts of the freshman admissions process. Letters and Science made up about eighty percent of Berkeley's freshman applicants, so the review was huge, but at least the Admissions Office was spared the added complexity of having to gather data and documents on the other four colleges.

For Berkeley, the OCR review was quite difficult and provoked high anxiety. Even the public announcement of the review was damaging because many observers assumed that there wouldn't be a review if there weren't something wrong. Much more important, however, are the workload increases that lawsuits and compliance reviews bring. Even if such a lawsuit or complaint is ultimately dismissed or if the university is found faultless, the workload burden and the high anxiety are extremely punitive in themselves. Someone has to prepare all of the summoned databases, gather the relevant—and often times irrelevant—documents and policies requested, and assemble the individual admission applications—oftentimes thousands and thousands of them. Everything has to be inventoried so that administrators know what they have sent and what they have not, and then everything has to be shipped.

Then the people being investigated have to help the investigators (or attorneys), who are clearly not their best friends, understand the admissions process. When the investigators pose their first questions, the people being investigated truly start to worry, because, in most cases, it's clear that these hostile critics don't understand all that much about how the admissions process actually works. It would be one thing— a significantly bad thing—to be found out of compliance by people who really understood the process and had mastered its intricacies and nuances. It would be another—a remarkably bad thing—to be found out of compliance by people who never did bother to fully understand the process but who made damaging judgments anyway, completely unencumbered by facts.

In the case of the OCR review, Berkeley spent much time trying to figure out who the key people would be, knowing that the key attorneys in the San Francisco Regional Office were supporters of affirmative action. It quickly became clear that most of the Reagan appointees in the Washington, D.C., OCR were not. It was also very clear that the awkward position of the San Francisco staff meant that there could be no direct or candid conversations between them and Berkeley's representatives. That meant that during much of the review, all of the parties conducted themselves as if they were part of some Byzantine court ceremony in which the slightest gesture, movement, or shift in posture might or might not be pregnant with meaning.

This complexity was compounded by the decision that the first phase of the investigation would have the Washington office performing an analysis of data on a large scale. Berkeley admissions staff spent a great deal of time in conference calls explaining codes and fields and their relationships to our actual selection process. Admissions staff patiently took OCR staff through the database time after time. It was often truly discouraging, after an hour and a half of discussion and explanation, to have an OCR staff person ask a really basic question that indicated he had missed the most fundamental points that Berkeley staff had been making. And no matter how ignorant the question or how much of an edge the OCR person may have developed, Berkeley staff could never appear to be exasperated, annoyed, impatient, sarcastic, hostile, or bored. In this equation, all of the power was on their side—and they knew it.

OCR repeatedly extended the full compliance review until it spanned six years. The last months of the review finally brought officials from Berkeley face to face with attorneys in the San Francisco office of OCR on April 25, 1995. OCR attorneys agreed that Berkeley could continue to admit students using the Academic Index Score (explained in Chapter 4) without reading their complete applications, but they wanted Berkeley to read all of the remaining applicants so that no student would be denied without having had a full reading. Berkeley admissions people agreed to make that change.

Finally, on March 7, 1996, Director of the Region IX OCR John Palomino issued the OCR Letter of Findings. It had taken almost another year after the April 1995 meeting in San Francisco, in part because the letter had to go through many levels of approval in Washington. The Letter of Findings found Berkeley's freshman admissions process in full compliance with federal law. Not only that, the Letter of Findings described that process as a model for other institutions. (This was the same process that Governor Wilson would so successfully attack at the July 20, 1995, UC Regents meeting, an event described in the next chapter.) The OCR investigation had lasted almost seven years. Long before the Letter of Findings, however, critics of affirmative action such as Dana Rohrabacher had given up on their strategy of destroying affirmative action by government agency.

OPENING A LOCAL FRONT

A third area of attack often comes from within a college or university, frequently a faculty member who opposes affirmative action and doesn't mind a bit of media attention. At Berkeley, such a thrust came from Vincent Sarich, a professor of anthropology. On April 4, 1990, Sarich wrote a letter to UC Regent William French Smith, enclosing an article Sarich had written, titled "The Institutionalization of Racism at the University of California at Berkeley." Smith had been appointed by Governor Ronald Reagan and was arguably the most conservative member of the Board, not an easy status to achieve then—or now, for that matter.

Sarich, who taught the large freshman Anthropology 1 course at Berkeley, was a quirky fellow who seemed to delight in being an iconoclast. In addition to vigorously opposing Berkeley's freshman admission policy, Sarich went further in his Anthropology 1 lectures and public appearances. At one of his public lectures, he carefully said, "Academic achievement and test scores may not be evenly distributed by race and ethnicity." The place went nuts. Several rows of Sarich groupies—very young white and Asian American students sitting at the feet of the master—applauded frenetically. Other students, including many African Americans and Latinos, booed and began shouting from the back of the room. Both sides thought Sarich had embraced the argument of Arthur Jensen and others that intelligence is correlated with race and that whites and Asians are genetically more intelligent than other peoples. In fact, Sarich had been most careful to say nothing at all about intelligence and to state a fact that has since been demonstrated in many research studies. The subject was so highly charged emotionally, however, that many people in the audience heard his first few words and filled out the rest with their own hungers and fears. Sarich genuinely loved the attention he was getting and was amused by how easy it was to whip folks into a frenzy—sort of like Richard Nixon holding up both hands in the peace sign.

During the next several months, Sarich became the first lightning rod for affirmative action at Berkeley. His letter to Smith began a messy and emotional debate over freshman admission at Berkeley that included dueling op-ed pieces first in the *San Francisco Chronicle* with Chancellor Heyman and then with Professor of English David Lloyd in *California Monthly*, the magazine of the California Alumni Association. Sarich's provocative statements in Anthropology 1, however, triggered a powerful reaction among many of his colleagues in what at the time was the notoriously fractured and dysfunctional Department of Anthropology. A department committee demanded to see his lecture notes for Anthropology 1 in order to determine whether he was fit to teach such an introductory course.

Sarich expanded the debate to include the issues of academic freedom and free speech, and Berkeley, unable to help itself, had to run through its usual, obligatory string of pontifications on these subjects. Finally, after a long, acrimonious struggle, the department decided that Sarich would not be allowed to teach Anthropology 1 by himself but that he might co-teach the course with another colleague who would present a different perspective on key issues. Sarich then seemed to lose interest in the entire matter, and he retired soon after.

THE NATIONAL WRITERS

A fourth stage in the attacks on affirmative action came in a dramatic escalation of media attention in the early 1990s. Writers such as Dinesh D'Souza with his rhetorical flamboyance, Thomas Sowell with his jarring bitterness, and, a little later, Shelby Steele, the most thoughtful and balanced of the legion of critics, either produced full-length books and/or found much more receptive audiences in mainstream newspapers and periodicals. Later in the decade, this group would by joined by Linda Chavez with her less-than-incompetent data staff at the Center for Economic Opportunity and Abigail and Stephen Thernstrom, who in thinly veiled condescension, in effect, wrote All of these nice little black and brown people are perfectly fine, but they're just not ready to play with the big white and Asian American kids.

Dinesh D'Souza published *Illiberal Education*, a critique of affirmative action in university admissions, in 1991. Chapter by chapter, the book rounded up the usual institutional suspects: Stanford, Harvard, Michigan, and Duke. Chapter 2, titled "More Equal Than Others," was devoted to Berkeley and the case of Yat-pang Au. Au had applied for freshman admission to Berkeley for fall 1987 and been denied.

At the time of his denial in March 1987, Au and his family had created their own little media blitz by going directly to Bay Area newspapers and television stations to protest Berkeley's decision—and to pressure Berkeley publicly into changing its decision. The Aus probably did feel deeply wronged, but it was also clear that the family, the father in particular, didn't at all mind the media attention.

Au was an outstanding student who had gone to Gunderson High, an undistinguished high school in San Jose, where he was valedictorian. For many years and for a complicated set of reasons, Berkeley has divided its freshman applicants into eighteen different pools, one for each of the four undergraduate colleges other than the College of Engineering and one for each individual major within the College of Engineering. Each of the eighteen applicant pools has a different degree of competition that is determined by the number of applicants, the qualifications of those applicants, and the number of spaces available to that particular program. Au had applied to Bioengineering, the most competitive major among the eighteen pools. Even by 1987, the competition for admission to Bioengineering and Electrical Engineering/Computer Science (EECS) had become extraordinary. Within the Bioengineering applicant pool, Au was, unfortunately, not particularly competitive. In fact, there were more than 125 students with higher Academic Index Scores who had also been denied admission to Bioengineering. There were also ten students from Au's high school with lower index scores who had been admitted to Berkeley, but in almost every case they had applied to less competitive programs.

D'Souza, capitalizing on the still-prominent Asian American admission controversy, used words like "seems" and "appears to" plus selected quotations from critics of Berkeley, such as Henry Der, to say, in effect, that Berkeley had a ceiling on the number of Asian Americans it would admit and enroll. He ignored the eighteen separate pools and their different academic qualifications, compared minority students to Au across those pools, and concluded that had it not been for the admission of minority students, Yat-pang Au would have been admitted to Berkeley. As point of fact, however, not a single African American, Chicano, Latino, or Native American student had been admitted to Bioengineering ahead of Au, in part because of the very small number of underrepresented minority applicants to that field and in part because of the intense degree of competition that had also knocked out Au. It was true that ten students from Gunderson High with lesser overall levels of achievement had been admitted to Berkeley, but that, as just noted, was largely the result of their having applied to less competitive programs at Berkeley.

In one way, the worst thing about D'Souza's attack on Berkeley wasn't his deliberate and malicious distortion of fact; it was Berkeley's paralysis in the face of that attack and the campus' subsequent inability to reply effectively. Although a range of different people at Berkeley in subsequent years made the case publicly over and over for affirmative action in print, in public speeches, and on radio and television, the campus never got out from under the feeling that it didn't do enough and it didn't do it well. This failure was most acutely concentrated when D'Souza spoke at Northgate Hall on the Berkeley campus in late 1991 as part of a national tour to promote his book. D'Souza gave a clever but rather canned speech—and no one in the audience, including a number of high-ranking administrators, had the nerve to take him on.

The other critic of affirmative action who was particularly irritating was Thomas Sowell, but only for a single, narrow reason. Sowell had come across a report (probably either "The Challenge Ahead: Improving Black Student Graduation," issued by the university's Task Force on Black Student Persistence in March 1987, or "Freshmen Persistence and Graduation Rates at UC Berkeley," produced in December 1986 by Gregg Thomson, the director of the Office of Student Research at Berkeley) that showed that African American freshmen who entered Berkeley in 1980 and 1981 had a five-year graduation rate of twenty-seven percent. (At that time, five years was the standard of measurement for graduation. The figures for the two years had been averaged according to the current practice at the time in the Office of Student Research.) Sowell seized upon this figure (it was horrible) and flogged Berkeley with it for more than fifteen years—even though graduation rates for African Americans at Berkeley have climbed steadily since that time (the six-year graduation rate for African American freshmen who entered Berkeley in fall 1996 was 65.7 percent, compared to a rate of 83.6 percent for the entire fall 1996 freshman class). That twenty-seven percent figure is puzzling because it is so much lower than the figure for any other year. The next cohort, for example, had a six-year graduation rate of 50.4 percent.

That 1980–81 graduation figure contributed to Sowell's persistent belief, more recently adopted by Abigail and Stephen Thernstrom, that affirmative action mismatches African American students with institutions that are too difficult for them, a position that Derek Bok and William Bowen have thoroughly refuted in *The Shape of the River*. The exasperating thing about Sowell, however, is not that he cited the twenty-seven−percent figure—if it's accurate, it deserves stern scrutiny— but that he clung to it for so long even when he must have known that the persistence and graduation rates for African American students at Berkeley were climbing. And Sowell can be quite harsh, as in his description of admissions officers in his review of *A Is For Admissions*: "What we have here is a bunch of shallow and petty people playing God."

CHANGING TACTICS: LEGISLATURES, LAWSUITS, INITIATIVES, GOVERNORS, AND PUBLIC INTEREST LAW FIRMS

Beginning about 1994, opponents of affirmative action became much more sophisticated—and much more successful—in the strategies they chose to attack affirmative action. One of these more polished approaches came through legislative bodies, including the U.S. Congress and state legislatures. In California, Assemblyman Bernie Richter (R., Chico) led the effort. Most recently in Congress, it has been Congressman Frank Riggs, from Northern California. So far, these efforts have not succeeded, although anti-affirmative action measures have lost by some appreciably close votes.

In the mid-1990s, Richter introduced Assembly Bill 2468 in the California State Assembly. AB 2468 stipulated that any admissions officer who could be shown to have considered race in any admission decision could be convicted of a felony and sentenced to a $1,000 fine and a year in state prison. The bill passed the Assembly Judiciary Committee by a vote of 9 to 4, then passed the Assembly Appropriations Committee, and in late May 1996 came to the floor of the full Assembly for a vote. By this point, the bill no longer included a one-year prison term. It needed forty-one votes to pass and failed on a 37 to 37 vote.

Another avenue of attack has been through lawsuits filed in federal court, many of them initiated or supported by the Center for Individual Rights. These cases, already described in Chapter 3, include the

Hopwood case in Texas in 1996, the *Gratz* and *Grutter* lawsuits against the University of Michigan, a lawsuit against the University of Washington that was decided in December 2000, and several lawsuits against the University of Georgia, some of which were settled in the fall and winter of 2000. The lawsuits in Texas and Georgia successfully overturned affirmative action in university admissions—until they, in turn, were reversed in 2003 by *Grutter*.

Several private organizations have also taken up the struggle against affirmative action. The most effective of these has been the Center for Individual Rights, under then-executive director Michael Greve. The Center was largely responsible for the end of affirmative action in Texas through the *Hopwood* case and caused considerable additional damage in Washington State and in Michigan through lawsuits it sponsored in those states. In San Francisco, the Pacific Legal Foundation has tried to be a western version of the Center for Individual Rights but with almost no success.

The most inept of these organizations has been the Center for Equal Opportunity, headed by Linda Chavez. In 1996, to take one example, the Center requested and got admissions data from UC Berkeley covering several previous freshman admission cycles. On October 10, 1996, the Center issued a press release announcing evidence of reverse discrimination in the 1993 and 1995 Berkeley freshman admissions processes based solely on differences in SAT I scores by race and ethnicity. The press release was timed to coincide with an appearance by Chavez on a panel discussing Proposition 209 that evening at Boalt Hall on the Berkeley campus. The press release made astonishing charges about Berkeley's freshman admissions process—astonishing because whoever did the data analysis for Chavez inadvertently lost more than 8,000 applicant files. The data the Center used was completely skewed and inaccurate. For fall 1993, the press release cited 9,949 freshman applicants to Berkeley. The actual number was 18,802. For fall 1995, the Center cited 12,194 applicants when the true number was 21,672. That same day, Jesus Mena, Berkeley's public information officer, issued a scathing press release in rebuttal. It was an embarrassing performance by Chavez and her staff.

So far, the most enduring attacks on affirmative action have been through the initiative process in both California with Proposition 209 and in Washington with Initiative 200. Both initiatives have ended affirmative action in the operation of public entities, including public higher education. In addition, Florida Governor Jeb Bush in 2000 ended affirmative action by executive order and then got the University Board of Trustees to adopt One Florida, which included his Talented Twenty Program that would admit the top twenty percent of the graduates of each high school to the public university system.

Surveying all of the ways that opponents have attacked affirmative action in university admissions and then looking ahead, it seems most likely that challenges with the greatest chances for success will come through initiative campaigns such as those in California and Washington and through lawsuits filed in federal courts, although the success of such suits will ultimately be heavily dependent on the composition of the U.S. Supreme Court. The next initiative battleground will almost certainly be Michigan in 2006, where former UC Regent Ward Connerly has already begun gathering signatures. Admissions policymakers who are framing policies and processes in light of *Grutter* should most anticipate and most concern themselves with the possibilities of initiative campaigns and federal lawsuits.

6 UNPRECEDENTED POLICIES: SP-1 AND PROPOSITION 209

Two of the most cataclysmic national events in the history of the struggle over affirmative action took place in California in 1995 and 1996. One was the vote by the Regents of the University of California in July 1995 to end affirmative action. The other was the passage of Proposition 209 by the voters of California in November 1996. The action of the UC Board of Regents and the decision by the voters of California were both wholly unprecedented actions by a university governing board or a state electorate. They shook the entire nation, and they still strongly influence the debate over affirmative action across the country.

BACKGROUND: THE BERKELEY MATRIX

As the criticism of affirmative action in university admissions became more sophisticated and more focused, many selective colleges and universities struggled to alter and refine their policies in order to minimize the likelihood that legal challenges might ensue. The difficulty was that in most cases policy-makers, including many campus attorneys, were not sufficiently experienced and not sufficiently versed in the legal and political issues to craft policies that had a good chance of surviving legal challenge. That was certainly the case with the University of Michigan, whose undergraduate admission policy was overturned by the U.S. Supreme Court in the *Gratz* decision in 2003. It was also true for UC Berkeley almost a decade earlier.

The Karabel Report, produced by Berkeley's faculty admissions committee in 1989, greatly advanced the sophistication and analysis of freshman admission policy at Berkeley. At the same time, however, it still used separate categories of applicants and it set numeric target ranges for the admission of each category. One of these categories was underrepresented minority students. These target ranges were flexible and were reviewed and adjusted from time to time, but sometime in 1991 attorneys from the office of the University of California General Counsel told Berkeley admissions officials the target ranges still gave the impression of separate admission tracks based on race and that they suggested de facto quotas. University attorneys urged Berkeley to move to a matrix system for its freshman admission policy, similar to a matrix that UCLA was already using.

The matrix was a grid with a top horizontal axis and a left vertical axis. The horizontal axis was a set of ranges of Academic Index Scores, starting at the maximum 8,000 and descending all the way to zero. The vertical axis contained combinations of diversity characteristics that were valued by the faculty admissions committee in keeping with UC Regents' policies. The highest rank was assigned to California residents who were from low-income families and were African American, Chicano, or Native American. (In fact, the highest rank was assigned to recruited athletes but the campus chose not to show them on the matrix for political—and cowardly—reasons. The next most highly weighted criterion after recruited athlete status was California residency.) It is also important to point out that, apart from recruited athlete status, no single characteristic could earn the highest ranking. Berkeley's notion of diversity was complex, and it took a combination of state residency, low socio-economic status, and underrepresented minority status to attain the top ranking. The campus also gave strong preference to low-income students regardless of race and less preference to underrepresented minority students who were from middle-

or high-income families. An important advantage of the matrix was that it allowed Berkeley to distribute all its freshman applicants into specific cells and then to make decisions by cell: admit, deny, or read.

At this time, Berkeley's admissions process was still heavily dependent on the use of its Academic Index Score, and the first fifty percent of the admissions spaces were filled on the basis of a linear ranking of applicants in descending AIS order. The first column along the horizontal axis of the Berkeley matrix was therefore set at the Academic Score cut point that identified the first fifty percent of the freshman admission spaces on a linear ranking by descending AIS. After that first fifty percent had been admitted, the Admissions Office would then admit some additional cells based on the combination of high AIS and high ranking on the diversity axis. The office could drop out a number of cells in the lower right as "not competitive" and then read the remaining cells—perhaps as many as 10,000 applicants, depending on the year—carefully and individually. Applications in the "read" cells were read twice by carefully trained readers using a scoring scale of 1 to 7, with the first score blocked from the second reader. If the two scores were more than a single point apart, the application was read by a senior reader to determine its final score. Applicants in the read cells were then admitted or denied at the conclusion of the reading process.

UC attorneys felt strongly that the matrix would give Berkeley a much greater degree of legal protection if its policy were to be challenged in court. The faculty admissions committee adopted the matrix format for the fall 1992 freshman admission cycle, and Berkeley used some version of this matrix from fall 1992 through fall 1997. The attorneys believed that the campus had made a major advance. In July 1995, that belief proved to be a major miscalculation.

SP-1

On July 20, 1995, the UC Board of Regents voted 14 to 10 with one abstention to end the consideration of race and ethnicity in University of California admissions. The July 31, 1995, issue of *Newsweek* carried on page 30 a remarkable color photo of California Governor Pete Wilson and the Reverend Jesse Jackson confronting each other during the July 1995 UC Regents meeting in San Francisco. The visual planes of the two men overlap. Jackson's hands are pressed together in front of him. Wilson's arms are spread wide palms up. Wilson is not backing down.

A person can learn a tremendous amount about the university and about California and about university politics at a Regents meeting, but, at times, it can be quite unnerving to see who has total responsibility for the finest public university system in the world. There are twenty-six members on the UC Board of Regents. The California Constitution established the Board as a constitutionally autonomous entity within the state, meaning that the Legislature cannot directly control the Board or the university. The Governor appoints eighteen Regents, seven serve *ex officio*, and the other Regents appoint a student Regent. The *ex officio* Regents include the governor, who is President of the Board; the lieutenant governor; the Speaker of the California Assembly; the State Superintendent of Public Instruction; the president and vice president of the University of California Alumni Associations; and the president of the University of California. The chair and vice chair of the system-wide faculty Academic Council sit as nonvoting members. The Board appoints the president of the university.

The UC Board of Regents is the most exclusive club in the state of California, even more so than the Bohemian Club with its notorious Russian River romps. In his recent book with its remarkably inaccurate title *Creating Equal*, Ward Connerly describes membership on the Board:

> A regent's term is 12 years, but it feels like a lifetime sinecure. You receive no salary, but the perks are world-class.
>
> From the outset, you are made to feel like minor royalty, cosseted by University administrators who look after you in the ritualized way of workers tending a queen bee. The board is steeped in tradition, and your colleagues initiate you into a ceremonial world that seems almost like a

secret society. Its plush world of power is second only to the State Supreme Court among such appointed entities in California.

Wilson appointed Connerly to the Board in 1993. Connerly is smart and quite articulate. Perhaps more impressive than anything, he is brilliant with the media—and he is astute enough to always return calls from reporters. He and Pete Wilson not only led the UC Regents to end affirmative action, but in December 1995 Connerly also rescued the California Civil Rights Initiative (CCRI) when it was foundering in its signature-gathering campaign, helped it qualify for the November 1996 ballot in California as Proposition 209, and then succeeded in getting California voters to approve it.

Appearing as a speaker or presenter at a Regents meeting is extremely difficult. The Regents have all the power—*all* the power. Some of them, like John Davies or Tirso del Junco, were capable of great arrogance, and many of them, like Sue Johnson or Velma Montoya or Stephen Nakashima or David Lee, either weren't very bright, struggled unsuccessfully with chronic confusion, or were completely unconcerned with facts or accuracy. Glenn Campbell, originally appointed by Governor Ronald Reagan and completing his second twelve-year term in July 1995, was so frail that people in the audience would glance at him from time to time just to see if he was still breathing.

One of the long-standing traditions of the Board is that it be as apolitical as possible—the Loyalty Oath controversy from 1949 to 1951 being one glaring exception. A second tradition is a sort of self-effacement; that is, the individual members do not use the university or their seats on the Board to call attention to themselves. A wonderfully ironic passage is included in Connerly's book, in which, describing his appointment to the Board, he says ". . . but neither he [Wilson] nor I had any idea that he had put me in a place that would soon become the cockpit of California's racial politics." Connerly's faux naïveté is amusing. He could have written the sentence more honestly: ". . . he had put me in a place that I would soon turn into the cockpit of California's racial politics."

It would be interesting to know what would have happened with the Board of Regents regarding affirmative action in 1995 had David Gardner not retired as president of the university in 1992, following the death of his wife Libby. It is certainly clear that the thrust and intentions of the Board changed in the early mid-1990s, in part reflecting the personalities of Ward Connerly and John Davies (and also, just behind the curtain, that of Pete Wilson) and in part reflecting a national trend of university governing boards to insert themselves into levels of university administration that they had in the past largely left to professional administrators. This much more aggressive stance by the Board was reflected in their choice for president of the university following Gardner's retirement. Jack Peltason was a remarkably low-key, easy-going man who had served with distinction as chancellor of UC Irvine. By the time he was appointed president, however, it was clear that he didn't have a great deal of energy and that he would manage the university rather than lead it. He was not an important participant in the Regents' discussions of affirmative action prior to their July 1995 vote. Gardner almost certainly would have been, and those discussions would have been something to witness.

In any event, Wilson, described by Howard Fineman in *Newsweek* as the "suburban avatar of the angry white male," was running for president of the United States against racial minorities, just as in 1994 he had run for re-election as governor against immigrants by exploiting Proposition 187, a measure on the November 1994 ballot that intended to severely restrict the rights and benefits of immigrants. There was some speculation that Connerly was angling for Secretary of Commerce or Secretary of Education in a Wilson presidential administration, although no one will ever be able to prove that.

The July 1995 meeting of the University of California Board of Regents was held in a building owned by the university in San Francisco's Laurel Heights. The building is on a hilltop and permits a high degree of security. It also has an auditorium with about 250 seats that slope down to the front, where there is enough room for an oblong table that can seat all twenty-six Regents, a couple of staff members, and one or two presenters. The nine campus chancellors, who have so much power on their individual campuses, all sit in the first or second row, looking as if they are attending obedience school. There is a large overhead screen for slide or PowerPoint displays and monitors near the table for those Regents who are seated in positions where they cannot see the large screen.

On July 20, building security was particularly tight. According to Kit Lively in *The Chronicle of Higher Education*, about forty students had held an all-night vigil outside the building, and hundreds more had come from all over the state to attend the meeting—and possibly disrupt it—or to demonstrate outside the building if they couldn't get into the meeting room itself. The university had imported university police officers from nearly all of the individual campuses. According to the *Los Angeles Times*, there were 500 demonstrators outside the meeting during most of the day.

In the auditorium where the meeting was to take place, there was a rope that separated the first five or six rows of seats that were reserved for invited guests and university staff from the remaining seats that were allocated to the public. Security staff had somehow decided which of the hundreds of people outside would be granted admission, and the spectator seats were full. Some mysterious protocol had ensured that the Reverend Jesse Jackson and a group of African American ministers from San Francisco had prime seats, and Jackson's presence increased the electricity in the already-tense meeting room.

In July 1995, all eighteen appointed Regents were Republicans. Governor Ronald Reagan appointed two of the original eighteen, Glenn Campbell and Dean Watkins. The seven *ex officio* included the governor, Lieutenant Governor Gray Davis, Speaker of the Assembly Doris Allen, State Superintendent of Public Instruction Delaine Eastin, President of the California Alumni Associations Judith Willick Levin, Vice President of the California Alumni Associations Ralph Carmona, and President of the University of California Jack Peltason. Although the governor is the president of the Board of Regents, this was the first meeting Wilson had attended since 1992.

Wilson was running determinedly for the Republican presidential nomination and leaning with all his weight on key Regents, especially the five that he had appointed, but the other *ex-officio* Regents made the outcome of the vote a little less certain than it might have been. Observers counting votes in the weeks preceding this meeting were fairly certain that Davis, Eastin, Willick, Carmona, and Peltason would all oppose Connerly and Wilson. In addition, student Regent Ed Gomez was an outspoken supporter of affirmative action. People were less certain about Allen, the only Regent of the twenty-six to miss this meeting, although she told the *Los Angeles Times* afterward that she probably would have voted with the governor. In any event, it looked as if there were at least six voting members of the Board who would vote against Connerly's motion, which had been labeled "SP-1" ("SP" for "special policy"). If all twenty-six Regents were present to vote, it would take thirteen no votes to defeat it (a tie would mean No). With twenty-five Regents present, it would still take thirteen No votes, since a tie would not be possible with an uneven number of voters.

Also sitting at the table as a Regent-designate, but not eligible to vote, was Richard Russell, president of the California Alumni Association (the alumni organization for the Berkeley campus) and the incoming vice president of the California Alumni Associations (thus becoming a voting member of the Board). Russell was also a strong supporter of affirmative action, and he and Ralph Carmona were close allies.

The Regents meeting began at 8:05 a.m. with Regent Clair Burgener presiding as chair. Governor Wilson made opening remarks, after which Burgener laid out the procedural rules for the meeting. That was followed by Remarks from Public Officials, speeches from a long parade of public figures, including former Speaker of the Assembly and Mayor of San Francisco Willie Brown; state Senators Tom Hayden, Diane Watson, and Tom Campbell; Assemblymembers John Vasconcellos, Barbara Lee, and Bernie Richter; Henry Der, chair of the California

Postsecondary Education Commission; and concluding with Reverend Jesse Jackson, who spoke and prayed for about forty-five minutes. According to Kit Lively, there were thirty-one of these folks and they were about evenly divided on the issue of affirmative action. It would clearly be a very full meeting.

Next came the public comment period, which included thirty-five people who had been chosen at random from the 140 who had signed up to speak. Six of these speakers supported Connerly's resolution; twenty-nine opposed it. The twenty-nine opponents included Amos Brown, Minister of the Third Baptist Church in San Francisco; Mario Obledo, former secretary of the California Department of Health and Human Services; Eva Paterson from the Lawyers' Committee for Civil Rights; and Dolores Huerta, from the United Farm Workers of America.

When the speakers had finally finished, the Board moved to consider SP-1. Although he was recovering from throat surgery and didn't have much of a voice, Wilson took charge of the discussion—not an encouraging sign. He began by showing on the large overhead screen the matrix used in freshman admissions policies at Berkeley. That was a bad sign.

The matrix, adopted for fall 1992 and described earlier in this chapter, was a grid that allowed Berkeley to arrange all its freshman applicants along two axes into specific cells.

In 1992, the matrix format had seemed eminently reasonable, but in the political climate and presidential race of July 1995—and particularly when it was flashed on the huge overhead screen by the governor of California—the matrix looked crude and politically naïve. Wilson immediately pointed out that non-California resident African American, Chicano, and Native American applicants ranked higher on the diversity axis than California residents from other racial and ethnic groups—that is, whites and Asian Americans. That was accurate. There were noticeably fewer non-California resident underrepresented minority students in the UC Berkeley applicant pools, and the campus wanted to be able to admit as many as possible, mostly to build the enrollment of underrepresented minority students at Berkeley but also in part to add to the complex idea of diversity that Berkeley valued.

HARDBALL

As Wilson was pointing out the injustice of Berkeley's diversity criteria, Regent Burgener announced that there had been a telephoned bomb threat and asked people to evacuate the building. An hour later, after the building had been searched, people were allowed back into the meeting room, and Wilson again took up the Berkeley matrix, making what seemed to be a carefully prepared campaign speech against affirmative action.

In a clever parliamentary move, however, Connerly then formally introduced SP-2, his measure to end affirmative action in hiring and contracting, rather than SP-1, his measure that focused on admissions. This action somewhat confused opponents of the two measures and resulted in an odd disconnection because all of the discussion that followed was still about the admissions measure. Regent-designate Russell spoke eloquently about what affirmative action had meant for him. Russell also said, in a pointed reference to Wilson, that he regretted that politics had intruded into what should have been a more neutral discussion of a complex issue. Regent Bill Bagley raised perhaps the most important issue. He asked why the Regents should plunge into a political morass by voting on this issue. Bagley pointed out that the voters of California would almost certainly decide the issue in November 1996 when the California Civil Rights Initiative—soon to be called Proposition 209 for that election—would almost certainly be on the ballot.

The debate continued for a long time. Finally—it must have been about 6 p.m.—Regent Howard Leach called for the question on SP-2. There was no objection, and Lee Trivette, Secretary of the Regents, called the roll. One by one the key Regents all voted with the governor and Connerly. The final vote was 15 to 10 in favor of SP-2. SP-2 wasn't going to change university practices appreciably because of federal laws governing hiring and contracting, but the fifteen votes meant that the suspense—whatever suspense there might have been—was over. The governor had SP-1 nailed. Of the eighteen appointed Regents, only Bagley, Roy Brophy, Alice Gonzales, and Tom Sayles had voted No.

Connerly then introduced SP-1. (The full text of SP-1 appears as Appendix I.) Brophy immediately moved to amend Connerly's policy, calling instead for the appointment of a task force on alternatives to current admissions practices instead of ending affirmative action. It was particularly ironic that Brophy should introduce such a motion because he had been one of the most outspoken critics of affirmative action prior to Connerly's joining the Board. Brophy, however, was also concerned about the effects of SP-1 on the search that was already underway for a new president of the university to replace Peltason, who was leaving his position in October. An intense discussion followed, but before Brophy's measure came to a vote, Regent Levin moved that a recommendation from President Peltason be substituted for SP-1. That motion was defeated 11 to 14. Regent Dean Watkins then called for the question on the Brophy amendment.

At this moment, people in the audience began jeering and chanting and moving down the aisles toward the front of the room. Police officers moved into the room from the doors on either side of the big table. Chair Burgener called a recess, and the Regents and other university officials began to file out of the room through those same doors. Police let the last of the university people pass through the doors and then sealed off the room with the rest of the audience still in there. Rev. Jesse Jackson linked arms with several other ministers and began singing "We Shall Overcome," and the rest of the room picked up the song. Many of the student demonstrators were quite pumped up and kept saying things like, "We shut them down!" and "We kicked ass!" The room was filled with a kind of hollow euphoria.

After about forty-five minutes, word somehow filtered into the auditorium that the Regents were about to resume their meeting in another part of the building. The meeting resumed at 8 p.m. in a large room on the second floor that had obviously been set up with tables and microphones at least a day earlier. There was a short debate about whether proper procedures had been followed in shutting down the original meeting room and whether the meeting should be moved back to that location. Regent Bagley suggested that the Regents officially declare a "finding of fact" that circumstances would not permit returning to the original room. The Board approved Bagley's suggestion and then voted 14 to 10 to continue the meeting where they were.

UCLA Chancellor Charles Young then addressed the Board and, on behalf of all of the chancellors, requested the Regents vote to retain affirmative action. Young was followed by Provost of the University of California system Walter Massey, who described his childhood as an African American growing up in Mississippi and asked the Regents to consider most carefully before rejecting the recommendations of all the leadership of the university other than the Board itself.

Brophy's amendment to head off SP-1 was finally seconded, voted on, and rejected 15 to 10. Bagley, quite upset, said that the Regents must at least affirm the value of diversity if they were going to pass SP-1. He began writing furiously on a piece of paper. When he had finished, he called Connerly over. Connerly read what Bagley had written, made a counter suggestion, nodded, and then read the six lines into the record as an amendment to both SP-1 and SP-2. Those six lines actually didn't amount to much, which is why Connerly agreed to them, but they became Section 9 of SP-1.

SP-1 was then voted on in a roll call vote. It passed 14 to 10 with one abstention. All of the Regents who had sided with Wilson and Connerly on SP-2 had also voted for SP-1 except Velma Montoya, who voted No on SP-1. The abstention was Bagley.

It was a painful moment. All nine of the UC chancellors had publicly supported affirmative action and had opposed the Regents' ending it. So had all of the senior leadership of the university in the Office of the President, and so had many faculty leaders. Farther down the administrative chain, so had all of the directors of admission. UCSF Dean of the School of Medicine Haile Debas had been one of the speakers during the Remarks from Public Officials portion of the agenda. As Amy Wallace and Dave Lesher reported in the July 21, 1995, edition of the *Los Angeles Times*, Debas said, "It would be an outrage if 13 or 14 Regents, acting alone, destroyed a historic instrument of social progress in a moment of political frenzy." Yet that was exactly what had happened, and almost every chancellor, vice chancellor, and director of admissions throughout the university knew that they would all be lumped together with the Regents in the public's perception of what had just taken place.

The meeting ended at 8:35 p.m., more than twelve hours after it had begun. Within the Board itself, the votes on SP-1 and SP-2 represented a major shift of power from the old-line Regents like Brophy and Bagley, who were accustomed to shaping Board opinion and to running the university, to the upstarts—particularly Connerly and Davies. Part of Brophy's support for affirmative action at this meeting—and therefore his opposition to Connerly—had much to do with his attempts to resist this shift of power.

Bagley's abstention would have been a No had he voted. That meant that SP-1 was decided by only two votes. That is, had two of the Yes votes been No votes and had Bagley voted, the count would have been 12 Yes and 13 No. The narrow margin of victory is all the more important to note, given the massive support for affirmative action among the chancellors and other senior administrators. Two votes have left an ugly stain on the University of California that, despite the Regents' subsequent reversal of SP-1 in 2001, will last a long, long time. Then-Lieutenant Governor Gray Davis, a member of the UC Board of Regents by virtue of his office, voted against SP-1. After the meeting had ended, Davis excoriated Governor Wilson for ending affirmative action: "He said this was a historic day. It is a historic day, but Pearl Harbor was a historic day that we don't look back on with any pride."

At the time, Bagley's abstention seemed to be the futile gesture of a defeated old man. A Regent who votes No on an issue, however, may not reintroduce that issue before the Board. By abstaining, Bagley positioned himself to reopen the issue if he ever thought he had the votes to overturn SP-1. To his credit, he worked fervently to do exactly that, until the policy was rescinded on May 16, 2001—but that was well after Proposition 209 had taken effect and was therefore a symbolic gesture rather than a substantive policy decision.

As it was intended to be, the entire day had been a powerful and impressive demonstration of Wilson's political skill and force. He had lined up his votes, held them in place (except Montoya), moved through the long day without faltering, and pushed through the outcomes that he had wanted. Reverend Jesse Jackson and a few other public figures had been allowed into the second floor room just before the final vote. Jackson had sat frowning in the front row as witness to and the moral conscience of the Board during this unprecedented time, but the Board had ignored him as Wilson rolled over everyone.

PUTTING OFF SP-1

In August 1995, one month after voting to end affirmative action, the Board of Regents named Richard Atkinson, the chancellor of UC San Diego, president of the university. The fact that he accepted the job immediately after the vote on SP-1 was a measure of how badly he had wanted it. Atkinson is a very smart man with erratic judgment who often chooses words most carelessly. Even as late as July 2000, he was quoted in *The Daily Californian* as saying, "The question now is can underrepresented minorities push out some of the Asians and whites." The Regents understood how much Atkinson hungered to be president and knew that the first question he would ask on most issues was "How will this play with the Regents?" In almost every instance, that proved to be true.

One of the rare exceptions occurred four months into his term as president when Atkinson did the boldest thing of his entire term. SP-1 was scheduled to take effect for fall 1997. Arguing that there wasn't enough time to revise publications and otherwise notify the university's varied constituencies, Atkinson unilaterally postponed the implementation of SP-1 for one year until fall 1998. His decision infuriated Governor Wilson and many of the Regents. Atkinson was summoned to Sacramento for a meeting with Wilson, and ten of the Regents authorized a performance review of Atkinson—after just four months in office. He was almost fired, and he was forced to compromise.

He agreed that SP-1 would take effect for fall 1997 for graduate admissions as originally intended by the Regents. He also had to give on undergraduate admissions but not much. He successfully argued that the soonest SP-1 could be implemented for undergraduate admission was for the spring quarter 1998. Because few of the campuses admitted students to the spring quarter—and Berkeley was on a semester calendar, so there was no spring quarter at Berkeley—there would be almost no effect on undergraduate admission until fall 1998, Atkinson's original postponement date. The Regents accepted this compromise on February 15, 1996. When that meeting ended, one Regent described Atkinson as having "eaten his crow."

Atkinson's argument about notification had little substance, but he is impulsive. He was frustrated and angered by the SP-1 vote and needed to do something to make himself feel less impotent. It was a remarkably bold act, and it gave the university one more year of affirmative action policy in undergraduate admission decisions for fall 1997. Berkeley, for example, enrolled a freshman class in fall 1997 that included 670 African American, Chicano, and Native American students. Those underrepresented minority students—the last class admitted to Berkeley using affirmative action—had a one-year persistence rate the following fall of 97.2 percent. That is, 97.2 percent of them returned to Berkeley for their sophomore year—compared to 97.0 percent for white students in that class.

PROPOSITION 209

When supporters began to gather signatures to qualify Proposition 209 for the California ballot in November 1996, the measure was known as the California Civil Rights Initiative. Once the California Secretary of State had certified the requisite number of valid signatures and authorized the initiative for that ballot, it was officially renamed Proposition 209, but it continued to be subtitled "the California Civil Rights Initiative." In a shrewd political move, the authors of the measure designated it as an amendment to the California Constitution. That meant that while it needed only a simple majority vote to pass as an initiative, it could only be changed in the future by a two-thirds majority of the electorate or the California legislature. The text contained only fifty-three words:

> Neither the State of California nor any of its political subdivisions or agents shall use race, sex, color, ethnicity, or national origin as a criterion for either discriminating against, or granting preferential treatment to, any individual or group in the operation of the State's system of public employment, public education, or public contracting.

Nicholas Lemann, in *The Big Test,* provides a careful and thorough description of the long election battle over Proposition 209. (Lydia Chávez does a similar job in *The Color Bind.*) The University of California is a major part of the story. UC Regent Ward Connerly took over the failing initiative campaign in December 1995 and succeeded in qualifying the initiative for the November 1996 ballot. Professor Jerry Karabel, author of *The Karabel Report,* was one of the leaders in the opposition to 209. Lemann has also noted that a radical-turned-conservative professor at Berkeley, Aaron Wildavsky, had been pivotal in putting Glenn Custred in touch with Tom Wood, a Berkeley Ph.D. in philosophy, through the National Association of Scholars. That collaboration resulted in Wood and Custred co-authoring the initiative.

Calling the initiative the "California Civil Rights Initiative" was both strategically brilliant, because some portion of voters would read "Civil Rights" and believe they were voting for something quite different from CCRI, and mocking, because CCRI truly was the exact antithesis of the goals of the civil rights movement. Wood and other supporters of

Central Islip Public Library
33 Hawthorne Avenue
Central Islip, NY 11722

Proposition 209 liked to quote Martin Luther King Jr., specifically his famous passage about "the content of their character." In a nasty little twist of the knife, Wood and Custred opened a small CCRI office on Martin Luther King Jr. Way, and they made certain that the office space was in a stretch that was within the Berkeley city limits.

The time leading up to the November election was similar in some ways to the time leading up to the July 1995 Regents meeting, as supporters of affirmative action constantly tried to gauge the chances that Proposition 209 would or could be defeated. Yet Proposition 209 passed by a margin of fifty-four to forty-six percent. That outcome reflected the deep and seemingly permanent division over race in this country. Had there been just a five-percentage-point shift (not impossible considering the number of voters who may have been deceived by the language and advertising campaign for Proposition 209), the measure would have been defeated fifty-one to forty-nine percent. Although Connerly told *The Daily Californian* as recently as July 2000, "You have to be living on another planet not to realize race preferences are dead," the truth is that California and the rest of the country remain deeply divided and that the critical ten-to-fifteen-percent of voters in the middle could change public policy.

WHY PROPOSITION 209 PASSED

Proposition 209 passed because Pete Wilson was running for president.

It passed because there are many people who dislike and resent African Americans, Latinos, and Native Americans.

It passed because many people are tired of African Americans, Latinos, and Native Americans pointing out all of the ways that American society works against them and pressing for the end of those social, economic, and educational barriers.

It passed because Ward Connerly, an articulate, charismatic African American, led the anti-affirmative action campaign. Had he not been African American, he almost certainly would have failed to overturn affirmative action in California. In crucial ways, Connerly's race gave many whites permission to indulge in and to speak publicly about not just their opposition to racial preferences but to express, in the guise of opposing racial preferences, their deep and abiding anger and resentment of African Americans, Latinos, and Native Americans.

It passed because many people truly believe that racial preferences are wrong and that a color-blind society should be the paramount social and legal value.

It passed because not enough people who support affirmative action voted, specifically African Americans and Latinos.

It passed because some African Americans, Latinos, and Native Americans feel their individual achievements have been devalued by affirmative action.

It passed because Connerly and other supporters of Proposition 209 won the Sound-byte War.

Several of these points require further comment. First, it is impossible to truly sort out or quantify among the opponents of affirmative action the mix of racial anger and resentment as opposed to high moral principle. In part, that is because some people don't even recognize that anger within themselves and in part because so many people have learned to lie publicly about their true feelings and beliefs regarding race.

Second, Ward Connerly's belief that race doesn't—or shouldn't— matter in American society is naïve and far off the mark. Given our history, race always matters in America, and, because of our history, it is a fundamental part of who a person is. The need to believe that it doesn't matter is a fundamental act of denial.

Third, the idea that affirmative action devalues the achievements of African Americans, Latinos, and Native Americans misses a fundamental point. Affirmative action in university admissions gives its beneficiaries an opportunity, not a degree. Affirmative action takes no midterms, writes no papers, endures no final examinations, and most certainly does not present students with 120 units and a bachelor's degree as soon as they arrive on campus. The beneficiaries of affirmative action earn everything they get once that opportunity has been given to them.

Fourth, the media's overwhelming dependence on sound-byte reporting clearly worked in favor of Proposition 209, and the backers of that measure were extremely skilled in crafting such messages. It takes more than eight seconds to respond to the tag lines "merit-based admissions" or "reverse discrimination," and neither the media nor the general public was willing to wait much longer than that before their attention began to waver. At the absolute minimum, it takes several minutes to explain how a careful admissions process defines merit as much more than just grades and test scores and considers everything an applicant has accomplished against all of the challenges and opportunities that particular student has faced.

"Reverse discrimination" was—and is—the most damaging of all the anti-affirmative action sound bytes, and it clearly strikes a nerve with many whites. It is fundamentally important to remember, however, that affirmative action is not another version of the racism that deliberately sought to exclude African Americans through segregation and Jim Crow laws. Affirmative action is not intended to keep out whites or Asian Americans in the way that segregation was intended to exclude blacks. At the same time, it is true that when there is a limited number of freshman admission places at a particular college or university and some of those places are filled in part by the consideration of race and ethnicity among applicants, there will almost certainly be fewer places for any group that is not included in the criteria for affirmative action. If that institution has a complex set of admissions criteria and if race is only one among many items considered, however, the charge of reverse discrimination simply does not hold up. It is far more accurate to say that affirmative action reflects the broader perspective of the greatest good for the greatest number. That is, some individuals sacrifice some benefit in order to promote a greater collective benefit to the society overall.

THE SHAPE OF THE RIVER

In 1998, just two years after the passage of Proposition 209 in California, Derek Bok and William Bowen published *The Shape of the River—Long-*

Term Consequences of Considering Race in College and University Admissions. The book analyzed both the broad social and the specific individual benefits of affirmative action as practiced in twenty-eight selective colleges and universities, four of them public. Bok and Bowen used an extraordinary database, called College and Beyond, built by the Andrew W. Mellon Foundation between 1995 and 1997, and they made a thorough, meticulously documented case for affirmative action in university admissions. College and Beyond tracked more than 45,000 students of all races who enrolled at those twenty-eight institutions in 1951, 1976, or 1989.

Bok and Bowen focused on African American students who had been admitted to these selective institutions, all of which employed race-conscious admissions policies. They found that these students performed as well academically as their white peers at these colleges and universities. *The Shape of the River* makes clear that the claim that minority students admitted through affirmative action are under-qualified or simply not prepared for the level of competition they will encounter in selective colleges and universities is unfounded, in spite of its constant repetition by critics of affirmative action, such as Thomas Sowell and Abigail and Stephen Thernstrom.

In addition, Bok and Bowen found that these African American students qualified for and successfully completed graduate and professional schools in much greater numbers than would have been the case had they not been admitted to these twenty-eight colleges and universities, and that in general these students contributed more to their communities and to civic life after college than their white peers. And, equally important, nonminority students in these institutions reported that the presence of significant numbers of minority students was fundamentally important to the value of their educations.

The Shape of the River has already influenced policy-makers and scholars and is frequently referred to in media articles discussing affirmative action. It was an important force in the legal defense of affirmative action in the lawsuits against the University of Michigan, and it may be so in the future for other institutions around the country.

Many supporters of affirmative action in university admissions felt overwhelmingly vindicated in 1998 by *The Shape of the River*. In July 1995, however, it was deeply painful for most students and staff of the University of California, after having helped lead the national struggle to integrate elite higher education across the country, to know that it was the university's own Board of Regents that had taken the first major step in thirty years to undo a social policy that had made truly important contributions to American society. It was equally painful to acknowledge that the voters of California, the most racially and ethnically diverse state in the country, had sixteen months later done a similar thing.

7 UNPRECEDENTED CONSEQUENCES

The end of affirmative action in admissions has the most profound effects on the most selective colleges and universities because these institutions, by definition, have more qualified applicants than they can admit and because, if they have practiced affirmative action, race and ethnicity will have played some role in the determination of who was admitted and who was not. At the graduate level in public university systems, it is the professional schools—medicine, law, and dentistry—that have been most affected when affirmative action has been ended. At the freshman level, it is the flagship public universities that have been most impacted. As citizens in Michigan and other states confront the possibility of ending the consideration of race and ethnicity in university admissions policies by initiative or other means, they should pay careful attention to the consequences of such actions at the public universities in California, Florida, Texas, and Washington. (Chapter 3 offers a description of the first-year effects of I-200 in ending affirmative action in Washington where the enrollment of African American, Latino, and Native American students dropped from 373 students in fall 1998, the last year before I-200 took effect, to 255 the following year, a one-year decline of 31.6 percent.) The effects in Florida and Texas are described in detail in the section on percent-by-high-school policies in Chapter 8. The most striking evidence of the damage inflicted by ending affirmative action in professional schools is found in those of the University of California. At the undergraduate level, the greatest damage happened at UC Berkeley.

SP-1 AND THE UC GRADUATE
AND PROFESSIONAL SCHOOLS

Immediately after its passage in November 1996, Proposition 209 became entangled in federal court. SP-1, the UC Regents policy ending affirmative action, however, was still in effect, and, although a compromise between President Atkinson and the UC Regents stipulated that SP-1 would be postponed until spring 1998 for undergraduate admission, the policy would still take effect for fall 1997 graduate and professional school admissions. That meant that no matter what happened to Proposition 209 in federal court, UC graduate programs could not consider race and ethnicity for fall 1997.

SP-1, however, had little effect on the admission of underrepresented minority students to graduate programs in specific academic departments, in part because there were already few such students who applied to those programs and in part because individual departments control their own graduate admissions and can essentially run that process as a private matter. The UC law and medical schools were another matter entirely, with the puzzling exception of the UC San Francisco Medical School.

In May 1997, the UC law schools released their fall 1997 admissions data and their expected enrollment figures, based on deposits submitted by admitted students. It was a shocking story. Ken Weiss, writing in the *Los Angeles Times* on May 15, 1997, noted that the number of African American applicants admitted to the UCLA School of Law dropped from 104 the preceding year to twenty-one, an eighty-percent decline. Latino admissions declined from 108 for fall 1996 to seventy-three for fall 1997, a thirty-two-percent drop. UC Davis, which already had extremely low minority enrollments, had a twenty-six-percent decline in African American admits from 1996 to 1997 and a twenty-one-percent drop in admitted Latino students for that period. At UC Berkeley's Boalt Hall, African American admitted students declined from seventy-five for fall 1996 to fourteen for fall 1997, an eighty-one-percent decrease. Chicanos/Latinos declined from seventy-eight to thirty-nine for that same period, a fifty-percent drop.

The actual enrollment figures for all three law schools were significantly below these admit levels because most of the African American and Latino students who were admitted to UCLA, Davis, or Boalt were also admitted to other outstanding law schools across the country. The most egregious figure was at Boalt where not one of the fourteen admitted African American students chose to enroll. The only African American in the fall 1997 first-year class of 270 students was a student who had deferred his enrollment from fall 1996. In the fall 1996 first-year class, there had been twenty African American students.

Boalt Hall, however, has had something of a spotty admissions history in recent years. In July 1990, the Office for Civil Rights had initiated a compliance review of Boalt's admissions practices following the disclosure that the law school maintained separate waiting lists based on race and ethnicity—an astonishing blunder, particularly for a law school. In November 1997, prompted by a complaint to OCR filed by the Mexican American Legal Defense and Education Fund (MALDEF), Boalt's faculty admissions committee voted to end an admission policy that had adjusted the GPAs of applicants on the basis of the undergraduate college or university they had attended. Each college had been assigned a rank based on how its students did on the Law School Admissions Test (LSAT). Boalt then established two cut points. Applicants from colleges and universities whose rankings were above the top cut were given additional credit in the selection process. Students from colleges and universities whose rankings were below the bottom cut were penalized. Applicants from institutions whose rankings fell between the two cuts were treated neutrally.

Boalt had established this policy fifteen years earlier in an attempt to reduce the effects of grade inflation. While it is certainly reasonable to assess the rigor of an applicant's preparation and academic achievements, this particular policy was a remarkably clumsy tool. It treated all applicants from the same college or university identically and it penalized disadvantaged students for attending institutions in cases where they may not have had a range of choices. There is no indication that the admissions committee differentiated among institutions within their band based on differences in grading practices from one institution to another or that the committee differentiated among applicants from the same institution by major or by professors taken.

The outcomes at UC law schools were strikingly similar to those at the University of Texas at Austin Law School where, for fall 1997 in the first year under the *Hopwood* decision, African American admits declined from sixty-five for fall 1996 to ten for fall 1997, an eighty-five-percent decrease, and Latinos declined from sixty-nine to twenty-nine, a drop of fifty-eight percent.

In August, the UC medical schools released their fall 1997 admission and expected enrollment data. These results were wildly uneven. According to *Los Angeles Times* writer Amy Wallace, African Americans admitted to the UCLA School of Medicine declined from twenty-one for fall 1996 to sixteen for fall 1997, but admitted Latino students increased from thirty to thirty-five for that same period. At UC Davis, the number of admitted African American students declined from eleven to nine (five of those, however, indicated they intended to enroll, up from zero the previous year). Admitted Latino students declined from thirty-one for fall 1996 to twenty-two for fall 1997. At UC Irvine, one African American student was accepted, compared to four the previous year, but indicated that he would not enroll, meaning that UCI would have zero African American students in its first-year medical school class. At UC San Diego School of Medicine, not one of the 196 African American applicants was accepted for fall 1997—compared to seven the previous year and eleven the previous year—a decline of exactly 100 percent. Latino admissions at UC San Diego declined from forty-two to twelve, a seventy-one-percent decrease.

The biggest puzzle was UC San Francisco, the most competitive of the UC medical schools and one of the most competitive in the entire country. At UCSF, admitted African American students actually increased from nineteen to twenty-one from fall 1996 to fall 1997. Latinos dropped by one student from thirty to twenty-nine for that same period. It was impossible to discern how UCSF could have had these outcomes without considering race and ethnicity, but opponents of affirmative action did not challenge the admissions process. Testifying at a Legislative hearing in Berkeley, the assistant dean of the medical school described the UCSF admissions process as "plucking suitcases off of an airport luggage carousel," an unfortunate and puzzling metaphor. One reason why opponents of affirmative action did not challenge the outcomes at UCSF may have been the staggering declines at most of the other UC medical and law schools. Perhaps attacking UCSF would have made them appear overbearing and vindictive.

The figures for University of California law and medical schools, apart from UCSF, were shameful, especially considering California's extraordinary diversity. How could the state and the university adhere to the claim that the University of California serves all California's peoples? And how could Boalt Hall, to take one example, claim to be preparing lawyers to practice law in California?

In the August 5, 2000, edition of the *Los Angeles Times*, Ken Weiss, then its education writer, profiled a remarkable young woman named Cristina Villarreal, who grew up in the tiny town of Orosi in California's Central Valley. The daughter of farm workers, she excelled academically in high school, served as senior-class president, and went to MIT, where she majored in chemical engineering but came home every summer to pick grapes. At MIT, she maintained close to a "B" average, played varsity softball, and founded the MIT chapter of the Society of Mexican Americans in the college of Engineering and Sciences. According to Weiss, Villarreal took the Medical College Admission Test (MCAT) without any of the preparation courses that most students pay to take. Intending to practice medicine in the rural communities of the Central Valley, she applied to every medical school in California and was denied by each. She then enrolled in a master's degree program in public health at Fresno State, became certified as an emergency medical technician, and prepared with even greater determination to apply to medical schools the next year. All of the UC medical schools rejected her again. Eventually the University of Southern California, a private institution not bound by SP-1 or Proposition 209, accepted her.

Villarreal also had other remarkable qualities. Measured against her accomplishments and qualities, it is instructive to read Ward Connerly's comment, quoted by Weiss in the May 15, 1997, *Los Angeles Times* story cited a few paragraphs above, on the sharp drops in law and medical schools minority admissions. Connerly said, "We are too politically correct to reach the conclusion: They are not as competitive to be lawyers and doctors. If we really want to help those black and Latino kids, we will give them some tough love and get them channeled into being able to compete."

We have to ask ourselves what it means for California when the reservoir of hope passes from the public University of California system to the elite private universities. In a comment describing the fall 1997 law school outcomes but which could apply to those of the medical schools as well, Richard Russell, who had been a nonvoting member of the UC Board of Regents in July 1995 when the Regents voted to end affirmative action, said, "It's obvious that the resegregation of higher education has begun." Russell was describing a monumental failure of will and public policy.

FRESHMAN ADMISSION AT UC BERKELEY

In discussing affirmative action, one must be careful to distinguish between *admission* and *enrollment*. Every college or university tries in the spring to admit the exact number of students that will yield the actual enrollment that the campus has determined it needs the following fall. No institution succeeds in getting all of its admitted students to enroll, and determining the number of students to admit each year is an imprecise process because many students get admitted to more than one college or university. Berkeley, for example, typically admits about 8,500 students to enroll a freshman class of about 3,500 students, a ratio that is called the "yield rate" in admissions jargon. (Berkeley's typical yield rate is between forty-one and forty-three percent, which is relatively high compared to those for most colleges and universities across the country.) The lack of absolute certainty in determining admit targets is why many colleges and universities employ the use of wait lists.

Although the enrollment and subsequent graduation of African American, Latino, and Native American students is the fundamental goal of affirmative action, most of the political and legal struggle is over who gets admitted—that is, who gets the chance to enroll at a particular institution rather than who actually does so. The following section on UC Berkeley therefore focuses on admissions figures rather than those for enrollment. (Filipino students have been excluded from these counts because in the late 1980s and early 1990s, the faculty admissions committee at Berkeley determined that Filipinos no longer met the criteria for "underrepresented" and gradually removed them from affirmative action consideration. The committee made a similar determination regarding Latino—as opposed to Chicano—students, who were gradually removed from affirmative action consideration in the early and mid-1990s. Latinos are included in the data counts that follow, however, because the Berkeley campus officially combines Chicano/Latino data and because Latinos cannot be disaggregated prior to 1997. In keeping with the statistical practices of the Office of Student Research at Berkeley, the base percentage calculations also exclude international students, who ranged from seventy admits in fall 1981 to a high of 250 for fall 1991 to 221 for fall 1997.)

THE YEARS PRIOR TO THE END
OF AFFIRMATIVE ACTION

From fall 1981, the year that Berkeley established its campus-wide Task Force on Minority Recruitment, through fall 1997, the last admission cycle in which race and ethnicity were considered, the admission of

African American, Latino, and Native American students climbed from 12.9 percent of the admitted class to 23.1 percent. During that seventeen-year period, this figure ranged from a low of 11.9 percent for fall 1982 to a high of 33.6 percent for fall 1989. The percentage of underrepresented minority students began a sharp increase in 1984, stayed relatively high from 1987 through 1991, and then fell back, ranging between 26.5 percent and 23.1 percent from 1992 to 1997. From one point of view, it's difficult to understand how such a furor could arise over an increase of 10.2 percentage points in the admission of African American, Latino, and Native American students over nearly two decades, particularly in light of the fact that 39.1 percent of June 1997 California public high school graduates were underrepresented minority students.

THE LAST CLASS

For fall 1997, Berkeley followed the same policy that it had employed for several years. The core of the admissions process has always been academic achievement, and admissions officers asked of every applicant these three questions:

1. What opportunities and what challenges has this applicant faced?
2. What has this student made of those opportunities and how has he or she responded to challenges and hardships?
3. Does this student have a reasonable chance to succeed at Berkeley?

If the answer to this last question were not a clear "yes," Berkeley would not admit that student.

Under that policy, the first half of each class was filled on the basis of a linear ranking by Academic Index Scores without reading applications, and the second half, as a result of the agreement with OCR, described in Chapter 5, would be filled after reading in full all remaining applications. In this process, readers considered all of an applicant's information. Since the mid-1980s, Berkeley had employed a complex definition of diversity, with particular emphasis on low socio-economic status, race and ethnicity (until eliminated for fall 1998), special talents (including the performing arts and athletics), geographical origin, and disability. Although the campus had weighted race and ethnicity heavily in this process when it was permitted to do so, the heaviest weights in fact went to California residency and recruited athletes. And all of these variables were considered in conjunction with an applicant's academic achievements. Ninety-seven percent of the fall 1997 admitted freshmen ranked in the top 12.5 percent of California's high school graduates.

For fall 1997, Berkeley received 27,151 freshman applications for 8,450 admission places—an admit percentage of 31.1 percent (the Admissions Office admitted an additional 2,500 fall freshman applicants to spring 1998). The campus' goal was to enroll a fall freshman class of 3,600 students. After admitting about 4,200 students by Academic Index Scores, admissions staff read all of the remaining 22,900 applicants at least twice. Counting third-reads and tie breaking, admissions staff completed in all about 49,000 reads over a period of eleven weeks.

Admitting 8,450 applicants to fall 1997 out of a total of 27,151 meant that Berkeley denied admission to more than 18,500 students (this figure, however, includes the 2,500 fall applicants who were offered admission in spring 1998). The pressure on the Admissions Office was exacerbated in part by the UC policy that gives additional grade points for honors classes; in part as a result of this policy, 11,924 of Berkeley's fall 1997 freshman applicants had GPAs of 4.0 or above. Although these students were not all straight-A students, they—and their parents—tended to think of themselves as "perfect" once they hit that 4.0 mark. The math was simple: no matter how Berkeley might have done things—even if the campus had admitted only applicants with 4.0s and up for those 8,500 fall spaces—the campus was going to deny several thousand applicants fall admission who had GPAs of 4.0 and above.

Berkeley admitted, on time and under great pressure, a remarkable group of students for fall 1997. This last class admitted under affirmative action was 6.8 percent African American, .8 percent Native American, 12.7 percent Chicano, and 2.7 percent Latino, a total, as already noted, of 23.1 percent underrepresented minorities. As noted earlier Berkeley no longer extended preference to Latinos but counted them because other UC campuses still gave that preference to them and therefore included them, and because counting them would make the declines that were to come under Proposition 209 the next year less severe. Asian Americans were 35.5 percent of the admitted class, whites 33.1 percent, and 6.1 percent checked No data/Decline to state on their applications. In addition, the campus admitted another 222 international students—about 2.6 percent of the total admitted class.

Is the 23.1-percent figure for admitted underrepresented minority students good or bad? That depends on your point of view. To opponents of affirmative action, 23.1 percent may have seemed outrageously high. On the other hand, it was a rather modest figure compared to the 39.1 percent figure for June 1997 California public high school graduates, and it was well below the 33.6 percent figure for UC Berkeley's fall 1989 freshman class. It was, however, a significant achievement considering the intense competition that year for admission to Berkeley and considering the low UC eligibility rates for underrepresented minority students. The 1996 California Postsecondary Education Commission UC Eligibility Study had found that only 2.8 percent of African American and 3.8 percent of Latino California public high school graduates were fully UC eligible, compared to thirty percent of Asian Americans and 12.7 percent of whites. The overall rate was 11.1 percent.

It's also instructive to note that the Asian American portion of the admitted class, 35.5 percent, was more than three times the proportion of Asian American/Pacific Islanders in the cohort of June 1997 California public high school graduates—11.3 percent—and that the percentage of whites in the admitted class, 33.1 percent, was considerably below the percentage of whites among the June 1997 California public high school graduates—46.3 percent.

Although this section focuses on admissions data, it's also worth looking at the fall 1997 freshman enrollment figures. As noted earlier, enrollment figures often vary widely from admission figures because no university succeeds in getting all of its admitted students to enroll. Figures also vary because different groups of applicants often enroll in significantly different patterns. The fall 1997 freshman enrolled class included 7.3 percent African Americans, .7 percent Native Americans, 11.1 percent Chicanos, and 2.3 percent Latinos, for a total of 21.4 percent underrepresented minorities. Asian Americans were 41.9 percent of the enrolled class and whites 29.1 percent.

Asian American students made up 35.5 percent of the admitted class compared to 11.3 percent of the state's 1997 public high school graduates. Whites made up 33.1 percent of the admitted freshman class compared to 46.3 of the state's 1997 public high school graduates. These differences in admit percentages are partly explained by the remarkably high proportion of Asian American high school graduates in California who achieve UC eligibility, by the high proportion of those students who apply to Berkeley, and by the fact that, among UC-eligible students, Asian Americans in general are more competitive for admission to Berkeley than whites.

Even more striking is the sharp imbalance in enrolled percentages: 41.9 percent for Asian Americans compared to 29.1 percent for whites. This difference is mostly explained by the fact that a much higher percentage of admitted Asian Americans (50.2 percent) chose to enroll at Berkeley for fall 1997 than the percentage of admitted whites (37.4 percent).

A significant amount of resentment of affirmative action at Berkeley by whites in general has clearly been based on the relatively small percentage of whites in the freshman class at Berkeley. Some whites attributed that small percentage to preferences given to minority students. It is true that without racial preferences there would have been an increase in whites (and Asian Americans) in the freshman class, but not to a significant degree—as the first-year class admitted under Proposition 209 would demonstrate. Even if one assumes that every underrepresented minority student admitted to Berkeley received some degree of preference (which was not true) and a person subtracts the 21.4 percent of the spaces that went to underrepresented minority students, that still leaves 78.6 percent of the spaces open. The biggest single factor in declining white enrollment was losing in the head-to-head competition with Asian Americans for the spaces that made up almost eighty percent of the total spaces available. It was an awkward position for those white critics of affirmative action who argued that the university should depend much more on academic criteria to admit its freshman class. It was and is primarily by those measures that whites have lost places to Asian Americans.

The percentages of whites and Asian Americans cited above, however, are somewhat misleading because of the "No data/Decline to state" category. For fall 1997, such students made up six percent of the admitted freshman class. For fall 1998, the first year under Proposition 209, they made up 15.7 percent. Gregg Thomson, director of the Office of Student Research at Berkeley, has looked at those students and concluded that they are almost entirely white and Asian American, which means that the percentages of whites and Asian Americans in the admitted freshman class—and the enrolled freshman class—at Berkeley, especially for fall 1998, are significantly higher than the university's data actually indicates. The category "White/Caucasian," for example, shows only a slight increase from 33.3 percent of the admitted class in fall 1997 to 33.8 percent of the admitted class for fall 1998.

The fact that Asian American students made up 41.9 percent of the enrolled freshman class at Berkeley compared to 11.3 percent of the 1997 California public high school graduates is a remarkable story of achievement and success. But Berkeley does not have the largest portion of Asian American enrollment in the UC system. According to the 2002–2003 *Introducing the University*, that distinction went to UC Irvine, where 51.6 percent of the undergraduate student body is Asian American. Berkeley was second at 39.2 percent, followed closely by UC Riverside at 38.9 percent, UCLA at 36 percent, UC San Diego at 35.1 percent, and UC Davis at 32.9 percent (these figures do not include Asian Americans who may have checked the Decline to State box or provided no data at all). Sarah Lubman, in a two-part February 1998 story in the *San Jose Mercury News*, noted that this pattern of achievement is a sensitive subject within California and that Asian American success certainly adds to the complexity of the demographic and racial and ethnic issues that the University of California system faces. Some careless observers have used the term "over-represented" to describe the enrollment of Asian American students at the University of California.

Critics of affirmative action frequently claim that the policy benefits only middle-class African American, Latino, and Native American students. At Berkeley and other University of California campuses, that charge was untrue. Here is the family income data for Berkeley's fall 1997 enrolled freshman class:

- The median family income for the class was $64,000. Twenty-five percent of the admitted class came from families that made $32,000 a year or less. Twenty-five percent came from families that made $100,000 a year or more.

- The median family income for Chicanos was $37,500; for African Americans $45,000; for Latinos $55,000; for Asian Americans $60,000; and for whites $88,000.

And what about those white and Asian American applicants who were allegedly wronged by affirmative action? For fall 1997, Berkeley admitted 1,676 African American, Native American, and Chicano freshman applicants (Latino students did not receive consideration under affirmative action and can be disaggregated from Chicanos for fall 1997) out of a total of 8,450 admitted students. At the absolute maximum, perhaps 1,400 of those 8,450 admission places were affected by the consideration of race and ethnicity—in some of those decisions, race and ethnicity counted only slightly; in others much more so.

Recall that Berkeley also admitted another 2,500 students to the following spring semester, including probably every one of those up to 1,400 white and Asian American students who may have been displaced by affirmative action. That meant that the enrollment of these deferred students at Berkeley was delayed by only four months. That would seem to be an acceptable social cost in return for the benefit to the larger society of a diverse student body at Berkeley. (With Proposition 209 in effect, many of the underrepresented minority students Berkeley would have admitted to fall are now admitted to spring. Unlike white and Asian American students admitted to spring, however, these students, despite intense recruitment, accept Berkeley's spring offer in significantly low numbers.) As former UCLA Chancellor Charles Young said, "Affirmative action is not something we do for minority students. It's something we do for all of us."

Another frequent criticism of affirmative action has been that African American, Latino, and Native American students are mismatched with the institutions to which they are admitted through affirmative action and that they therefore do not succeed there. Berkeley's graduation rates, however, are among the highest they have ever been for all ethnic groups. These are the six-year graduation rates for students who entered as freshmen in fall 1996: African American 65.7 percent, Asian American 87.5 percent, Latino 73.2 percent, Native American 78.8 percent, and white 86.4 percent. The overall six-year graduation rate for that freshman class is 83.6 percent. It's interesting to note that the graduation rates for underrepresented minority students at Berkeley today are far higher than the graduation rates for the nearly all-white freshman class of 1955, when only forty-eight percent of the entering freshman graduated within six years.

The six-year graduation rate for African American students in particular varies considerably from year to year. Nevertheless, the gap between the rates for African American and Latino students, on the one hand, and white and Asian American students on the other has narrowed sharply over the past twenty years, a fact that is particularly impressive considering differences in family income and parental education levels by racial or ethnic group, two variables tied directly to college persistence. And, although most attention has focused on the differences in graduation rates between underrepresented minority students and whites and Asian Americans, one could also raise similar questions about the difference in graduation rates at Berkeley between whites on one hand (86.4 percent) and Chinese Americans on the other hand (91.0 percent), a gap of almost five percentage points.

The campus' one-year persistence rate for fall 1997 freshmen was ninety-seven percent—that is, ninety-seven percent of the freshmen who entered that year returned for their second year. That is a remarkable rate for any institution, particularly a public university. Contained within that overall percentage figure is an intriguing fact: the one-year persistence rate for African American and Chicano fall 1997 freshmen, the last year of affirmative action at Berkeley, was .1 percent higher than the rate for fall 1997 white freshmen.

The overall rise in graduation rates at Berkeley is, in part, the result of a major shift in the institutional culture of the university. Over the past thirty years, the campus, along with many other flagship public universities, has gradually abandoned its Darwinian, sink-or-swim attitude toward its undergraduates and has sharply increased its commitment to the success of all students. The narrowing gap in graduation rates between underrepresented minority students on the one hand and white and Asian American students on the other is almost certainly the result of stronger and better academic preparation among many African American, Latino, and Native American students combined with a determined effort by the university to be more welcoming, inclusive, and supportive. Much of this effort has been driven by the critical masses of African American, Latino, and Native American students who have enrolled at Berkeley and who have helped change its culture. Indeed, the presence of these critical masses has also contributed in many other ways to the sharply increasing graduation rates for underrepresented students.

The fall 1997 freshman class is a positive story. Still, it may be that Berkeley pushed too forcibly, especially from 1988 through 1991, and that the campus' early admissions polices were clumsy. It's also clear, however, that critics of affirmative action deliberately distorted how things worked at Berkeley and that such distortion contributed to Berkeley's becoming the national target for opponents of affirmative action. In any event, first the UC Regents and then the voters of California ended affirmative action. At the freshman level, that ban took effect for fall 1998.

The compromise on the implementation date of SP-1 between President Atkinson and the Board of Regents following the Regents' passage of SP-1 and then, immediately following the passage of Proposition 209, the legal entanglements of the proposition in federal court meant that the first full undergraduate admission cycle to be affected by the bans on affirmative action would be fall 1998.

After long and careful deliberation beginning in 1995, the UC Berkeley faculty admissions committee had approved a freshman admission policy to take effect for fall 1998, which, with the possible exception of the University of Virginia, would be unique among large public universities. Using criteria that had no formulas or fixed weights, Berkeley would read every single fall 1998 freshman application at least twice in a carefully developed and monitored comprehensive reading process.

In each reading, an applicant would be assigned an academic score (on a scale of 1 to 7) and a comprehensive score (on a scale of 1 to 5). The second reader of a file would not know the scores assigned by its first reader. Instead of formulas or fixed weights, the faculty admissions committee instructed readers to base approximately seventy-five percent of the academic score on the courses taken by an applicant, the grades earned in those courses, and scores on the required SAT I and SAT II tests, but also to consider carefully such things as the pattern of grades over time, the senior year course load, academic honors and distinctions, and scores on Advanced Placement tests. All of the academic assessment would be measured against what was available in a particular applicant's high school curriculum.

The comprehensive score would be based on the academic record but also on all other information in the file with emphasis on intellectual curiosity, motivation, tenacity, the demonstrated ability to overcome hardship, and extraordinary achievement. This part of the process was similar to the reading process the Admissions Office had employed the previous year with the major exception that it would not consider race and ethnicity.

Instead of filling the first fifty percent of its admit spaces by index as the campus had done the previous year, Berkeley would rank all of its applicants by final comprehensive academic score and fill the first fifty percent on the basis of the highest academic scores. Admissions officers would then rank all of the remaining applicants by their comprehensive scores and admit the rest of the class.

In essence, Berkeley was moving to the admissions practices of selective private colleges and universities. There were, however, three exceptions to this statement. The first exception was that instead of using a single overall score for its applicants, the Admissions Office would continue to use two separate scores. That was because UC Regents policy, as already noted, required that at least fifty percent and no more than seventy-five percent of the admit spaces be filled "solely on the basis of academic achievement." (The language in quotation marks is taken from SP-1.) The remaining spaces were to be filled on the basis of academic achievement and supplemental criteria. In July 1996, President Atkinson and Arnold Leiman, the chair of the university's Academic Council, issued "Guidelines for Implementation of University Policy on Undergraduate Admissions," which had been crafted by a university task force of senior administrators and faculty. These guidelines, included as Appendix 2, contained the undergraduate admission selection criteria that faculty on each campus could use in crafting their campus selection policies under SP-1. They were broad, comprehensive, and flexible and included both academic and other considerations. The fifty-to-seventy-five-percent policy meant that each campus, including Berkeley, would admit part of its students in one way and part in another. Berkeley's faculty admissions committee had decided that the campus would fill fifty percent of its spaces on the basis of a comprehensive academic review and the remainder on the basis of a comprehensive review of academic achievement and personal characteristics and achievements.

The second exception to the private university model was another

Regents policy, this one known as Admission by Exception. Admission by Exception, which was formerly called Special Action, meant that each campus could enroll up to six percent of its freshman class (and six percent of its transfer class) with students who were not UC-eligible. At Berkeley, these students included recruited athletes, students with outstanding talent in the performing arts, disabled students, and students who had overcome severe disadvantage and showed great promise. Because of the degree of competition for admission to Berkeley in recent years, the campus had enrolled no more than three percent of its freshman class under the Admission by Exception policy. In establishing the Admission by Exception reading pool, admissions officers reviewed not only UC-ineligible applicants but also UC-eligible applicants who were unlikely to be admitted in the regular admission review. The faculty admissions committee wanted to ensure that the campus did not pass over more deserving UC-eligible applicants to admit ineligible students. Students in the Admission by Exception pool were sent a supplemental questionnaire and also invited to submit letters of recommendation. Because private universities do not have the specific minimum eligibility requirements that the University of California uses, they do not have a formal, somewhat separate review process for "ineligible" applicants.

The third exception was a one-year moratorium on the new admission policy granted to the College of Engineering by the faculty admissions committee. Engineering was the only one of the five undergraduate colleges at Berkeley that had succeeded in getting its faculty to serve as admissions readers. In the late spring of 1997, Bill Webster, associate dean of the college, had begun to worry about building faculty support for the new freshman admission policy because it would replace faculty readers with professional admissions officers. Webster had wanted to be certain that his faculty would both support the new policy and have a role in training our readers because the new policy required a volume of reading well beyond what faculty could take on.

At the beginning of the fall 1998 outreach cycle in September 1997,

Berkeley administrators worried that qualified underrepresented minority students would not apply to Berkeley because of all of the negative publicity surrounding Proposition 209. The admissions staff was determined to do everything it could to encourage such students to consider Berkeley, and the outreach staff worked tirelessly throughout California. The result was a 10.7 percent increase in freshman applicants, including an aggregate increase of 11.3 percent for African American, Chicano (as opposed to Latinos), and Native American students. Overall, however, the number of freshman applications increased from 27,151 for fall 1997 to 30,042 for fall 1998, an increase of 10.7 percent. With 8,443 fall admission places, the freshman admit percentage would be 28.1 percent, and the campus would turn away 21,600 applicants, including almost 7,000 applicants with GPAs of 4.0 and above.

Without affirmative action, the hammer came down hard in the admissions process. Berkeley admitted only 247 African American freshmen compared to 562 the previous year, a decline of 315 students or fifty-six percent. Chicano admits dropped from 1,045 in fall 1997 to 466 for fall 1998, a decrease of 579 students or 55.4 percent. Native American admitted students dropped from sixty-nine in fall 1997 to thirty-one for fall 1998, a decline of thirty-eight students or 55.1 percent. Overall, African American, Chicano, and Native American admitted students went from 1,676 for fall 1997 to 744, a decrease of 932 students or 55.6 percent. The admission of Latino applicants, who were not included in affirmative action preferences for fall 1997, nevertheless declined from 221 for fall 1997 to 180 for fall 1998, a drop of 18.6 percent. Among the students denied fall 1998 admission were 6,979 with GPAs of 4.0 or better, including 754 African American, Chicano, Latino, and Native American students. Even though Berkeley knew such losses were coming, it was very painful. The campus that had prided itself on setting the benchmark for colleges and universities across the country had now lunged in a damaging direction.

There were also many stunned white and Asian American applicants and parents. There had been a fairly widespread assumption that the end of affirmative action would mean that the admission of white and Asian American applicants to Berkeley would be much easier. It is true that more white and Asian American freshman applicants were admitted to Berkeley for fall 1998, especially if one accepts the research that indicates nearly all of the "No data/Decline to state" applicants were white or Asian American. With 30,042 applicants for 8,443 fall admission places, however, competition was intense, and the admit percentages were still quite low both overall and for whites and Asian Americans as separate subgroups.

The fall 1998 freshman enrollment figures reflected the admissions figures. When the campus completed its enrollment census in late October 1998, African American, Chicano, and Native American students made up 9.1 percent of the enrolled freshman class. That 9.1 percent was a sharp drop compared to the 19.1 percent figure for the fall 1997 enrolled freshman class. African American students made up 3.5 percent of the enrolled freshman class, Chicano students made up 5.2 percent, and Native American students were 0.4. The sharp drop in admitted African American, Chicano, and Native American freshman applicants in April had somewhat prepared the campus and the rest of the state for the enrollment figures, but it was truly sobering to see the percentage of African American, Chicano, and Native American enrolled freshman decrease by 52.4 percent.

Unless Berkeley could do something dramatic to change these outcomes in coming years, the undergraduate presence of African American, Chicano, and Native American students at Berkeley would be cut by more than half by fall 2002 as each cohort admitted under Proposition 209 replaced much larger graduating cohorts admitted prior to the implementation of 209. It was a dismal prospect for the flagship public university in a state where by June 2002, 41.9 percent of the state's public high school graduates would be African American, Hispanic, and Native American (Chicanos and Latinos are not broken out separately in the California State Department of Finance projections).

The subject of recruited athletes and big-time college sports is complex and deeply intertwined in the culture of those colleges and universities that are determined to compete in Division I of the NCAA. William Bowen and James Shulman have pointed out the conflicting values and the institutional and societal costs of such sports programs in *The Game of Life*. So has Garry Trudeau in "Doonesbury." In one panel, Walden College signs a most lucrative contract with a prominent sports equipment company. In return, Walden agrees to rename its teams the Fighting Swooshes. It's a small price to pay, after all, for such snazzy uniforms.

As noted earlier, even when Berkeley was able to practice affirmative action, the strongest degree of preference in the admissions process was given to California residents and to recruited athletes. One of the results of Proposition 209 was a sharp increase in the resentment of the preference given to athletes. Pedro Noguera, then a professor in the School of Education, worried publicly on a number of occasions that in two or three years the only African American undergraduate students at Berkeley would be athletes. In fact, in the first three admission cycles conducted after Proposition 209 took effect—fall 1998, fall 1999, and fall 2000—recruited African American athletes made up 19.1 percent, 19.8 percent, and 14.9 percent, respectively, of the African American students in those freshman classes at Berkeley (the actual numbers varied from twenty-two in fall 2000 to twenty-five in fall 1999). Because of the high visibility of football and men's basketball, in which there are large numbers of African American athletes, many people assume that recruited athletes are overwhelmingly African American. At a place like Berkeley, however, which operates twenty-seven different men's and women's intercollegiate teams, the overwhelming majority of recruited athletes are white. The twenty-two recruited African American athletes just cited for fall 2000, for example, made up just ten percent of the total number of recruited athletes that enrolled as freshmen that year.

There were 140 white recruited athletes, who made up 63.6 percent of the total 220 recruits.

Middle-income African American students were not the only African American students to benefit from affirmative action at Berkeley, and they received a more limited degree of preference than did African American students from low-income families. Nevertheless, the biggest losses in African American freshmen at Berkeley under Proposition 209 were among middle-income students. There is a danger that over time the overwhelming majority of African American students at Berkeley may be either disadvantaged students or recruited athletes. That would offer students and everyone else on campus a limited and skewed perspective on African American experiences in this country.

Some critics of affirmative action believe that the end of such admittance practices will mean the end of the stereotype that African American students at Berkeley must have benefited from affirmative action and that they will now be viewed as having "earned" their way into Berkeley. Given the history of race in this country, however, it is more likely that the affirmative action stereotype will be replaced by two others: "You must have come from really difficult circumstances" or "Which team are you on?"

ENROLLMENT DIFFERENCES BY GENDER

It is also relevant to look at patterns of enrollment by gender, especially among African American and Latino students. This issue has just begun to be examined on a national level, and there is a public disagreement regarding the decline of male students as a percentage of total undergraduate enrollments in the United States. Andrew Brownstein, writing in the November 3, 2000, issue of *The Chronicle of Higher Education*, notes that part of the disagreement is whether the decline in male enrollment affects all males, as Tom Mortenson, a senior scholar at the Center for the Study of Opportunity in Higher Education, argues or whether the declines are found mostly among low-income students of all races and among African Americans, as Jacqueline King, director of the

Center for Policy Analysis for the American Council of Education, claims. At Berkeley, female undergraduate students outnumbered men for the first time in fall 1998. That event was particularly noteworthy because Berkeley has a College of Engineering in which the enrollment is overwhelmingly male. By fall 2003, females made up fifty-four percent of the undergraduate enrollment, the highest non-wartime percentage at Berkeley ever.

The patterns at Berkeley, however, vary significantly by race and ethnicity. For fall 2003, Native American males made up 39.2 percent of the Native American undergraduates enrolled at Berkeley (51 of 130). Of the 924 African American students enrolled, 347, or 37.6 percent, were male. For Latinos, 1,055, or 43.1 percent, of the 2,450 students enrolled were male. For Asian Americans, 4,194, or 43.9 percent, of the 9,557 enrolled students were male. (Among Asian American subgroups, only 326 of 876 or 37.2 percent of Filipino students were male.) For whites, however, 3,459, or 49.8 percent, of the 6,951 enrolled students were male. The imbalances among Native American, African American, Asian American, and Latino males and females at Berkeley, in particular, are a cause of institutional concern. It is especially important to determine over time if across the country an overwhelming majority of African American, Latino, and Native American males are not entering and graduating from college. The social and economic consequences of such a possibility are complex yet crucial to the well-being of the country.

The sharp decline in middle-income African American freshmen at Berkeley as a result of Proposition 209 makes it more likely that the imbalance between African American men and women will continue and perhaps increase because low-income African American women appear (from available data) to attend college in much larger numbers than low-income African American males. At the same time, male African American athletes, mostly because of football, make up about two-thirds of all recruited African American athletes at Berkeley and may somewhat offset this imbalance. With the relatively low percentage of African American males among the total African American undergraduate population, recruited African American male athletes may make up as much as one quarter of all African American male undergraduates.

THE RIGHT AND THE LEFT: REACTIONS TO THE FALL 1998 FRESHMAN ADMISSION OUTCOMES

When affirmative action in university admissions is ended abruptly, as in California, Florida, and Texas, the political landscape changes radically. It is as if a giant hand has turned the political kaleidoscope and all of the pieces of colored glass have formed an entirely new pattern. Instead of being attacked by Republican state legislators for racial preferences, universities are attacked by Democrats who accuse them of not doing enough to compensate for the end of affirmative action. In California, for example, state senators Theresa Hughes and Tom Hayden held hearings in which they excoriated the University of California. Legislators and other policy-makers begin casting about desperately for alternatives—particularly percentage plans that guarantee university admission to a certain percentage of graduates from each high school in a particular state. In California, Democrats in the Legislature announced that outreach was the solution and began pouring millions and millions of dollars into such programs. Critics of admissions tests, specifically the SAT I, become mobilized and more virulent, arguing that the tests will now become even larger barriers to the admission of underrepresented minority students. Civil rights groups file lawsuits either against universities on behalf of minority applicants denied admission or against states on behalf of poor and minority students trapped in disadvantaged high schools.

In California, the sharp drops in African American, Chicano/Latino, and Native Americans students admitted to Berkeley and UCLA produced radically different reactions from opponents and supporters of affirmative action. Many opponents, including Ward Connerly, expected Berkeley and UCLA to cheat in order to prevent the admit figures from dropping significantly. When those campuses released their fall 1998 freshman admit results, most opponents of affirmative action were rather subdued, although one or two of them claimed that the sharp drops only confirmed how prominent race had been in the university's earlier process. Connerly and other critics of Berkeley were embarrassed that the sharp declines in African American, Chicano/ Latino, and Native American admits and registrants predicted by admissions officers did in fact occur. In July 2000, Connerly told Anne Benjaminson, a writer for *The Daily Californian*, "I really thought that there would be a drop in the number of underrepresented minority students at UCLA and Berkeley and Davis and San Diego, I really thought that. I did not, however, think it would be as dramatic at Berkeley and UCLA as it was." Partly because of these declines (and partly because they had thus far won), critics of affirmative action in California were somewhat quiet for the next four or five years.

On the other hand, supporters of affirmative action were harshly critical of Berkeley. In the first few days after the fall 1998 results were released, long-time coalitions among staff and faculty at Berkeley who supported affirmative action began to crack, especially for people in admissions. Many campus staff had thought the admissions officers would figure out something. There was even a little of "They're cool. They'll make it happen." But there wasn't any way to make it happen under Proposition 209, and the letdown for many was severe. One staff counselor on campus with whom the Admissions Office had worked for many years was furious that her daughter had been denied. She told people, "Now, it's personal!" It was painful for people in admissions to hear friends and colleagues say or imply "You didn't try hard enough" or "You weren't clever enough" or "You didn't have the courage and the will to maintain your commitment to underrepresented minority students." The most exasperating comment, which was often heard, was "You should have broken the law." It is remarkably easy for people to recommend that others break the law.

And underlying some of the criticism was the suspicion that admissions officers didn't really try or that they were relieved not to have to try or that they could now truly come down hard on underrepresented minority applicants, which is what they had wanted to do all along.

These charges were similar to arguments heard over the years that the lawyers for the University of California hadn't really tried their best in the *Bakke* case because the university had, in fact, wanted to lose.

As noted earlier, Berkeley, for somewhat complicated historical and political reasons, had traditionally distinguished statistically between Latino and Chicano students. The faculty admissions committee in the early 1990s decided to phase out affirmative action consideration for Latino students just as the Committee had done in the late 1980s for Filipinos. This phasing out had resulted in a drop in Latinos as a percentage of the freshman class, a process that had been completed before the fall 1998 admission cycle. Hoping to mitigate the political damage from the first year of Proposition 209, Vice Chancellor for Undergraduate Affairs Genaro Padilla decided that Berkeley would no longer count—and report—Latinos and Chicanos separately. That meant that the decline in Chicano students under Proposition 209 would be masked somewhat because there probably would not be a similar decline in Latinos, who had already had affirmative action consideration removed.

This decision reflected one side of the emotional schizophrenia that existed regarding the likely statistical outcomes under Proposition 209. On the one hand, many campus administrators perversely hoped for sharp drops in underrepresented students as an indictment of the anti-affirmative action wing ("We told you so!"). At the same time, many staff fervently wanted to maintain diversity at Berkeley and to protect political alliances and even personal relationships that some of them had formed with minority and civil rights constituencies ("See? We did everything we could!"). It was impossible to reconcile these two impulses.

THE BERKELEY PLEDGE

Almost as soon as the Regents passed SP-1 and SP-2 on July 20, 1995, Chancellor Chang-Lin Tien announced that he was establishing a major new outreach initiative called the Berkeley Pledge. The Pledge stated that Berkeley would do everything it possibly could under the law to help disadvantaged students, especially African American, Latino, and Native American students, become eligible for the university and to help them get admitted. The plan was to build special relationships with key schools that had high-minority enrollments and eventually to develop a pipeline of highly qualified minority students who would apply to the University of California. Tien had been eager to do something in the face of the July 20 Regents vote, and the Pledge was his answer.

Tien announced the Berkeley Pledge on September 7, 1995, at Fremont High School in Oakland, joined by the superintendents of the Berkeley, San Francisco, and West Contra Costa school districts and a representative of the superintendent of Oakland Unified. He also provided $1 million from the university to support the Pledge. The press conference drew substantial media attention, and it was clear that Tien had touched a nerve by offering hope to low-income and minority students, families, and schools that had felt completely disenfranchised by the Regent's vote to end affirmative action. The Pledge had some early, well-publicized successes. In February 1998, for example, U.S. Secretary of Education Richard Riley toured Berkeley Pledge schools with Chancellor Robert Berdahl, who by then had succeeded Tien, and described the Pledge as a model program to preserve diversity on college campuses through stronger partnerships with K-12 schools. Yet Berkeley had been operating other, notably successful outreach programs for many years, and the Pledge, which turned out to have more symbolic importance than substance, soon lost much of its momentum and was eventually absorbed into those other outreach programs.

THE DAMAGE OVER SIX YEARS

By fall 2003 UC Berkeley had completed six admissions cycles under Proposition 209. During that period, the freshman enrollment of African American students dropped from 257 in fall 1997, the last year under affirmative action, to 149 in fall 2001, a decline of 108 students or forty-two percent. As a share of the freshman class at Berkeley, African American students declined from 7.3 percent to 4.2 percent, a drop of 42.5 percent. During this period, the lowest enrollment figure for African American freshmen was 126 in both 1998 and 1999. The fall 2003 figure of 149 students represents only a slight recovery from that remarkably low point. Of even greater concern is the fact that preliminary enrollment figures for fall 2004 indicated that the enrollment of African American freshmen would be well below one hundred students.

The freshman enrollment of Latino students dropped from 472 in fall 1997 to 393 in fall 2003, a decline of seventy-nine students or 16.7 percent. As a share of the freshman class at Berkeley, Latino students declined from 13.5 percent to 11.1 percent, a drop of 17.8 percent. The lowest enrollment of Latinos over this span of time occurred in fall 1998, the first year under Proposition 209, when the figure was 271 students, more than two hundred fewer than in fall 1997. Latino freshman enrollment has recovered more rapidly than that of African American students in part because there continues to be a steady increase in the number of Chicano high school graduates in California (they were projected to make up 34.5 percent of the state's June 2003 public high school graduates, according to the California Department of Finance); because the university's new Eligibility Index formula, a table that combines grade-point averages with SAT I and SAT II scores to determine minimum UC eligibility, benefited large numbers of Chicano students; and because the university's Top Four-Percent eligibility policy, which will be discussed in the next chapter, has also benefited them.

The freshman enrollment of Native American students dropped from twenty-three in fall 1997 to sixteen in fall 2003, a decline of seven students or 30.4 percent. As a share of the freshman class at Berkeley, Native American students declined from 0.7 to 0.5 percent, a drop of 28.6 percent, although the raw numbers and percentage-point differences are so small that calculating percentages for those changes seems overly dramatic. The lowest freshman enrollment of Native American students during this period was fourteen in 1998 and again in 2002. However, it is important to note that, for reasons the campus hasn't been able to understand, Native American freshman enrollment dropped sharply from fifty-two students in fall 1996 to the twenty-three students already noted for fall 1997, even though affirmative action was part of both of those admission cycles.

The cumulative effect of these six years under Proposition 209 are, of course, reflected in the overall composition of the undergraduate student body at UC Berkeley. As each post-Proposition 209 freshman class has replaced a senior class admitted under affirmative action, the presence of African American, Chicano, and Native American undergraduate students at Berkeley has continued to contract.

African American students have gone from 1,270 students (6.1 percent of undergraduates in fall 1997) to 924 students in fall 2003 (4.1 percent of all undergraduates), a decline of 27.2 percent. That 4.1 percent figure falls far short of the percentage of African American students—7.3 percent—among the June 2003 public high school graduates in California, as projected by the California Department of Finance.

The decline in Latino students has also been sharp—down from 2,771 undergraduates in fall 1997 (12.8 percent of all undergraduates) to 2,450 students in fall 2003 (10.6 percent of all undergraduates), a drop of 11.6 percent. This decline was much steeper in the first two years of Proposition 209 but was tempered somewhat by increases in the number of entering Latino freshmen in fall 2000 and 2001. Latino undergraduate enrollment at Berkeley, however, remains far below the percentage of Latinos among California's most recent public high school graduating class—where "Hispanics," as noted above, were projected to have made up 34.5 percent of those graduates in June 2003.

Native American undergraduates have declined from 243 in fall 1997 (1.2 percent of all undergraduates) to 130 in fall 2003 (.6 percent of all undergraduates), a decrease of 46.5 percent. The number of Native American students enrolled at Berkeley and at the other UC campuses is so small that it is easy to overlook their importance. Indeed, Native American students are often left out of the national discussion of affirmative action altogether. It is fundamentally important, however, not to overlook these students in the state—and the nation's—struggle toward a more equitable society. Annie Nakao, writing in the February 13, 2002, *San Francisco Chronicle,* points out that California has the largest Native American population of any state—628,000 people, according to the 2000 Census. That figure is 15.3 percent of the 4.1 million people who identified themselves as Native American in that counting. And contrary to a widespread perception, most Native Americans live in urban centers. The two largest concentrations in the country are not located on reservations in the wide-open western spaces but in New York City and Los Angeles.

In the aggregate, the enrollment of underrepresented minority students at Berkeley has gone from 4,284 students, 19.7 percent of the undergraduate student body in fall 1997, to 3,504 students, 15.6 percent of the undergraduate student body in fall 2003. Put another way, that is a loss of 780 students, a decline of 18.2 percent, over a period when the total undergraduate student body has grown from 21,738 students to 23,206, an increase of 1,468 students or 6.8 percent.

SPINNING THOSE NUMBERS

Another pronounced effect of the end of affirmative action is that various interested parties begin to bend numbers into politically expedient configurations. When the UC Office of the President released the UC system-wide fall 2002 freshman admit numbers in early April 2002, for example, the university made a point of emphasizing that the percentage of underrepresented minority students in the fall 2002 admitted class—19.1 percent—was, for the first time, higher than the figure for fall 1997—18.8 percent—the last year of affirmative action. Piper Fogg quoted Ward Connerly in the April 19, 2002, issue of *The Chronicle of Higher Education*: "I don't mean to gloat, but I told you so." In their spin work, both the university and Connerly, however, deliberately ignored the fact that the figures for Berkeley and UCLA were still far below what they had been for fall 1997. According to Fogg, the comparative figures for Berkeley were 15.9 percent for fall 2002 (this count included both Latino and Chicano students) versus twenty-two percent for fall 1997. At UCLA, the total of 1,675 underrepresented minority students was still well below the 2,010 admitted for fall 1997.

What those fall 2002 numbers reflected as much as anything was the continuing shift of underrepresented minority students from Berkeley and UCLA to the other, less competitive UC campuses, namely UC Riverside and UC Irvine. UC San Diego, the third-most competitive UC campus for freshman admission, also has remarkably low numbers of African American, Latino, and Native American students, but that campus had not been nearly as effective as Berkeley and UCLA in enrolling underrepresented minority students—particularly African American students—when affirmative action was permitted, so the drops at UCSD after Proposition 209 took effect were not nearly as sharp as they were at the other two campuses.

In May 2002, the university released its preliminary fall 2002 freshman deposit counts. That data showed that of the 950 African American freshmen who committed to attend a UC campus, 232—almost twenty-five percent—would enroll at UC Riverside. The next closest campus was UCLA with 158 African American students, while Berkeley had 125. UC San Diego was at the bottom of the list for African American freshman deposits with fifty-four. UC Riverside also had freshman deposits from 955 Chicano/Latino students, more than twenty percent of the total for all eight campuses and far more than UC Santa Barbara, which was next with 708. UCLA had 668 Chicano/Latino deposits, and Berkeley was the last of the eight campuses with 390. A few years earlier, someone in the university's administration invented a repugnant euphemism for this growing segregation, calling it "the cascade effect." That is, in this quaint metaphor, students of color are cascading from Berkeley and UCLA to UC Riverside in a kind of lovely, polychrome waterfall.

The end of affirmative action at public universities in California has resulted in a strong tendency toward a segregated University of California system, a system in which there are almost no African American, Latino, and Native American students in the UC law and medical schools and a system in which African American, Latino, and Native American undergraduate students are increasingly concentrated at UC

Riverside and at UC Irvine, two of the least-competitive campuses in the system, while Berkeley and UCLA have become increasingly white and Asian American. Californians and the state's policy-makers have to ask themselves what message they are sending to the students and parents of California if the freshman class at Berkeley is 12.9 percent— the campus estimate for fall 2004—or ten percent or eight percent African American, Latino, and Native American, at the same time that the California Department of Finance projects that students from those racial and ethnic groups will make up more than fifty percent of the state's public high school graduates by the 2009–10 school year.

Some observers have said, "What's the big deal? At least at the undergraduate level, the overall UC minority enrollment is about what it was before Proposition 209." But it does matter—first, because the education of all of the students at Berkeley and UCLA is diminished by the declining numbers of African American, Latino, and Native American students on those campuses, and, second, because, as Chapter 1 highlights, access to prestigious graduate and professional schools, internships in Sacramento or Washington, D.C., and job interviews with the most influential private companies or public-sector organizations are determined to a significant extent by where a person has gone to college. Derek Bok and William Bowen in *The Shape of the River* arrived at similar conclusions. If leading corporations or public-sector organizations want to interview prospective employees but are only willing to visit twenty colleges or universities, which twenty are they almost certain to choose? It isn't that a student can't get admitted to Harvard Law School or the Stanford Medical School from UC Riverside; it's just that it's more difficult to do so than it is from Berkeley or UCLA.

The previous year, Connerly had made a similar boast to that he made in 2002, pointing out that UC overall had admitted more underrepresented minority freshmen than it had in fall 1997. Statistically, that was true in terms of raw numbers—but only because the university had admitted about 10,000 more freshman students overall for fall 2001 than it had for fall 1997. As a share of the total number of admits, Connerly's claim was clearly inaccurate. And all of this numbers spinning deliberately ignored the fact that the number of African American, Hispanic, and Native American students graduating from California public high schools had increased by 29.3 percent, from 105,121 in June 1997, when they made up 39.1 percent of the public high school graduates in the state, to 135,903 in June 2002, when they made up 41.8 percent of the public high school graduates in California. The gap between the total fall 2002 UC systemwide undergraduate enrollment of African American, Latino, and Native American students—16.5 percent—and that 41.8-percent figure is enormous. The University of California is, after all, a public university supported by the taxes paid by all of the state's citizens.

It wasn't until April 20, 2003, that Richard Atkinson publicly told the full story about Proposition 209 in an opinion piece published in *The Washington Post*. Writing in support of affirmative action and the University of Michigan in its two cases before the Supreme Court, Atkinson finally pointed out how damaging Proposition 209 had been to the enrollment of African American, Latino, and Native American students at Berkeley and UCLA, the two most prestigious—and most competitive—campuses in the UC system. Atkinson's candor, however, was years late in coming, and, because he had announced many months earlier his intention to retire in October 2003, carried little political risk.

STRUGGLING TO FIND SOLACE

The fall 2003 undergraduate enrollment figures reflect the considerable damage done by Proposition 209 over six years. However, the modest gains in underrepresented minority freshman enrollment in the five years since the precipitous drop in fall 1998, achieved in the face of immense negative publicity regarding Proposition 209 and the cutthroat competition with other colleges and universities for admitted African American, Chicano, and Native American students, are important achievements for Berkeley. They reflect dedicated and widespread outreach work all over the state as well as the care and commitment required to read every single freshman applicant at least twice in order to be certain that the campus was making the fairest admissions decisions possible. Those modest gains also have to be measured against the fact that from fall 1997 to fall 2003, freshman applications to UC Berkeley increased from 27,151 to 36,414, a gain of thirty-four percent, while the number of admissions places remained relatively stable. That means that the degree of competition for admission to Berkeley increased sharply over that period.

The most current admissions and enrollment figures for underrepresented minority students, however, make it absolutely clear that it may not be possible to recover from the damage of Proposition 209, especially for African American and Native American students.

8 PIES IN THE SKY

Socio-Economic Affirmative Action and Percent Plans

When a court or voters end affirmative action, legislators, governors, university officials, and other policy-makers begin casting frantically about for some policy that might be deemed legal and that would achieve essentially similar enrollment outcomes that affirmative action had achieved. That is certainly what happened in California, Texas, and Florida—and what would almost certainly happen across the country if the United States Supreme Court were to abolish affirmative action.

It isn't just the supporters of affirmative action who seek substitute criteria because of their continuing commitment to racial and ethnic diversity; often it is some of the same people who pushed adamantly for the end of affirmative action. The motives of these people are often complex. Some of them seem eager to want to prove that they are not racist now that they have succeeded in undoing affirmative action. Some of them may believe that there are no viable substitutes and are happy to encourage such a futile public policy pursuit. Others argue that they are not against racial and ethnic diversity but that they oppose the consideration of race and ethnicity as a means of achieving diversity.

In one sense, there is something oddly illogical about trying to find a direct substitute for race without considering race. Some of the conversations on this subject in California recall the scene in *Through the Looking Glass* when Humpty Dumpty snaps at Alice, "When I use a word, it means just what I choose it to mean, neither more nor less." It is as if people tiptoe around the 800-pound gorilla in the center of the room, trying to find a substitute for race without admitting they are trying to find a substitute for race in order to avoid being accused of trying to find a substitute for race.

SOCIO-ECONOMIC AFFIRMATIVE ACTION— AND ITS LIMITS

In states where affirmative action has been abruptly ended, the first alternative to the consideration of race and ethnicity in university admissions has almost always been socio-economic affirmative action— that is, additional consideration to applicants from low-income families.

Socio-economic affirmative action gives students from poor families—and usually from poor schools—access to colleges and universities that they might not otherwise consider and adds complexity to an institution's definition of diversity. It can also, of course, significantly change for the better the life chances of the students it affects. In a series of speeches at the University of Virginia in 2004, William Bowen, co-author of *The Shape of the River* with Derek Bok and co-author of *The Game of Life* with James Shulman, called for additional consideration for low-income students on the part of selective colleges. In the April 16, 2004, edition of *The Chronicle of Higher Education*, Peter Schmidt quotes Bowen: "Allegiance to this country's ideals requires that American higher education do more than it is doing at present to support the aspirations of high-achieving young people from modest backgrounds who want to be welcomed within the walls of what are still seen by many as 'bastions of privilege.'"

Almost everyone, it seems, supports additional consideration for applicants from low-income backgrounds and almost everyone seems to agree that such a criterion is an important part of the notion of diversity. The difficulties are that the idea has long been a part of the admission policies of most selective colleges and universities and that, in many parts of the country, it will not achieve the same racial and ethnic outcomes as affirmative action has achieved.

Following the end of affirmative action in both California and Texas, Democratic legislators and other policy-makers in both states suddenly discovered the idea of replacing race and ethnicity with economic status—as if admissions officers and policy-makers had never conceived of such a possibility. Many selective colleges and universities, however, have long considered socio-economic status as part of their complex definition of diversity. At UC Berkeley, to take one example, that has been true for almost forty years, beginning with the first Educational Opportunity Program in the country there in 1965.

It isn't that colleges and universities haven't considered socio-economic status in their admissions processes. It's more that they have been uneven in such consideration across the country. Bowen and his research associate Martin Kurzwell analyzed the 1995 entering classes of nineteen selective colleges and universities, almost all of them private. According to Amy Argetsinger, in the April 13, 2004, issue of *The Washington Post*, Bowen noted that only 3.1 percent of the students in those entering classes came from lower-income families in which neither parent had attended college. In a study of the fifty top-national universities published in the March 2004 issue of *Postsecondary Education Opportunity* and briefly referred to in Chapter 1, Tom Mortenson of the Center for the Study of Opportunity in Higher Education found that most elite private universities had relatively modest numbers of low-income students (as measured by recipients of Pell Grants): Harvard—6.8 percent, Princeton—7.4 percent, Brown—9.7 percent. The six universities with the largest percentages of Pell Grant recipients were all University of California campuses: UCLA—35.1 percent, UC Berkeley—32.4 percent, UC Irvine—31.5 percent, UC Davis—28.5 percent, UC San Diego—28.3 percent, and UC Santa Barbara—24.8 percent. Here is an important set of statistics: the total cost of education for the 2004–05 academic year at UC Berkeley was $21,538. Berkeley's fall 2004 enrollment included 2,191 undergraduates who came from families with annual incomes below $20,000—that is, more than two thousand students came from families with annual incomes that were less than what it took to pay for that academic year at UC Berkeley.

The explanation for the UC rankings is, of course, complex. Part of it is state and institutional will. Although they are being sharply eroded, the state of California and the university itself have historically had substantial financial aid policies through the state's Cal Grant program and UC's University Grant program. A third part of the explanation is less admirable: there are significantly large numbers of remarkably poor children in California—twenty-five percent of the state's children, according to at least one study, live below the federal poverty line. And a fourth part of the explanation is that among those poor children in California are sizeable numbers of Asian American students who nevertheless achieve outstanding academic records.

While Bowen argues for greater inclusion of low-income students, he is careful to say that such consideration should not replace the consideration of race and ethnicity in university admissions. According to Schmidt, Bowen's research indicates that if race-based affirmative action were replaced by socio-economic preferences in the nineteen institutions he studied, the enrollment of minority students would drop from 13.4 percent to 7.1 percent. Argetsinger noted in her *Washington Post* article that Bowen waited until the University of Michigan cases were decided before releasing the results of his study in order not to dilute or distract from the case supporting affirmative action.

On the other hand, Richard Kahlenberg, author of *The Remedy: Class, Race, and Affirmative Action* (1996), has long been one of the strongest proponents of class-based affirmative action but, unlike Bowen, he argues that it can achieve the same racial and ethnic diversity of African American, Latino, and Native American students as race-conscious affirmative action. That is a much more difficult proposition because immigration patterns have complicated the demographics of poverty in many parts of the United States. In numerous states, relatively large populations of low-income immigrants from Asia exist. In California, to take one example, such an economic affirmative action policy does not come close to enabling an institution to obtain a racially integrated freshman class.

What it will do, absent the ability to also consider race among low-income students, is result in a sharp increase in the admission of low-income Asian American students with only slight increases in African American and Latino students. While there are certainly large numbers of poor African American and Latino students in California, there are also very large numbers of low-income Asian American students, and among poor students in California, Asian American students have much higher levels of academic achievement than any other racial or ethnic group. Because the core of a selective admission policy is academic achievement, low-income Asian American students are much more successful in gaining admission to selective colleges and universities than low-income students from any other racial or ethnic group, including whites.

Because research shows that race and economic class compound disadvantage in America for African Americans, Latinos, and Native Americans, it isn't enough simply to consider socio-economic status if the goal is to mitigate the end of race-based affirmative action in university admissions. The results of economic affirmative action in admissions may lead to sound and desirable outcomes, but economic affirmative action will not solve the problem faced by colleges and universities in states with complex population patterns where affirmative action has been ended.

PERCENTAGE PLANS

After socio-economic affirmative action, the next policy reaction to the end of affirmative action has been to adopt so-called "percentage plans." Texas, Florida, and California have all officially embraced different versions of such a policy, and Pennsylvania flirted briefly with the idea. These policies all guarantee to admit or to make university-eligible students who rank in a specific percentage at the top of their high school classes, and they all focus on the individual high school as the basis for admission or eligibility in addition to or in place of some sort of statewide pool. Texas set its cut-point at ten percent; Florida, at Governor Jeb Bush's insistence, set its figure at twenty percent; and California set its percentage marker at four percent. Such policies, in effect, shift university eligibility from a statewide pool to an individual high school pool.

Texas. Almost as soon as the Fifth Circuit Court issued the *Hopwood* decision in March 1996, Democrats in the Texas Legislature introduced HB 588, a bill that guaranteed students graduating in the top-ten percent of their high school a place at the public university campus of their choice. This bill was passed by the Legislature and signed by the governor in June 1997, to be implemented with the class entering in fall 1998. The enrollment results were unimpressive the first year of the ten-percent policy, but when UT Austin added scholarship incentives to top ten-percent students at high schools with a history of low enrollment at the flagship university, the freshman class returned to the same proportion of minority students that was present prior to *Hopwood*. Carl Irving points out in the winter 2003 issue of *National CrossTalk* that the fall 2003 freshman class at UT Austin was four-percent African American, the same mark as in 1996, the last admission cycle before *Hopwood* took effect. Hispanic (the term used in the article) freshmen made up sixteen percent of the class, two percentage points above the figure for 1996. At the same time, Irving notes that those figures are unimpressive compared to the overall population figures for the state where 11.5 percent of the population is African American and thirty-two percent is Hispanic.

It is an unpleasant irony that the success of the top ten-percent policy depends almost entirely on the fact that most high schools in Texas are still largely segregated. As Marta Tienda and Sunny Niu point out in the January 23, 2004, issue of *The Chronicle of Higher Education*, there is a significant legal question as to whether the Texas Top Ten-Percent plan is truly race-neutral because it depends so heavily on residential segregation.

Both UT Austin and Texas A&M (and the Texas Legislature) face a dilemma in the near future as the number of students in the top ten-percent approaches and then exceeds the admissions capacity of the two institutions. Irving suggests that the top ten-percent policy may have to be revised by the Texas Legislature, although whether and how to do so is a highly contentious matter. This dilemma will be complicated by the different choices currently being made by the two universities regarding the consideration of race in admissions. UT Austin is in the process of restoring the consideration of race and ethnicity to its admissions policies for fall 2005. On the other hand, Robert M. Gates, the president of Texas A&M, announced in December 2003 that A&M would not consider race and ethnicity in its admissions decisions despite the Supreme Court ruling in *Grutter*. These significantly separate directions set up the possibility of a contentious and highly political collision between the two flagship institutions over the next few years.

As Tienda and Niu note, there has been a good deal of opposition to the ten-percent plan, mostly from affluent parents who are afraid that their children will be shut out of UT Austin or, to a lesser extent, Texas A&M. Jonathan Glater, in the June 13, 2004, edition of *The New York Times*, quoted Governor Rick Perry, who said of the ten-percent policy, "I really don't see how it has worked the way people projected it would work. And I think, across the board, Texans see it as a problem." Critics of the policy claim that it is driving many quite-good-but-not-great students (those who just miss the top ten-percent cut in their high-performing high schools) to out-of-state universities and that many of these students will be permanently lost to Texas.

One part of the battle over the ten-percent law is clearly a class struggle between affluent, suburban families on the one hand and families, teachers, and administrators from poorer and rural high schools that began to send students to UT Austin for the first time under the 1997 law. Glater quotes Cherri Franklin, the principal of the public junior and senior high school in Marfa, Texas, who says, "The State of Texas has done a great thing by offering this opportunity to get our most gifted students into a challenging educational setting. And the rich people don't want them there."

Within that ten-percent band of students, first-choice campus demand has thus far not exceeded the capacity of UT Austin. In part, that is because UT Austin has deliberately enrolled significantly larger freshman classes since the *Hopwood* decision. Prior to the *Grutter* decision, had the university arrived at a point where it would have had to select among eligible students, it would have faced a much more complicated dilemma. As Tienda and Niu note, almost seventy percent of Austin's 2003 freshmen ranked in the top ten percent of their high schools. As that figure gets closer to 100 percent, there will be less and less room to admit those quite good students who just miss the top ten-percent cut-point in their high-performing, affluent high schools. If, beginning in fall 2005, the university admits significant numbers of African American and Latino students from its non-ten–percent freshman applicant pool in part on the basis of race or ethnicity, that will reduce the number of spaces available to nonminority applicants from those high-performing, affluent high schools who just missed the ten-percent cut-point in their schools, and that, in turn, will create a serious political problem.

The situation at Texas A&M is different from that at UT Austin because of President Robert Gates' announcement that A&M would not consider race and ethnicity in its admissions. Instead, Gates has chosen to continue down the convoluted path of trying to increase the number of African American and Latino students at A&M without considering race: targeting specific high schools for special consideration in admissions, establishing special scholarships, hiring a vice president for diversity, and setting up outreach and recruitment centers in areas of the state with heavy minority populations. He was forced to abandon one such attempt in March 2002 in the face of heavy criticism and political pressure, an event discussed in more detail in the next section of this chapter.

Tienda and Niu also point out that African American students made up less than three percent of the fall 2002 entering freshman class at A&M and that Hispanic students were less than ten percent. Those figures are well below the figures for the fall 1996 freshman class (3.4 percent and 11.5 percent, respectively), which was the last class admitted before *Hopwood* took effect, and a dismal record for a public university in a state where, as noted above, 11.5 percent of the population is African American and thirty-two percent is Hispanic. But the most important question is what will happen in Texas politics and Texas society if A&M remains an overwhelmingly white institution while UT Austin continues to increase its African American and Hispanic enrollments through affirmative action, much more closely reflecting the population of the entire state where, as Irving points out, Hispanics are expected to become the majority in just twenty years. The possibility of A&M becoming some sort of isolated white outpost is quite real.

Florida. As noted in Chapter 3, Florida's public universities in 2000 adopted a policy called One Florida (also referred to as The Talented Twenty Program). Legal challenges prevented One Florida from taking effect until mid-July 2000 for the fall 2000 semester that was to begin just a few weeks later. By mid-July, however, the University of Florida had completed ninety percent of its fall 2000 admission decisions in a process that had still included affirmative action. The university also added a number of minority scholarships that would be permissible even under Florida One. In many ways, this admission cycle in Florida was similar to the fall 1997 admission cycle in California. Because of legal challenges to Proposition 209 in California and a subsequent series of conflicting federal court decisions, Proposition 209 was in effect, not in effect, then in effect but too late to affect the admission decisions that fall 1997 cycle.

This uncertainty in the middle of an extraordinarily complex operation is an admission director's nightmare. Admissions officers at the University of Florida and at Florida State had a very anxious time waiting until late July to see what would happen with One Florida. They were, however, smart enough—and lucky enough—to complete almost all of their freshman admissions as early as possible in the cycle and were thus able to consider race before One Florida took effect.

The fact that UF was able to consider race in most of its fall 2000 freshman admission decisions and the establishment of new minority-targeted scholarships resulted in a nineteen-percent increase in Latino freshman enrollment and a thirty-three–percent increase in African American freshman enrollment. At an August 29, 2000, press conference, Governor Jeb Bush announced the University of Florida numbers and added that minority freshman enrollment had risen by twelve percent overall at the state's ten public universities. Bush neglected to mention that ninety percent of the UF decisions had been made considering race, prior to One Florida taking effect. In fact, according to Jeffrey Selingo in *The Chronicle of Higher Education*, Bush attributed the gains in African American and Latino freshman enrollment to the Talented Twenty Plan. "I've spent the last ten months getting blistered by people who didn't believe we could do this," Mr. Bush said of his Talented Twenty policy. "Today, I can tell you that our word has been kept."

That naked political move put enormous pressure on the University of Florida for the next admission cycle, fall 2001, when One Florida truly did govern the entire process. Predictably, there were sharp drops in African American freshman enrollment at UF. Writing in the August 14, 2001, electronic version of *The Chronicle of Higher Education*, Susannah Dainow noted that the University of Florida at Gainesville expected its fall 2001 African American enrollment to drop from twelve percent of the freshman class the previous year to seven percent. There were two primary reasons for this huge decline. First, in past years, many of the African American students admitted to Gainesville came from impressively strong high schools where they might have ranked in the top twenty-five or thirty percent of their classes but not in the top twenty percent. Under One Florida, these students were no longer eligible for the university system. Second, unlike UT Austin with the ten-percent policy, the University of Florida did not have the capacity to admit all freshman applicants in the top twenty percent of their high schools. The university's inability to consider race when deciding among applicants in the top twenty percent also contributed to those declines in African American and Latino freshman enrollment at UF. Given the dishonest claims he made for One Florida at that August 29 press conference a year earlier, it was interesting to watch Governor Bush transparently attempt to distract attention from the results at the flagship campus at Gainesville by pointing out that minority enrollment had risen at the other ten public universities in the state. It was the same cascading argument, described in the preceding chapter, that some University of California officials had used to duck the issue in that state.

Ignoring the outcome for African American students at UF, Bush rephrased his comments from a year earlier: "Many were the critics in late 1999 and early 2000 who claimed that diversity would plummet absent racial quotas and race-based admissions. With all due respect, they were incorrect then, and they are incorrect now."

One can even argue that affirmative action helped decide the outcome of the November 2000 U.S. presidential election. Jeb Bush's success in enacting One Florida succeeded in keeping a Ward Connerly ballot initiative out of Florida and therefore kept the issue of affirmative action out of the presidential campaign there. If the Bush campaign advisors were correct that Connerly would have cost George Bush votes in Florida, Jeb Bush's One Florida ploy enabled his brother to stay close enough in the state of Florida vote count that the U.S. Supreme Court could then decide the election for him.

CALIFORNIA: THE TOP FOUR PERCENT OR UC-ELIGIBILITY IN THE LOCAL CONTEXT (ELC)

In California, where the state Master Plan for Higher Education calls for the University of California to admit the top 12.5 percent of the state's high school graduates, policy-makers and academics proposed various percent plans following the passage of Proposition 209 in November 1996. The first of these alternative proposals came from Rodolfo Alvarez, a professor of sociology at UCLA, and Richard Flacks, a sociology professor at UC Santa Barbara. The Alvarez-Flacks plan was somewhat complex, but its essence was to replace the current statewide eligibility criteria with a policy in which the top six percent of the graduates of each high school in California would be deemed UC-eligible.

Because the University of California is constitutionally autonomous, State Senator Theresa Hughes then introduced a constitutional amendment in the California Senate that would have defined UC-eligibility as the top 12.5 percent of the graduates in each public high school. Then-Lieutenant Governor Gray Davis followed by introducing a plan of his own under which the top two students from each high school would be guaranteed a place at the university, although no one other than Davis took that proposal seriously. Other university faculty suggested a policy that would deem the top four percent in each high school UC-eligible, and in early May 1997 UC President Richard Atkinson said publicly that he liked the Top Four-Percent idea.

Some of the impetus for these proposals came from the ten-percent policy adopted in Texas. With the highly respected Master Plan in place, however, the possibility of moving from a statewide eligibility pool in California to a pool defined by each high school represented an enormous policy shift with potentially huge consequences. Because of the disparities among high schools, some disadvantaged high schools might have only three or four percent of their seniors eligible for UC based on the statewide criteria. At the same time, there were a significant number of affluent public high schools where twenty-five percent or more of the senior class was UC-eligible and where most of those students actually ended up enrolling at one of the eight UC campuses. Pam Burdman, writing in the *San Francisco Chronicle* on November 13, 1997, calculated that if the Hughes 12.5-percent policy were adopted, for example, the number of students eligible for UC from Lowell High School in San Francisco would drop from about 250 to eighty-five. Telling the parents of Lowell High or those in Danville, Lafayette, Orinda, Brentwood, or La Jolla that in the future only 12.5 percent of the graduates from each of their high schools would be UC-eligible would have been political suicide. This, of course, is exactly the same problem with which Texas is now struggling.

After the election in November 1998, Davis, now calling himself the education governor, claimed the university's four-percent proposal as his own and began to refer to it publicly as "my four-percent policy." He mounted a forceful campaign among the UC Board of Regents and appointed three new Regents in time for them to vote on his proposal. As the Board got closer to voting on the Top Four-Percent policy, which was officially renamed by the university "Eligibility in the Local Context", there was a theater-of-the-absurd quality to the public discussion, in that nearly everyone who supported ELC denied that building minority enrollment was one of the goals. The Board passed the policy in March 1999, to take effect for freshman applicants to the university fall 2001.

The top four-percent policy did not replace the pattern of courses, grades, and test scores that determined the top 12.5 percent of high school graduates statewide. Instead, the new policy would be added to the existing requirements to provide an alternative avenue to UC eligibility. In order to distinguish ELC from the existing criteria that would continue in effect, the university then renamed those criteria "Eligibility in the Statewide Context."

ELC took effect for entering freshmen in fall 2001. That year there was a significant increase in the number of Chicano freshmen enrolling in the UC system, from 2,668 in fall 2000 to 3,039 in fall 2001—in raw numbers a gain of 13.9 percent. The university immediately trumpeted this percentage figure, publicly attributed full credit for this gain to ELC, and declared victory. Yet there was more to this story. Fall 2001 was also the first year that the university's new Eligibility Index (a table that combined grade-point average and SAT I and II scores to determine UC eligibility) took effect, which contained a significant advantage for many Chicano/Latino students. The revised Index doubled the weight of the three SAT II tests that UC required. Many Chicano and Latino students whose first language was Spanish took the SAT II Spanish exam as their third SAT II test and made remarkably high scores. In addition, the university as a whole enrolled more freshmen than in the previous year (30,495 in fall 2001 compared to 28,560 the previous fall, an increase of 6.8 percent), and there were more Hispanic (the state's official term) California public high school graduates that year than the previous year (104,538 compared to 100,658, an increase of 3.9 percent, according to the California Department of Finance, although the 2001 figure was a projection). Any careful analysis has to consider these facts as well, and it would have been difficult to tease out the effects of ELC alone, particularly on underrepresented minority students, because the university couldn't collect racial and ethnic information from the ELC transcripts submitted by participating California high schools since the transcripts sent to UC do not contain that information.

In May 2002, the university released a report evaluating the first two years of ELC. Because that report focused on actual applicants to UC, rather than on the students made eligible under ELC, the report was able to track race and ethnicity because the UC application does ask for that information. As Jeffrey Selingo pointed out in the May 31, 2002, issue of *The Chronicle of Higher Education*, this report was much more restrained in the claims it made for ELC. Selingo noted that the program helped rural students more than it helped Latino and African American students. Rural students made up fourteen percent of the 10,908 students admitted under ELC compared to 6.4 percent of the 50,000 students in the traditional statewide applicant pool that is based on grades and test scores. Latino students benefited more than African American students, but their gains were quite modest. They made up 17.3 percent of the applicants guaranteed admission under ELC compared to 15.7 percent of the traditional eligibility pool. African American students made up only 2.8 percent of the ELC applicant pool compared to 4.7 percent of the statewide eligibility pool.

The increased participation of rural students in the university is probably a good thing for the state overall, but the university gave no explanation why rural students benefited more from ELC than other groups. It may be, however, that the new policy provided just enough incentive to attract a significant number of rural students who otherwise might not have considered the University of California as a possibility. It may also have been that a much higher percentage of rural high schools gathered and sent in the required transcripts in order to participate in ELC than urban schools with large Latino and African American enrollments where often there are few or no counselors.

The primary goal of most of the percent-plan proposals in California was to make up for the losses in African American, Latino, and Native American students at the university that Proposition 209 had caused. As the first two years of ELC indicate, however, it is unlikely that ELC will add many underrepresented minority students to the university over time. Many of the students made newly eligible in the future are likely to be white students from small rural high schools. Even in predominantly African American or Latino high schools, as Ken Weiss pointed out in the May 12, 1997, *Los Angeles Times*, there is often "a sprinkling of Asian Americans or others who make up a disproportionate number of top achievers."

One reason why ELC will turn out to have a noticeably limited effect is because in most of the high schools in California, far more than the top four-percent of the senior class achieves UC eligibility. The number of students who would not have been UC-eligible under the existing criteria but who will now be UC-eligible under ELC is therefore likely to be small. The most optimistic estimate by the university was 3,500 students. The actual number will almost certainly be much lower.

Unlike Texas, California does not guarantee top four-percent students the campus of their choice. A most important variable in the effect of ELC, therefore, is how much admissions preference, if any, individual UC campuses assign to ranking in the top four percent of a particular high school. For fall 2001, the faculty admissions committee at UC Irvine, to take one example, decided the campus would admit all top four-percent freshman applicants. That figure resulted in the admission of well over 4,000 students, a few of whom may not have had adequate preparation to succeed at the university—one student admitted to Engineering at UCI, for example, had a 3.9 GPA but an SAT I total of 600. It will be important to track the academic performance at UC of those students ranking in the top four percent of their high schools but failing to qualify among the top 12.5 percent of UC-eligible students statewide.

It will also be important to see if Irvine and the other five selective UC campuses maintain, increase, or reduce the degree of preference to ELC applicants over the next few admissions cycles. It's conceivable, though admittedly unlikely, that in future years ELC students who were not otherwise UC-eligible could be offered admission only to UC Riverside and UC Santa Cruz, the only two UC campuses that are even close to being able to admit all UC-eligible freshman applicants.

And, finally, there is the question of cost versus benefit. ELC is quite expensive for the university to administer, in part because the university has to evaluate thousands and thousands of transcripts each year during the summer for students who will be seniors that fall in order to determine who ranks in the top four percent in each high school— transcript evaluations that would not have to be done without ELC. In addition, ELC imposes a significant workload on each high school which must identify the top ten percent of its junior class (the university requires each participating high school to send transcripts for the top ten percent of its junior class, from which the university then determines the top four percent), print accurate transcripts for these students, and ship them to the UC Office of the President in Oakland. A significant cost/benefit question is how much money is spent for each student who is made UC-eligible under ELC who would not have been eligible under the existing eligibility criteria. It will then be important to learn how many of those students in fact applied to UC, were admitted, and chose to enroll. The per-capita expenditure for each student who enrolls may be shocking.

In any event, it will be impossible to evaluate accurately how many African American, Chicano, Latino, and Native American students were made eligible for the university through ELC because, as noted above, the transcripts sent by California high schools do not identify the race or ethnicity of high school students. The university does send all ELC students a postcard asking about their interest in UC and—oh, by the way—their race or ethnicity. Unless the university crosschecks the race and ethnicity of ELC students with some other database, however, it will have to depend on the highly questionable postcard survey data to estimate the effect of ELC on underrepresented minority students.

RISING OPPOSITION TO
X PERCENT-BY-HIGH-SCHOOL POLICIES

As higher-education policy-makers have had a chance to study the percent policies put into place in California, Texas, and Florida, critics have emerged from both supporters and opponents of affirmative action. Essentially, they raise four objections. First, if such policies succeed in achieving racial diversity in a particular state, that is almost certainly because that state has a highly segregated public-education system. Second, in a particular state with some integrated, high-performing high schools, underrepresented minority students in those schools with strong academic records who don't quite make the percent-plan cut-off will be denied admission to universities to which they would have been admitted in the past and where they have historically succeeded. This argument applies equally to white students from affluent high schools where more than the percent-plan cut-off have traditionally been admitted to public universities and succeeded there. Third, many of the students made eligible under a percent plan in low-performing high schools may have significantly weaker academic preparation, may require additional, and costly, academic support (a "bridge" summer session, academic support services during the regular academic year), and may be less likely to succeed at the university. Shelby Steele, who opposes affirmative action, made this latter point in the February 7, 2000, edition of *National Review*, although Tienda and Niu claim that this has not been true in Texas. Fourth, percentage plans do nothing to ameliorate the damage to minority enrollments at the professional graduate-school level in law schools and medical schools.

In the June 2, 2000, issue of *The Chronicle of Higher Education*, Jeffrey Selingo pointed out the role of segregated public-school systems in the success of percent policies and then went on to demonstrate who would be displaced by One Florida. Selingo contrasted a Latina student from Edison Senior High in Miami with a 2.9 GPA and no AP classes who would be eligible under One Florida with an African American woman from Palmetto Senior High with a 3.9 GPA, three AP classes already completed, and three more in her senior year, plus Calculus, who would not be eligible. He also quotes a young woman from El Camino High, a high-performing school in Los Angeles, who, in commenting on the Top Four-Percent Policy in California, raises the chronic issue of different grading standards from one school to another: "Schools need to be rated because four percent punishes students at schools like El Camino. I know people at other schools who don't work nearly as hard for a 4.0." Even though almost every high school student in the country believes that "the other schools" are a lot easier, this issue is still important.

A more serious challenge to percent policies came from the United States Civil Rights Commission. Writing in the April 10, 2000, issue of *The Chronicle of Higher Education*, Patrick Healy reported that Commission members voted 6 to 2 the previous week to approve a statement characterizing the criteria in class-rank plans as "hollow and regressive replacements for the use of racial preferences to admit some minority students." Mary Frances Berry, the chair of the Commission, followed in the August 4, 2000, issue of *The Chronicle of Higher Education* with an opinion piece which elaborated on the Commission's objections to such policies. She noted that the Florida plan does not give students the right to a particular campus and rightfully implies that underrepresented minority students will end up shunted away from the flagship campuses, much as has happened in California under Proposition 209. She also pointed out how minimal the effect of California's ELC policy was likely to be. Finally, Berry also made the point that such policies do nothing to help with the problem of underrepresented minority enrollment in graduate programs, especially in law and medical schools.

On January 28, 2004, however, Christopher Jennings, an assistant to Peter Kiransow, another member of the United States Civil Rights Commission and an opponent of affirmative action, sent out a questionnaire on affirmative action policies and practices to a group of forty selective public and private colleges and universities. The questionnaire, printed on Commission letterhead, gave the impression that these institutions were under some form of scrutiny by the Commission—and created a small furor. Writing in the electronic version of *The Chronicle of Higher Education* on February 13, 2004, Peter Schmidt quotes Commission Chair Berry: "I am outraged that opponents of affirmative action would go to these lengths to mislead people, to collect information that they will use to attack affirmative action. It is illegal, immoral, and unethical, in my view, for a special assistant to a commissioner to send a survey to colleges and universities that will be led to believe that this is the U.S. Commission on Civil Rights undertaking the survey."

How the tension among commissioners over the admissions policies and practices of colleges and universities following *Grutter* works out may have a significant effect on the future of affirmative action. It also will be important to see if the Commission undertakes formal challenges to class-rank polices, especially those in Florida and Texas, and to see how challenges to those policies from the Commission and other bodies develop in conjunction with the decisions universities make to consider race and ethnicity in their admissions policies.

Opponents of affirmative action raised the sharpest objections to percent policies in Texas as the result of a policy tentatively approved in early December 2001 by the Texas A&M University System Board of Regents. That policy would have admitted to the Texas A&M system the top twenty percent of the students from about 250 carefully selected Texas public high schools (in addition to the top ten percent from all other public high schools in the state under the existing law). Although the list of 250 high schools carefully included some schools that an A&M official described as "white, non-Hispanic high schools," the policy provoked harsh opposition from Ward Connerly and Linda Chavez, among others, who claimed that the A&M plan is a direct surrogate for race and a blatant attempt to resurrect affirmative action. As Jeffrey Selingo noted in the January 11, 2002, issue of *The Chronicle of Higher Education*, final approval of the policy would depend on an opinion from Texas State Attorney General John Cornyn as to whether it violates the *Hopwood* ruling. On March 1, 2002, however, the university announced that it was postponing the policy while it studied possible modifications to the original plan.

Selingo also pointed out that some observers were worried that this controversy would re-focus attention on the state's Top Ten-percent law as well. Had this Top Twenty-Percent policy been formally adopted, it does seem likely that opponents of affirmative action would have formally challenged such criteria in court as direct surrogates for race. Such a case would be carefully watched across the country, particularly in California and Florida. And, clearly, the outcome of such a case would depend heavily on which court and which judges heard it.

In terms of legal importance, the most telling criticism of percent plans came from Justice O'Connor in her majority opinion in *Grutter*:

> The United States advocates "percentage plans," recently adopted by public undergraduate institutions in Texas, Florida, and California to guarantee admission to all students above a certain class-rank threshold in every high school in the state. Brief for United States as *Amicus Curiae* 14-18. The United States does not, however, explain how such plans could work for graduate and professional schools. Moreover, even assuming such plans are race-neutral, they may preclude the university from conducting the individualized assessments necessary to assemble a student body that is not just racially diverse, but diverse along all the qualities valued by the university.

Finally, it is important to emphasize that percentage plans work to increase the admission of African American, Latino, and Native American students only in states where there is pronounced residential segregation by race and ethnicity—and where large numbers of low-income immigrants, especially from Asian countries, are absent.

9 MORE PIE
Outreach! Transfer!

OUTREACH IS THE ANSWER!

Just as many policy-makers in California, Florida, Texas, and Washington rushed to embrace socio-economic affirmative action and percent plans as a solution to the problems created by the end of affirmative action, so too did they suddenly discover outreach programs. The problem with this approach was that most outreach programs are superficial and not particularly effective, that, at least in some states, they have already been in existence for many years, and that the truly effective programs are labor-intensive and therefore quite expensive.

Several years ago, the University of Michigan established an outreach center in central Detroit in order to recruit African American students from inner-city high schools. Following the *Hopwood* decision, the University of Texas and Texas A&M established outreach centers in the Rio Grande Valley to do the same thing for Latino students. The idea in both cases was that admissions or outreach staff could visit high-minority high schools regularly, identify promising minority students, and encourage them to apply. Many of the most recent supporters of outreach naïvely believed that all that was needed was an effort to inform low-income, rural, and minority students about the opportunities available to them at their state universities.

As the University of California has learned over forty years, however, simply holding a college information/motivation meeting once a month isn't worth much over the long run. Disadvantaged students need frequent, rigorous academic support in middle school and in high school over a long period of time—Saturday College most weekends of the school year and residential summer programs on university campuses—to compensate for the low quality of education in many low-income and minority schools and to help them close the achievement gap with affluent students whose parents went to college and who know how to provide their children with every possible academic, economic, and political advantage. Such students need direct, personal help in order to identify which colleges to visit and which colleges to apply to, and they need strategic advice on filling out college applications, including application essays. Their parents need information and support, too, and some students need personal and emotional support to compensate for the frequent lack of such qualities at home. Both students and parents need information on financial aid and help in applying for it.

At the federal level, Upward Bound has provided the kind of program just described across the United States, but the individual Upward Bound programs can serve only a limited number of freshmen-through-senior students—usually about 105, for example, in the program operated by UC Berkeley. In a state with the population of California or Texas, Upward Bound can reach a relatively small number of students. At the state level, California—particularly the University of California—has been the national leader in the development of intensive outreach programs over the past forty years, and the state's experience is instructive.

As soon as the University of California Regents passed SP-1 on July 20, 1995, the Board of Regents itself, the university's senior administration, and Democrats in the California Legislature announced that university outreach programs were the best way to prevent the predicted drop in African American, Chicano, and Native American enrollments. Even the Regents who had voted in favor of SP-1 wanted to prevent such a decline. In addition to a task force on admissions criteria, the Board also established the University of California Outreach Task Force, a high-level group of business, community, and university leaders that began to meet in February 1996 and issued a forty-six-page report in July 1997. At the same time, the Regents and, especially, the Legislature began a process that would greatly increase funding for UC outreach programs.

The UC Outreach Task Force report surveyed current University of California outreach programs and recommended a four-point strategy for the future: school-centered partnerships, academic development programs, informational outreach, and university research and evaluation. The first point urged each UC campus to "work intensively with a select number of regional partner schools to help improve opportunities for college preparation and to foster a school culture that promotes academic success and high educational standards." The second called for expanding "existing effective academic development programs such as the Early Academic Outreach Program (EAOP), the Puente Project, and the Mathematics, Science, Engineering, Achievement program (MESA)." The third point called for an intensified short-term informational campaign "to provide better and more timely information to students, families, teachers and counselors to improve planning and preparation for college." The last point called for "harnessing the University's research expertise more systematically" and applying rigorous evaluation processes to existing and new outreach programs.

The Task Force's recommendations were reasonable enough but were unlikely to accomplish much other than provide a foundation for the university's request for more outreach money from the Regents and the Legislature. The reason the recommendations were unlikely to result in significant change is that the university had already been engaged in aggressive outreach programs for thirty-five years, starting, as noted above, with the first Upward Bound program in the country at Berkeley in 1964 and the first Educational Opportunity Program, also at Berkeley, in 1965. In the ensuing years, the university had added on all of its campuses, in addition to the programs named above, an Immediate

Outreach Program that focused on seniors, a number of community college transfer programs, and a substantial number of campus-specific programs. At Berkeley, for example, these campus-specific programs included the Professional Development Program under Uri Treisman, the Academic Talent Development Program, Project SEED, the Berkeley Pledge, the East Bay Consortium, the Educational Guidance Center, and a several programs through the School of Education and the Lawrence Hall of Science.

The University of California's outreach history is, in fact, extraordinary. The academic development programs in particular are nothing less than an attempt to repair the damage caused by California's public policies toward people and schools in low-income and disadvantaged areas. Many people have argued that fixing these schools in this way is not at all the university's responsibility, particularly when the university money that goes to outreach programs could also be going to support faculty research, undergraduate education, and graduate students, but the university has aggressively filled an extraordinary need that no other entity, including the state legislature, has been willing to take on.

Effective outreach programs, as noted above, are expensive and labor intensive. University officials had long claimed that its outreach programs were quite successful, but that claim had been difficult to prove because many of the programs had never done adequate evaluations. Part of the reason for this lack was that it is almost impossible to identify and track a control group. For many years, advocates for these programs could only say, "Imagine how much worse things would be if we weren't here."

It wasn't until July 2001 that the university established the University of California's All Campus Consortium for Research for Diversity (ACCORD), the most ambitious project yet to document the effects of the university's outreach programs. Jeannie Oakes, a professor of education at UCLA who heads ACCORD, testified at a joint Legislative hearing in January 2004. Oakes pointed out UC outreach participants account for thirty-six percent of current African American UC freshmen and forty-seven percent of Latino UC freshmen. She also noted,

"Outreach participants complete the a-g college preparatory course-work [the pattern required for UC] at four times the rate of similar students not in outreach programs—40.1 percent compared to 9.5 percent."

Critics claim that most of these programs have simply selected the best students in the schools where the programs operate. That may well be true, although it also seems reasonable to work with the students who have the best chances of succeeding. It is both important and fair to question how far can an outreach program move a student academically over a two or three year period. An outreach program that helps a student go from a 2.5 freshman-year GPA to a 3.5 junior-year GPA has managed a remarkable achievement. The problem, of course, is that depending on a range of other factors, a 3.5 GPA may not be competitive for UT Austin, the University of Florida at Gainesville, UCLA, or UC Berkeley.

The biggest reason why "Outreach is the answer!" seemed naïve from the beginning is that the university's outreach programs had already reached a significant portion of the students who were most accessible to them and who had the greatest chance of becoming UC-eligible or, perhaps, competitive for the most selective UC campuses. There are certainly thousands and thousands of disadvantaged students in California who could benefit greatly from UC outreach programs. However, because these students are scattered across an expansive geographic area, the cost of reaching them with the required intensity of academic and personal support makes it seem unlikely that university outreach programs are realistically going to be able to do a great deal more than they have already been doing. There is also something completely out of whack in attempting K-12 school reform backward through university-based outreach programs.

When the Outreach Task Force plan was presented to the UC Board of Regents on July 17, 1997, the Board agreed to double UC spending on outreach. The goal was to increase the number of UC-eligible African American and Latino high school graduates from 4,200 to 8,400. Amy Wallace, writing in the *Los Angeles Times*, noted that the plan would "target 50 underachieving or 'educationally disadvantaged' high schools across California, as well as about 100 middle schools and 300 elementary schools." She also noted that the plan sought "to increase minority enrollment without using affirmative action."

Many people have focused on the social cost of Proposition 209, but a significant public policy issue, which no one has thus far explored publicly, is the dollar cost of Proposition 209. According to the UC 2001–02 budget document, released in early November 2000, the first big increase in post-209 spending occurred in 1998–99 when the state appropriated an additional $33.5 million for expanded university outreach activities and the UC Regents added $5 million to that amount for a total of $38.5 million. For 1999–2000, the state added another $17.3 million and the Regents another $1.5 million for a second increase of $18.8 million. For 2000–01, the figures are $78.8 million from the state and $1 million for the Regents. The three-year total in *new* outreach money is $137.1 million—$129.6 from the state and $7.5 million from the Regents.

And there's more. The university's budget for outreach in 1997–98 was $32.4 million. If one adds to this base all the new programs and the cost adjustments they include, the total State of California/UC funds available for outreach in the 2000–01 UC budget total $184 million. The university has also secured outside funds for outreach from federal and private sources and from in-kind matching requirements that the state imposed on K-12 and the community colleges as conditions tied to the allocations to the university. The 2001–02 budget document estimated this amount at $144.2 million for 2000–01. The total amount of money available for outreach in 2000–01, therefore, was $328.1 million. That figure for 1999–00 was $178.5 million, and in 1998–99, it was $137.3 million. That's a total of $643.9 million.

A footnote to Display 2 in the 2001–02 budget document noted that the university's Outreach Task Force identified a total of $60 million from all sources spent on outreach in 1995–96. Subtracting that $60 million as a base-budget figure for each of the three years since the big increases began, one sees that the new money spent on outreach for 1998–99, 1999–00, and 2000–01 totaled $463.9 million. (Because of slight inconsistencies in budgeting from year to year, that figure may not be precise, but it is quite close to the actual total.) The State of California, the University of California, and many other agents have spent nearly a half-billion dollars to mitigate the effects of Proposition 209. That is a staggering cost.

It is important to point out that it wasn't just the supporters of affirmative action who supported and voted for these expenditures. As with the Board of Regents itself, many of the people who voted to end affirmative action were also concerned about what would happen to the enrollment of African American, Latino, and Native American students at the University of California. Many opponents of affirmative action, therefore, supported the massive investment in outreach.

The expectations of the California Legislature for the success of increased outreach, perhaps based on desperate hope and a lack of alternatives, were most unrealistic. At the same time, however, the leadership of the University of California chose not to engage in a public discussion of the complex challenges and the realistic possibilities for increased outreach and instead quietly accepted the millions and millions of dollars of increased funding. Along with the money from the Legislature, however, came an unspoken but not-so-subtle threat: "Okay, here's the money. But you better make this thing work." And almost immediately after the Legislature had allocated the money to the university, legislators began demanding, "Is it fixed yet?" During a Legislative hearing in Sacramento in April 2001, key legislators, furious over what they saw as a lack of progress in underrepresented minority enrollments at UC, threatened to withhold as much as $100 million from the university's budget until the problem was solved. By not explaining the clear limits of outreach from the beginning, the university had left itself vulnerable.

GOODBYE TO UC OUTREACH

These enormous sums of money for outreach came when California was unbelievably flush, carrying as recently as early 2001 a budget surplus of $12 billion. The combination of the technology-sector economic collapse, an energy mess, and the effects of the events of September 11, however, not only wiped out that $12 billion but created a huge budget shortfall, first projected at $12 billion in January 2002 by Governor Davis, then raised to $17 billion by the Legislative Analyst a month later, reassessed yet again by the Legislative Analyst in late April at $22 billion, and finally determined to be $23.6 billion in May 2002. As *The Chronicle of Higher Education* pointed out even before the April reassessment, that was "the biggest decline in revenues since World War II." Imagine a $35.6 billion swing over a period of slightly more than one year. Most Californians went into deep shock, and everyone dependent on state funding lobbied like crazy just to preserve core functions in the 2002–03 state budget.

California's budget crisis, of course, has continued. Before he was recalled in November 2003, Gray Davis and the Legislature cut UC outreach funding by fifty percent for the 2003–04 year. Governor Schwarzenegger then proposed cutting the remaining fifty percent in his budget for 2004–05. At the end of the 2004–05 budget process, Democrats in the Legislature were able to restore most of that proposed cut, but the cumulative effect of these two years of cuts has been the evisceration of UC outreach programs. Two governors and the California Legislature have gone from believing "Outreach is the answer!" in 1996 to "Outreach is so unimportant that we can eliminate it almost completely" in 2004. That is a stunning shift in such a remarkably short time.

More important, cutting UC outreach completely is almost certainly going to have a sharp, negative impact on the preparation of African American, Latino, and Native American students for the University of California and therefore on the enrollment of those students at the university. It will compound the damage already caused by Proposition 209 to the enrollment of such students at UC, particularly at UC Berkeley, UCLA, and UC San Diego. Admissions officials at UC Berkeley, for example, believe that the fifty percent outreach cut for 2003–04 strongly influenced the sharp drop in fall 2004 African American freshman applications, which declined from 1,704 for fall 2003 to 1,542 for fall 2004, a drop of 9.5 percent. As of late spring 2004, according to Michelle Locke of the Associated Press, Berkeley had received fall deposits from just ninety-eight African American freshmen, although the final figure was slightly higher. California is about to learn what, some years ago, had just been speculation on the part of the university's outreach programs: "Imagine how much worse things would be if we weren't here."

But even before the state reversed its position on outreach, it was naïve and foolish to think that the solution to the gross social inequities in California that begin even before birth and that lead to such disparate outcomes by race, ethnicity, and economic class could be University of California outreach.

HI-VOLTAGE ZAP

Prior to that funding reversal by the state, UC outreach programs had already suffered a major setback by the California Supreme Court. On November 30, 2000, the Court issued a decision in a case called *Hi-Voltage Wire Works v. City of San Jose* that profoundly affected an important dimension of UC outreach. This decision eliminated a targeted outreach program conducted by San Jose on the basis that outreach programs focusing on race, ethnicity, and gender are not permitted under Proposition 209. The seven justices were unanimous in rejecting the San Jose program, but there was a sharp difference of opinion among the seven regarding what sort of outreach might be permissible under 209. University of California attorneys spent considerable time studying the decision and then concluded that, under it, University of California outreach and recruitment targeted specifically to African American, Latino, and Native American students was no longer permissible.

That was a major setback for UC campuses. At Berkeley, for example, targeted outreach has been vital since the passage of Proposition 209 and may have prevented even greater declines in the enrollment of African American, Latino, and Native American students. The campus built a database of prospective African American, Chicano, and Native American students by gathering data from its own outreach officer school visits, UC outreach programs, direct inquiries to the Admissions Office from prospective students, Visitor Center records, and the Student Search Service of the College Board. Through the Student Search Service, Berkeley, like other colleges and universities all over the country, would buy the names and other information of students who had taken College Board tests such as the SAT I and who had agreed to have their information released to colleges and universities. Berkeley then began a comprehensive set of activities—sequenced mailings, receptions, telephone calls, invitations to visit UC Berkeley, Cal Day activities—a whole range of actions to inform these students about Berkeley, to let them know that Berkeley was interested in them, and to build some sort of relationship with them over time in hopes that they would apply to Berkeley and, if they were admitted, would choose to enroll there. These activities reached underrepresented minority students before they applied to Berkeley, after they applied but before admissions decisions had been made, and after they had been admitted. (In differing degrees, Berkeley conducts similar recruitment activities for students who are being considered for Regents' and Chancellor's Scholarships—the most prestigious scholarships the campus offers—students interested in the physical sciences, and, depending on the year, students interested in other academic areas that the campus administration has determined need support.)

The authority for these targeted recruitment activities for underrepresented minority students had come from a memorandum from Deputy General Counsel Gary Morrison to Provost and Senior Vice President C. Judson King, dated March 16, 1998, and conveyed to UC chancellors on April 8, 1998, by General Counsel James Holst. In that memo, Morrison wrote, "informational outreach targeted to under-represented minorities is permissible as it is consistent with a reasonable interpretation of what is a 'preference' in 'the operation of public education' under Proposition 209." Morrison carefully distinguished between informational outreach and *developmental outreach* that provides "special academic enrichment opportunities." The modest gains in the freshman enrollment of African American, Chicano, and Native American students that Berkeley has gained since the first year that Proposition 209 took effect are almost certainly due to a significant degree to these outreach and recruitment efforts.

The core of this issue is what the phrase "preferential treatment" in the language of Proposition 209 means legally. According to Morrison, there was no agreed-upon definition and there is no definition in case law. The *Hi-Voltage* decision begins to build that definition, but it may also require at least one more court case that specifically addresses the meaning of the "preferential treatment." If targeted outreach continues to be impermissible and if the state in essence eliminates outreach programs, the enrollment of African American, Chicano, and Native American students at the University of California, especially at Berkeley and UCLA, will almost certainly drop sharply.

In the meantime, following the passage of Proposition 209, private universities in California and both public and private universities from outside California have greatly increased their recruitment in California of African American, Latino, and Native American high school seniors. On September 24, 2000, historically black colleges and universities held their second annual Application Day in the San Francisco Bay Area, admitting on the spot large numbers of African American students and offering many of them scholarships. In the November/December Berkeley High School PTSA Newsletter, the school's college advisor at that time, Rory Bled—one of the best in the country—wrote, "Bates, Dartmouth, and Mt. Holyoke are bringing underrepresented students from BHS to their campuses, and more colleges will do so in the spring. In the aftermath of Proposition 209, colleges across the United States are enthusiastically recruiting our students of color."

This shift of underrepresented minority students from the University of California to out-of-state colleges and universities and to private universities within California was documented by the UC system-wide faculty admissions committee (BOARS or the Board of Admissions and Relations with Schools) in its September 2003 report to the UC Board of Regents. According to Tanya Schevitz, writing in the September 20, 2003, *San Francisco Chronicle*, "High-achieving African American, Latino and American Indian students who were accepted into the University of California system are increasingly choosing to attend elite private institutions, such as Stanford, Harvard, and Yale. . . ." The report points out that these losses have occurred since the passage of Proposition 209. Citing the report, Schevitz says, "The trend is especially pronounced among African American, Latino, and American Indian students who were turned away by UC Berkeley and UCLA but admitted to less prestigious UC campuses."

Within California, the biggest beneficiaries of Proposition 209 have been the University of Southern California and, to a lesser extent, Stanford. In an unmistakable irony, Stanford and USC, the traditional bastions of white privilege in California, are now far more racially diverse than Berkeley and UCLA, the traditional engines of opportunity for the sons and daughters of the working and middle classes.

These increased opportunities for underrepresented minority students at private and out-of-state colleges and universities may be good for those students—but they are not necessarily good for California. The declining enrollments of African American, Latino, and Native American students at many UC campuses mean that the education of the students enrolled on those campuses is diminished by the absence of a significant minority presence in the classroom, in residence halls, in study groups, and in all of the other places university students learn from and about each other. And many of those students who attend out-of-state colleges and universities will not return to California in a time when California desperately needs educated citizens and leaders who reflect the state's remarkably diverse population.

In addition to socio-economic affirmative action, percent plans, and outreach, states that have ended affirmative action have also attempted to increase the transfer of African American, Latino, and Native American community college students in order to offset the drop in the freshman enrollment of those students. In part, that is because in many states, community colleges enroll significant numbers of minority students—the California Postsecondary Education Commission, for example, calculates that eighty percent of the African American, Latino, and Native American students enrolled in college in California attend one of the state's 109 community colleges.

The issue of increasing community college transfers to public universities in states that have ended affirmative action is complex. For one thing, states differ enormously in the degree of control they can exercise over their four-year universities. In Florida, for example, the Legislature years ago imposed a common course-numbering system on all public colleges in the state. Under that numbering system, a student at any Florida community college knows that a course with the title and number "English 10" will be accepted as the equivalent of that same course offered at any four-year public university, where that course will also have the same title and number. In California, however, the constitutional autonomy of the University of California has enabled its faculty to fight off legislative attempts to impose a common course-numbering system on all public colleges in California. Potential transfer students have to be careful and, in many cases, quite determined in order to discern course equivalencies, particularly at the University of California. UC Berkeley, for example, has a separate transfer agreement with each California community college, listing which courses, if any, will satisfy the freshman reading and composition (English 1A-1B) requirement. From some community colleges, no courses are accepted. At others, a student has to take a precise sequence of courses—often more than the two that Berkeley requires of its own freshmen. The result is a massive bureaucratic apparatus that is cumbersome, inefficient, and intimidating to many students.

A second issue is that four-year colleges and universities within the same state often have remarkably different prerequisites and general education requirements for the same major. Transfer students often must prepare for the possibility of transfer to several four-year institutions, depending on the degree of competition for the major they wish on each campus, their own qualifications, and variables within their own lives. When each of those four-year institutions has a different set of transfer requirements or when their requirements overlap only partially, preparing for transfer is quite complicated.

A third issue is the difficulty four-year colleges have had in identifying potential transfer students early in their community-college careers so that admissions and outreach officers can advise students about course selection, course equivalencies, and admission requirements. Most community colleges have not had a data system that enabled them to identify early on those students with the intent and the potential to transfer. In California, for example, it wasn't until fall 2000 that California community colleges were able for the first time to send potential-transfer-student data to the University of California. Out of some two million students enrolled in what at that time was the state's 107 community colleges, about 25,000 were identified as having met potential-transfer-student criteria.

This early identification of potential transfer students is also important because of a fourth issue. The quality of transfer advising varies enormously from one community college to another and from one counselor to another within the same community college. Some of this unevenness is a question of institutional will. Santa Monica College and Diablo Valley College, to take two California examples, have made transferring the central core of their mission, and they are highly effective transfer institutions. Within a particular community college, counselors vary widely in how thoroughly they have learned the intricacies of transfer information. In community colleges that transfer small numbers of students to four-year institutions, it may even be unrealistic to expect counselors to master the complex body of material they need to know in order to be effective transfer counselors for the few students who do aspire to transfer.

A fifth factor is that many four-year colleges, especially those that are selective, are in general unaccommodating to part-time undergraduate students, even though many community college students go to college part-time for legitimate reasons. Budget pressures have forced many four-year colleges and universities to put increasing pressure on their students to take a full academic load each term and to graduate as quickly as possible in order to make space for other students. Because many potential transfer students have full-time jobs, families, or other obligations, they have much less mobility than unencumbered students who are nineteen or twenty years old. That means if it is extremely difficult to gain admission to the four-year public university campus nearest to them in the major they want, they may be much more likely to choose a private college or university, rather than consider another public campus much farther away, or they may just give up. In California, it seems clear that one reason why roughly four times as many California community college students transfer to California State University campuses than to UC campuses, beyond the fact that CSU has twenty-three campuses compared to eight for UC, is that the CSU campuses serve part-time students hospitably.

A sixth factor is that transfer admission to flagship public university campuses—and to many other public universities as well—has in many cases become almost as competitive as freshman admission. For fall 2003, for example, UC Berkeley admitted 26.1 percent of its 10,378 transfer applicants compared to 23.9 percent of its freshman applicants. At UCLA, the figures were 40.1 percent for transfer applicants and 23.6 percent for freshmen. UC San Diego admitted 57.2 percent of its transfer applicants compared to 37.4 percent of its freshman applicants. UC Irvine admitted 64.2 percent of its transfer applicants compared to 53.8 percent of its freshman applicants.

In addition, an overall transfer-admit percentage may mask the competition for the most popular majors, such as electrical engineering, computer science, business administration, and, in many cases, those in the social sciences. The transfer competition for these programs at many public universities is severe. That is certainly true, for example, at UC Berkeley, and, in the case of business administration, the problem is compounded by the fact that there is only one other undergraduate business administration program in the UC system, at UC Riverside. In addition to the specific majors just listed, many African American, Latino, and Native American students want to major in programs in the social sciences, programs that frequently turn away many qualified applicants because of the competition for admission.

CALIFORNIA: A SPECIFIC CASE

Ever since the adoption of the Master Plan for Higher Education in 1960, there has been a working partnership between the University of California and the California State University systems on the one hand and the community colleges on the other. The partnership between UC and the community colleges, however, goes through distinct cycles of close attention and seeming neglect. Throughout the 1990s, the university worked diligently to increase the number of community college students transferring to the UC system, and those efforts received a sharp boost following the passage of Proposition 209 in November 1996. Despite long-term, elaborate outreach and recruitment efforts by all eight of the UC general campuses, however, the enrollment of California community-college transfer students at UC declined for much of that period. According to *Information Digest 2001*, a publication produced by the University of California Office of the President, in fall 1993, 8,846 students transferred from the state's then-107 community colleges to the eight undergraduate UC campuses. That number climbed slightly to 9,019 in fall 1995, declined to 8,359 in fall 1998, and then rose steadily to 10,381 in fall 2002, the most recent year for which data is available. That 10,381 figure was only 1,535 students more than the figure for fall 1993.

For African American, Latino, and Native American students, transfer enrollments to UC have been very low. For fall 2002 (the most recent data available), all 107 California community colleges transferred to all eight UC campuses a total of 277 African American students—an average of 2.6 students per community college. That 277 figure was a significant increase over the 185 figure for fall 1998—but still well below the 314 African American transfers in fall 1995. Thirty-six of the 277 African American transfers came from just two community colleges—Santa Monica College and Laney College in Oakland. Only four other California community colleges transferred at least ten African American students to the entire UC system. These figures are not just the result of where African American students are concentrated. They also reflect the determination of those particular community colleges, but there are other factors, discussed later, that influence these low numbers. The trend line for African American community-college transfer students is particularly disheartening to UC administrators—and has been for at least fifteen years.

For Chicano/Latino students, the number of fall 2002 transfer students enrolling at UC was 1,566, an average of less than fifteen students per community college. Riverside Community College and Santa Monica College accounted for 134 of those students, almost ten percent. That 1,566 figure represents a steady increase from the 1,054 Chicano/Latino transfers in fall 1998, but the actual number is quite small when one considers the population of California and the enrollment of Chicano/Latino students in California community colleges.

The transfer enrollment figures for Native Americans are even more disheartening than those for African American transfer students. The high figure prior to the passage of Proposition 209 was 111 Native American transfer students in 1995. In 1996, the last year before Proposition 209 took effect, the number was ninety-nine. From there, the enrollment of Native American transfer students plunged to fifty-three in 2000 and then rebounded somewhat in 2001 to seventy-five (the last year for which Native American transfer data is available).

It seems unlikely that UC and the community colleges will be able to sharply increase the numbers of African American, Chicano/Latino, and Native American transfers to UC. Proposition 209 has, of course, eliminated the consideration of race and ethnicity in transfer admissions as well as at the freshman level. That law particularly affects the

UC campuses that are the most competitive for transfer admission, just as it has at the freshman level. At Berkeley, engineering majors, the business major, and majors in the social sciences have a much lower admit percentage than the overall 26.1 percent transfer-admit percentage. Although the base transfer numbers are smaller, Proposition 209 has meant proportional drops in underrepresented minority transfer students similar to those for African American, Chicano, and Native American freshman.

Proposition 209 has also had another effect. Since its passage, as noted earlier, private universities in California and both public and private universities from outside California have sharply increased their recruitment in California of African American, Latino, and Native American high school seniors. Underrepresented minority students who have completed a college-prep curriculum and have a GPA above 2.0 are quite likely to be recruited by and admitted to four-year colleges and universities outside the UC system rather than consider attending a California community college.

In part because this intensive recruitment skims off underrepresented minority students graduating from California high schools with grade-point averages all the way down to 2.0, a high percentage of African American, Chicano/Latino, and Native American students who do attend community colleges have to do remedial coursework—often the same classes they struggled with in high school—before they can enroll in transfer-level courses, the so-called "transfer track." That, in turn, means that they have to spend more than two years at a community college—often another full year or more—in order to complete the first two years of transferable course work. In general, there is much less financial aid available in community colleges than from four-year colleges and universities, a situation made much worse by recent steep increases in California community college fees. For these and other reasons, it is difficult for many students to maintain academic momentum in the atmosphere of a community college.

There is another complicated issue in community college transfer: the extraordinary unevenness in transfer rates among community colleges. For fall 2002 in California, ten of the 107 community colleges provided 3,797 of the 10,381 students who transferred to UC—or 36.6 percent. Seventeen of the 107 colleges provided more than fifty percent of the 10,381 total. At the same time, Feather River Community College and Palo Verde Community College transferred zero students; Taft College transferred two; Barstow Community College, Lassen College, and West Hills Community College transferred four; and Compton College transferred five.

Even though all of the UC campuses already offered some form of transfer guarantee program, the University of California in recent years proposed a series of innovative transfer programs. These programs, unfortunately, have not proven successful. In September 2000, UC President Atkinson announced an initiative called Dual Admissions that he hoped would increase the number of community college students transferring to the university, particularly African American, Latino, and Native American students. This proposal was another effort based on class rank that would focus on those students in each California public high school who fall between the top four and top 12.5 percent of their graduating class but who are otherwise not UC-eligible according to the statewide criteria. These students would be identified by the university prior to their senior year in high school and would be admitted simultaneously to a community college as freshmen and to a UC campus as juniors, provided that they completed the specified UC requirements during their time at community college. According to Atkinson in a letter to Michael Cowan, the Chair of the Academic Council, "After satisfactorily fulfilling their freshman and sophomore requirements at a community college, they would complete their upper-division studies at the UC campus to which they were admitted earlier."

Dual Admissions seemed sound in theory but, like ELC, it turned out to be cost-prohibitive to administer and quite cumbersome. UC staff had to review high school transcripts during the summer in order to identify dual admission candidates. That meant instead of asking high schools to provide transcripts for the top ten percent of their rising seniors, as ELC currently does, the university now asked high schools to provide transcripts for perhaps the top eighteen to twenty percent of their upcoming seniors. That is both a work and a financial burden on California high schools. And it isn't the affluent high schools that had to worry about Dual Admissions because in most of them more than 12.5 percent of the senior class qualified for UC on the basis of the statewide criteria. It was the disadvantaged high schools that bore the burden, many of which didn't even have counselors.

When Governor Schwarzenegger proposed his 2004–05 state budget in January 2004, he included a much reduced and modified version of Dual Admissions that was called the Eligible Dual Admissions Program (EDAP). Because he was proposing yet another set of budget cuts for the University of California, the Governor's program would divert UC-eligible applicants to UC to California community colleges for two years with a guarantee of admission to a particular UC campus as juniors. That program was then renamed the Guaranteed Transfer Option (GTO). It was offered to 7,600 fall 2004 UC-eligible freshman applicants for whom—for the first time since the implementation of the state's Master Plan in 1960—there was no room in the University of California system. Only about thirteen percent of the 7,600 students accepted the GTO offer, and turning away those UC-eligible applicants created a political furor. Democrats in the Legislature were so angry that UC President Robert Dynes had struck a deal with Governor Schwarzenegger to reduce fall 2004 freshman enrollment without including them in the discussion that they forced the university in the final stages of the budget negotiations to offer fall 2004 admission to the students who had accepted the GTO offer. All eight UC campuses were required to take a portion of these students. In the case of UC Berkeley and UCLA, these were students who, for complicated reasons, would not have come close to being admitted to those campuses as freshman applicants for fall 2004.

It is certainly true that California's community colleges offer all students the opportunity to complete the first two years of a four-year college degree for significantly less money than the same two years would cost at a University of California or California State University campus. Furthermore, the opportunity to start fresh no matter how badly a person might have done in high school—the so-called "forgiveness policy"—is a truly enlightened public policy that has enabled thousands and thousands of Californians to complete college at any age. Nevertheless, it is important to recognize that for a student who needs remedial work it takes a tremendous amount of determination and grit to persevere through two and a half or three years of community college—perhaps more—before being able to transfer, especially if that student has to work a lot of hours or raise children or both. Given the realities of community college transfer, it is naïve to think that community college transfer can undo the damage done by Proposition 209.

SYMBOLIC POLITICS AS OPPOSED TO SUBSTANTIVE POLICIES

California's approaches to outreach and transfer are either naïve or deliberately superficial, and there is no policy discussion of the true causes of the widening inequities in California and across the country. The state and university polices on ELC, outreach, and transfer are hugely expensive, cumbersome, and unlikely to yield greater participation in the university or greater racial and ethnic diversity following the damage of Proposition 209. They also seem to have been developed without any consideration to the practical issues of how much work they will require, how the work will actually be done, and who will do it.

The University of California has endured a strenuous ten years. Governor Pete Wilson and key members of its Board of Regents pushed it into the center of the nation's bitter struggle over affirmative action. The university has been and is pressured severely by members of the California Legislature, especially the Latino Caucus, to increase African American, Chicano/Latino, and Native American enrollments following the passage of SP-1 and Proposition 209, and many of these legislators have directly threatened the University of California budget as punishment for failing to increase those minority enrollments. The senior administration has also had to deal with a number of difficult Regents who voted to take away affirmative action, the only workable tool for achieving some degree of racial and ethnic diversity within the University of California, and who then said, "Fix it by some means other than by the one thing that will fix it."

Assuming that a majority of California citizens want California's public universities to reflect the population of the entire state, these policies are actually harmful because they give the impression that serious steps are being taken and that the problems they address may be solved. In that way, they raise hopes for outcomes that are unlikely to be attained, and they spend millions and millions of dollars that might have gone to help mitigate the real causes of the problem. Whether the goal of fully integrated public universities can be achieved without affirmative action is a critical public-policy question. As former UC President Richard Atkinson wrote in his April 2003 opinion piece in *The Washington Post*, "Without affirmative action, this is an intractable problem." Other states should draw important lessons from California's experience.

10 POGO: WE HAVE MET THE ENEMY . . .

BLAMING K-12

The Education Trust and other advocacy groups have for some time argued that the long-term solution to the achievement gap between African American, Latino, and Native American students on the one hand and white and Asian American students on the other lies in greatly improving the schools attended by low-income and minority students across the country. With the end of affirmative action in several states, this argument has gained in intensity as an important way to overcome the damage to college and university enrollments of African American, Latino, and Native American students that the end of affirmative action has caused.

Most of us would agree that fixing these schools would be at least a partial solution to the problem and that such reform should be an important public policy goal. The difficulty is that gross disparities among public schools occur almost entirely along lines of race and economic class and have been identified for decades. Advocates for educational improvement, university faculty in schools of education, civil rights attorneys, and social activists of one kind or another have all pushed to change this set of inequities for many years.

In May 2000, the American Civil Liberties Union (ACLU) filed a class-action lawsuit against California on behalf of students attending eighteen highly disadvantaged schools across California. That suit, called *Williams et al. v. State of California*, was amended on August 2000 to add another forty-six schools. In describing the schools named in the *Williams* lawsuit, Mark Rosenbaum, the ACLU attorney who also filed the suit, said, "This is the 'Mississippification' of California's schools, a separate and unequal system for the have-nots. These are the schools a government would create if it didn't care about all its children." As if to demonstrate the truth of Rosenbaum's claim, then-Governor Gray Davis, in an astonishing move, filed a counter-suit against these schools and school districts, claiming that they were responsible for their own degradation.

Which children was Rosenbaum referring to? The ACLU points out that the eighteen schools listed in the original filing of the *Williams* lawsuit are 96.4 percent students of color, compared to fifty-nine percent statewide. In January 2003, The Civil Rights Project at Harvard University issued a report by Erica Frankenberg, Chungmei Lee, and Gary Orfield called *A Multiracial Society with Segregated Schools: Are We Losing the Dream?* That report found that America's public schools are being re-segregated:

> The nation's largest city school systems account for a shrinking share of the total enrollment and are, almost without exception, overwhelmingly nonwhite and increasingly segregated internally. These twenty-seven largest urban systems have lost the vast majority of their white enrollment whether or not they ever had significant desegregation plans, and today serve almost one-quarter of our black and Latino student population.

The report referred to such schools as "apartheid schools." California is certainly part of this process: in 1998–99, the San Francisco Unified School District, with 61,042 students, was 12.2 percent white. For Los Angeles Unified School District—with 695,885 students—the figure was 10.5 percent. For the Oakland Unified School District, the figure was 5.8 percent.

Writing about a similar report issued by The Civil Rights Project in June 1999, Richard Lee Colvin began his story in the *Los Angeles Times* with this sentence: "Segregation in the nation's public schools is accelerating, with the trend particularly notable among Latinos in California. . . ." Colvin noted that the 1999 report found that, nationwide, "nearly 70 percent of black students and 75 percent of Latinos attend schools that are predominantly black, Latino, or Native American" while the average white student attended a school where eighty percent of the students were white. "In California," Colvin added, "ethnic isolation is even greater, with more than 40 percent of Latino students and 35 percent of African Americans attending schools that are 90 percent or more minority."

For several years, commentators from all over the United States have been saying, "K-12 has failed." But they don't mean "K-12." They actually mean *public* K-12. And they don't mean all public K-12. They mean public K-12 in the Bronx, not Nassau County; in Chicago, not New Trier; in Boston, not in Brookline; in San Francisco, not Marin County. They mean some rural and almost all-inner-city-public K-12—the schools from which we have deliberately stripped funding; the schools that have the most teachers on emergency credentials because they're forced to pay the lowest teacher salaries; the schools that deal with the poorest kids in America—and, given the number of kids and families in deep poverty in the United States, that's saying something.

LEADING THE PLUNGE DOWNWARD: CALIFORNIA

On May 8, 2000, the California Teachers Association (CTA) held a rally on the steps of the state capitol in Sacramento for higher teacher salaries. CTA President Wayne Johnson was one of the keynote speakers. He noted that California has the seventh largest (now the fifth) economy in the world and that the state's budget surplus that year would be $13 billion. "Despite that wealth," he said, "we rank only fortieth in educational funding, over $1,000 per student per year below the national average. California now ranks forty-ninth in class size, fiftieth in computers per students, fifty-first [sic] in library services." Johnson went on to say that when he started teaching in 1962, California ranked sixth in funding. "I have watched the thirty-eight-year funding slide! A slide from sixth to fortieth. It has been painful to watch." Johnson might also have cited the California State Standards for English: "National Institutes of Health studies indicate that students who are behind in reading in grade three have only a 12 to 20 percent chance of ever catching up." What Johnson did not say is that these data are aggregate numbers for all California's public schools. Given the disparities among affluent and poor schools in California, imagine how bad the data must be for, say, the poorest forty percent of California's schools. One teacher at the rally carried a sign that said, "Dare to be Average!"

Although it may be tempting for people in other states to say that these issues are California's problem, California school children make up thirteen percent of the total public-school enrollment in the United States. The scale of California means that what happens there will affect the rest of the country. Johnson noted that California has by far the largest public school system in the United States—six million students, compared to Texas, the second largest with 3.8 million students. He also noted that the racial and ethnic diversity of California's schoolchildren is astonishing. "There are 164 native languages spoken in California schools. There are 101 native languages spoken in the Fresno Unified School District. California has more limited and non-English speaking children than thirty-four states have enrollment. The Los Angeles Unified District has more students than twenty-nine states, eighty percent of them are poor, seventy percent are limited English speaking."

Pedro Noguera, formerly a professor in the School of Education at UC Berkeley and an elected member of the City of Berkeley School Board a few years ago, points out that the starting annual salary for a prison guard in California is $46,000. At the time of the CTA rally in Sacramento, the beginning annual salary for a teacher in the Berkeley Unified School District was $28,800. That is, in California we often pay teachers in our poorest school districts about half of what we pay a prison guard. At the CTA rally in Sacramento, a man waved a sign that said, "Will teach for food."

In California, the first thing most people said after learning of the damage to minority enrollments at Berkeley and UCLA under the first year of Proposition 209 was this: "K-12 has failed." But they didn't mean public K-12 in Piedmont, Orinda, Los Altos Hills, Danville, Brentwood, La Jolla, or many other similar places. They meant public K-12 in Richmond, Oakland, San Francisco, Los Angeles, San Diego, and most parts of the Central, Salinas, and Imperial Valleys.

As they do in affluent areas in the rest of the country, public schools in places like Orinda and Brentwood do remarkably well. The salary scales for their teachers are relatively high, almost every one of their teachers holds a state-standard teaching credential, and in general children come to school well-fed, adequately clothed, with decent medical and dental care, and from parents who are economically and educationally able to devote time and attention to them. The passage of Proposition 13 in 1978 was a major force in stripping public schools throughout California of adequate funding, but well-off communities, as they almost always do, have found their own ways to compensate, often by passing local tax initiatives for their own school districts.

It isn't simply that the schools in these communities get better public funding, they get better private funding as well. At San Ramon Valley High School just a few years ago, to take a single example, parents felt the American Literature classes for juniors were too large when school opened. Working together, they raised enough money within just a few days from parents of juniors—in effect, they taxed themselves—to enable the high school to hire another English teacher. It wasn't just the $50,000 or so that the parents raised that was impressive. It was also that some of those parents had the organizational skills, the will, and the political sophistication, as well as the financial capacity, to achieve such a goal in such short time.

The differences in financial strength among school districts in California, particularly the higher salary scales in affluent communities, helped undercut what could have been a much more significant educational reform in California: the reduction of class size to twenty students in kindergarten, first, and second grade (third grade was added soon after, then English and math classes in ninth grade). Class-size reduction, surprisingly, was a Pete Wilson initiative. What happened was that reducing class size in these three grades throughout California created thousands of additional teaching positions. Demand quickly outstripped supply, so the affluent districts lured away many of the most experienced and credentialed teachers from the lower-paying districts, and the lower-paying districts ended up hiring thousands of new teachers who possessed emergency teaching credentials only.

According to Nanette Asimov in the December 7, 2000, *San Francisco Chronicle*, the Center for the Future of Teaching and Learning reported that there were 37,000 teachers working in California on emergency permits during the 1999–00 school year. That was a thirteen-percent increase from 32,700 in 1998–99. The Center also reported that fourteen percent of California's teachers—one in seven—have either no credential or hold an incorrect credential for the subjects they are teaching. Finally, the Center noted that the vast majority of these teachers work with the urban students requiring the most attention. Asimov pointed out that a year ago the Center had issued its first report, "a scathing look at how California's poorest children got the least-prepared teachers."

In addition, schools in affluent areas in general had more land, so they could bring in portables or, in many cases, build another permanent building without cannibalizing other parts of their plant. Poorer schools had to chop up libraries, music rooms, and auditoriums or drop portables into the middle of their already-small playgrounds to accommodate their extra classes. As Lori Olszewski, who writes for the *San Francisco Chronicle*, notes, the playgrounds of some of these schools now look like trailer parks. It may be that every school in California benefited from class-size reduction, but the affluent schools, as they always seem to do, benefited more and suffered less.

One family that moved from Berkeley to Orinda during the summer a few years ago learned about these differences immediately. Before the public schools had even started in September, a parent volunteer for the Education Foundation of Orinda, the fund-raising arm of the Orinda public schools, called them. The Foundation raises money for four elementary schools and one middle school in the Orinda Union School District plus Miramonte High School, a total of about 3,700 students. The caller told the new arrivals that their "expected contribution" to the Foundation would be a little over $500 for each of their two kids. According to the July 25, 2000, edition of the *San Francisco Chronicle*, the Foundation raised $620,000 for the 1999–00 school year. According to the Foundation, its goal for 2000–01 was $770,000— that's for the *public* schools in Orinda. The television special *First to Worst*, broadcast in February 2004, reported that the foundation raised over $1 million in its most recent campaign, more than $1,000 for each child in the Orinda schools.

The City of Orinda and the City of Oakland would share a common boundary along the spine of the Berkeley Hills, if it weren't for a half-mile-wide strip of Sibley Volcanic Regional Preserve running between them as a kind of demilitarized zone. When an Oakland public school holds a silent auction to raise money, the top item may well be a pair of tickets to an Oakland Raiders or San Francisco 49ers football game. When the Orinda schools recently held their silent auction, one of the items was lunch with Steve Young, then the quarterback for the 49ers. That wasn't even the top item in the Orinda auction. The top item was a week at someone's mountain house in Switzerland.

According to Diana Walsh, writing in the November 5, 2000, *San Francisco Examiner*, the Portola Valley School District, which is located south of San Francisco and has only two schools, raised $1,050,000 at its auction in October 2000. One family paid $10,000 for a soccer clinic with Julie Foudy, co-captain of the American women's national soccer team. Another family paid $7,500 for an Australian shepherd puppy (plus one vet visit, a training class, and a dog bed). Other families paid $5,000 for their child to act as principal for a day at the elementary school and $5,000 for the same opportunity at the middle school. In a similar auction in the nearby Las Lomitas School District, two families paid $6,000 each for front-row seats and parking at the eighth-grade graduation the following June.

The headline for the school auction article helps explain why our public conversation on school inequities is so shallow and dishonest: "Auction fever hits schools." The title should have been "Why some public schools are so much better off than others" or, better, "Understanding the huge inequalities among public schools." Walsh's article is quite long—forty-three column-inches. Only in the last paragraph is there any mention of other, poorer school districts: In nearby Redwood City, with a much larger school district, the public education foundation was able to raise only $42,000 in its spring 2000 auction.

In early November 2000, a group of private-school parents complained that when they wanted to use Berkeley public school facilities for their sons' private lacrosse team, they had to pay to do so and, worse, the grass on the sports fields was often too long and poorly maintained. A Berkeley Unified School district representative explained as politely as possible under the circumstances that Berkeley Unified had cut its maintenance/landscaping budget over the years in order to fund academic programs and paltry salary increases for teachers, and that there was now only one person assigned to maintain the grounds of thirteen schools. One of the reasons so many disadvantaged schools look so awful is that when a district doesn't have enough money to pay for all of its core needs, maintenance is the least crucial and most likely thing to reduce or put off. The problem is that schools and landscaping deteriorate rapidly. The general public then sneers at the slum-like facilities, and it becomes extremely difficult to build public support for restoration because it appears as if the district just didn't take care of what it had.

It is certainly true that a few districts, notably Oakland Unified, Richmond Unified, and, most recently, San Francisco Unified, have been grossly mismanaged and have wasted critical resources. Richmond (now the West Contra Costa Unified School District) was devastated almost single-handedly by then-Superintendent Walter Marks, and San Francisco, according to the November 12, 2001, *San Francisco Chronicle*, may have misspent as much as $100 million from four bond issues. Yet pointing to these few districts is like Richard Nixon pointing at those infamous welfare queens in the 1970s. There may be some of them out there, but focusing on them allows people to ignore all of the actual suffering that is going on in those schools and those communities.

In one of the great ironies of American geography, the City of Piedmont is completely surrounded by the City of Oakland. Piedmont High and McClymonds High in west Oakland are 3.15 miles apart. You could walk from one to the other in about an hour—it's downhill from Piedmont—but only if you were completely crazy. No one who knew the urban geography/sociology would do that because, as you got close to McClymonds, you would be right in the middle of one of the most dangerous drug-war combat zones in America—and that, too, is saying something.

Both high schools enroll about 850 students. At Piedmont High, the average annual family income is $92,000; at McClymonds, it is $19,000. At Piedmont High, one percent of the students are Limited English Proficiency; at McClymonds, the figure is fourteen percent. At Piedmont High, one percent of the students are eligible for free federal meal programs; at McClymonds, the figure is fifty-three percent. At Piedmont High, one percent of the students are from families on Aid to Families with Dependent Children (AFDC—or welfare); at McClymonds, the figure is eighty-two percent.

At Piedmont High, four percent of the teachers hold emergency teaching credentials; at McClymonds, the figure is sixteen percent. Piedmont offers twelve Advanced Placement courses; McClymonds offers two. Of all the students who took AP exams at Piedmont High in 1998, eighty-nine percent received scores of three or better, thus earning their takers college credit. At McClymonds, the figure was zero percent. Not one student scored three or higher on a single AP exam in 1998. The mean SAT I score at Piedmont High in 1998 was 1,243. At McClymonds, it was 681. For fall 2000, sixty-seven students applied to UC Berkeley from Piedmont High; from McClymonds, six students applied to Berkeley.

And what is the connection between the data on the two high schools two paragraphs above and the data in the preceding paragraph? The socio-economic data goes a long way toward explaining the school curriculum and performance data. Although they are only three miles apart, these two high schools might as well be on different planets. In May 2004, Nanette Asimov profiled Piedmont High and McClymonds as part of a feature story in the *San Francisco Chronicle* on the fiftieth anniversary of the *Brown v. Board of Education* Supreme Court decision. That article, titled "Segregation by Income," generated a letter from a parent in Piedmont, who wrote in part:

> Contrary to the implications of this article, Piedmont receives less government funding than the districts in Oakland and Berkeley. That's why the parents need to do so much fund raising. We vote to tax ourselves with school bonds, we fund-raise constantly, we take time off from work to work in the classrooms, coach the teams and drive on field trips.
>
> Piedmont has great schools. It's not magic and it's not discrimination; it's just hard work.

The same contrast exists between Miramonte High in Orinda and Castlemont High just over the hills in east Oakland and between scores and scores of other high schools throughout the United States. According to Joshunda Sanders in the May 17, 2002, *San Francisco Chronicle*, the C.P. Bannon Mortuary near Castlemont High in East Oakland has a staff member, Cecelia Lambert, whose formal title is funeral director for homicidal deaths. In the last decade, Lambert has buried forty-five people, half of them black and all of them under twenty-five years old. Mourners now customarily make funeral T-shirts with a picture of the dead person printed on the front. And in the surrounding neighborhoods, Sanders notes, the new threat is "Don't make me put your face on a T-shirt."

WE HAVE MET THE ENEMY . . .

The massive disparities between America's urban and suburban schools did not happen by accident. It is simply dishonest to say that public K-12 has failed. The truth is that, as a society, we have all failed a huge proportion of our K-12 schools all over the country by stripping them of money. That, in turn, has forced those schools to hire less qualified teachers, to have gross shortages of school supplies and textbooks, and to watch their buildings, playgrounds, and landscaping deteriorate to the point of wretchedness. These were almost all deliberate public policy decisions made through the initiative process, as with Proposition 13 in California; or by state Legislatures, which chose to put state tax revenues into other parts of the state budget (prisons, for example) or to cut taxes; or by the federal government. And somehow a majority of Americans—or their elected representatives, many of them determined to get re-elected—have chosen over and over again not to raise taxes to support adequately all public K-12 schools.

And California is certainly not the only state to refuse to raise taxes to support its public schools and colleges. In February 2004, almost sixty percent of the people who voted in a special mail-ballot referendum in Oregon opposed Measure 30, which would have temporarily raised state income taxes in order to finance, in part, higher education. Writing in the February 5, 2004, electronic edition of *The Chronicle of Higher Education*, Peter Schmidt noted that the defeat of Measure 30 meant that the state's university system would have to cut its budget another 2.6 percent, following a nine-percent cut in the previous biennium and an eleven-percent cut in the first year of the current biennium.

In March 2000, 51.2 percent of the voters in California voted against Proposition 26, an initiative that would have changed the majority needed to pass school bonds throughout California from a two-thirds majority to a simple majority. According to Lori Olszewski in the October 23, 2000, edition of the *San Francisco Chronicle*, California voters approved just over half of the school bonds presented to them over the past fourteen years, totaling $18 billion. Had a simple majority been required instead of the current two-thirds, another $13 billion in bonds would have succeeded.

Six months later, however, the California ballot in November 2000 included Proposition 39, a measure similar to Proposition 26 but which specified a fifty-five percent majority for approval of school bonds instead of the existing two-thirds majority. Astonishingly, Proposition 39 passed fifty-three to forty-seven percent. Although a fifty-five percent majority is difficult to achieve, it is immensely easier than a two-thirds majority, and the passage of Proposition 39 may be the most important thing to happen for public K-12 since Proposition 13 was passed in 1978.

The other encouraging event in the November 2000 California election was the smashing defeat—seventy-one to twenty-nine percent—of a school voucher initiative called Proposition 38. This measure would have given parents in California an annual $4,000 voucher to apply toward private schooling for their children. As Luis Huerta pointed out in an October 19, 2000, Open Forum piece in the *San Francisco Chronicle*, $4,000 would barely be enough money to help low-income families afford the cheapest private high schools. (Catholic high schools average $4,000 a year in tuition.) What the vouchers would have done is given affluent parents whose children are already in $8,000 to $18,000-a-year private schools a $4,000 per year subsidy. And vouchers might pull enough high-achieving kids out of low-performing schools to leave those schools much worse off than they were.

The defeat of Proposition 38 by such a margin is encouraging. It seems less likely that California voters will approve vouchers in the future. President Bush, however, has pledged to pursue vouchers at the federal level. Vouchers will further erode our already-strained sense of national community and purpose by further weakening the single-most unifying force in our nation—public schools. If vouchers are ever approved, they will be a massive body blow to public education in this country, like that delivered by Proposition 13 to the public schools in California in 1978, the effects of which the state's children are still feeling.

Finally, it is important to note that in August 2004 Governor Schwarzenegger, to his credit, negotiated a settlement of the *Williams* lawsuit discussed earlier in this chapter. In the first year under that agreement, California would provide $138 million for extra materials to the state's lowest-performing schools and $50 million to repair rundown, crumbling, low-performing schools. Reactions to the settlement varied widely, as James Sterngold reported in the August 14, 2004, edition of the *San Francisco Chronicle*. ACLU attorneys were delighted, and one of them, Mark Rosenbaum, described the agreement as a civil rights watershed. "The face and the culture of the California educational system," said Rosenbaum, "will never be the same." Others were less optimistic. Scott Plotkin, executive director of the California School Boards Association, said, "It will take more than counting textbooks and inspecting bathrooms to provide a better education for students who need and deserve extra help." Given the woeful conditions in the state's lowest-performing schools and the large number of those schools, the first-year dollar amounts do not seem to be anywhere near what it will actually take to bring those schools up to even a moderate level of adequacy.

WE COULD BE A LITTLE MORE HONEST ABOUT ALL THIS

As stark as the disparities among affluent and poor schools are, however, they are just one set of symptoms of a much larger set of inequities. On November 2, 2000, the California Association of Realtors released information that stated only thirty-one percent of Californians can afford to buy a median-priced home. That figure was a five percentage-point decline from the previous year and compares to fifty-three percent nationwide.

Children Now, a child advocacy group in Oakland, issues an annual report on the status of children in California. The group's 2000 report, released on October 19, 2000, pointed out that 19.8 percent of the children in California live at or below the federal poverty level (a number of other studies put the figure at twenty-five percent). The federal poverty level for a family of four at the time of this study was a gross annual income of $16,450. By 2003, the federal poverty mark had risen slightly to $18,400 for a family of four. Imagine trying to live as a single person on $18,400 a year, let alone provide for a family of four. The

Children Now report further notes that forty-seven percent of California's children live at or below twice the poverty level. This latter benchmark is a more accurate estimate of poverty, particularly in California where the cost of living is so high. A detailed census of the homeless in 2003, profiled by Rick DelVecchio in the November 7, 2003, *San Francisco Chronicle*, revealed that in Alameda County 6,215 adults and children were living on the streets or in temporary housing, more than sixty percent of them in Oakland and Berkeley. In that article, Louis Chicoine, executive director of the Tri-City Homeless Coalition, described "an atrocious growth" of homeless families in the suburbs of Alameda County.

The Census Bureau reported on September 27, 2000, that nationally the percentage of children living in poverty was 16.9 percent. Marian Wright Edelman from The Children's Defense Fund calls this our national shame. How can we allow so many children—and adults—to struggle at this level when collectively we have so much of the world's wealth? More important, how can we tacitly accept the definition of poverty as a family of four living at or below $18,400 a year?

We all know the disadvantages faced by poor kids long before they reach their money-starved, public school kindergarten classes. They begin before birth with poor or no pre-natal care, and the disadvantages pile up rapidly: poor or no medical and dental care during infancy and childhood, not enough healthful food to eat, too much time in front of a television because childcare is so costly, limited English skills in many cases, dangerous neighborhoods in many cases, parents who may work two or more jobs apiece just to cling to subsistence—or one parent or no parents but a grandmother or aunt or foster parent, parents or guardians who don't speak English, parents or guardians who are too tired to read with their kids, parents or guardians who don't understand public school bureaucracies and don't know how to advocate for their children, or, worse, parents or guardians who are angry and shamed by their inability to provide for their families, who abuse alcohol and drugs, who are depressed, who are physically or emotionally abusive, who have simply given up.

Not surprisingly, some or all of these factors often combine to produce what Elizabeth Burr and Bruce Fuller and others describe as "parental stress, family conflict, and harsh parenting" in an article titled "Early Education and Family Poverty." Perhaps even worse than abject neglect, the harshness and cruelty with which many children are treated sentences them to a life of underachievement and misery and the likelihood that they will perpetuate that harshness and cruelty on others who are more vulnerable than they are—classmates, younger children, or their own children down the line. Harsh parenting, of course, isn't confined to the poverty stricken, and there are many parents, uncles, aunts, grandparents, and foster parents who do a miraculous job raising kids in remarkably difficult circumstances. Nevertheless, the combination of forces described in the paragraphs above makes it so much more likely that harsh parenting will be added to the mix of pain and dysfunction.

It is woefully naïve or just plain dishonest to believe that public schools—especially the public schools from which we have stripped money, supplies, and qualified teachers—can—or even should—make up for the deprived social and economic conditions out of which come so many of their students and the damage caused by years of harsh and cruel treatment. In fall 2000, Meredith Maran published *Class Dismissed: A Year in the Life of an American High School, a Glimpse into the Heart of a Nation.* The book follows three students through their senior year at Berkeley High in 1999–00 but uses the contradictions and tensions of Berkeley High to explore public schools across America. One of the most telling sections comes about a third of the way through the book when Maran quotes James Traub from "Schools Are Not the Answer," his cover story in *The New York Times Magazine*: "How powerful can this one institution be in the face of the kind of disadvantages that so many ghetto children bring with them to the schoolhouse door, and return to at home?"

Across the country, our public conversations almost never go to the real underlying causes of school inequities. Even a tough-minded, smart columnist like Peter Schrag, who had an editorial column in *The*

Sacramento Bee on August 4, 1999, attacking the disparities in California public schools, didn't push beyond the schools to describe the true problem. And *The New York Times* truly missed the point in a May 20, 2000, editorial in which the writer concluded that the decline in African American, Chicano, and Native American freshmen at Berkeley and UCLA is "largely because the high schools in black and Latino neighborhoods routinely fail to offer the advanced placement courses that are readily available in white neighborhoods and that are taken into account when the elite college make admissions decisions." The true miracle is that as many African American, Latino, and Native American students manage to not only endure their family, community, and school circumstances but to achieve despite them and that so many of them, often because of affirmative action, do manage to succeed in college and well beyond.

K-12 SCHOOL REFORM!
THE DELUSIONAL AND THE DISHONEST

When school reform does get attention in the United States, the notion is much too simple. The essence of George W. Bush's No Child Left Behind reform program is one-dimensional: set testable standards, test heavily, reward high-performing schools, and punish low-performing schools.

That notion is also the heart of school reform in many of the individual states. Almost as soon as Proposition 209 had passed, the golden hills of California began to ring with cries of "Fix K-12! Fix K-12!" Governor Gray Davis, describing himself as "the education governor," set public school reform as his top priority. But his version of school reform, like that of George W. Bush, was to set testable standards, test heavily, reward high-performing schools, and punish low-performing schools.

California's standardized test scores result in an Academic Performance Index (API), which is calculated for each school in California. API scores were released for the first time in early October 2000. The stakes were high: according to Duke Helfand and Jessica Garrison in the October 5, 2000, *Los Angeles Times*, the California state budget for 2000–01 contained $677 million to award to schools, teachers, and other staff for achievement gains. Guess what? Eighty percent of the highest performing schools qualified for award money—including all of the schools in San Marino, La Canada, and Agoura Hills. Only sixty-two percent of the lowest-performing schools qualified for the awards. Like Pete Wilson's class-size reduction policy, this policy dispropor-tionately benefits the most affluent schools in California. Helfand and Garrison quote Arthur Fields, the principal of Horace Mann Elementary School in Beverly Hills: "There's nothing wrong with our getting the money," said Fields. "I think it's fair."

Davis' school reform policy with its emphasis on standardized tests and its entrepreneurial focus on individual cash awards to schools and teachers was surprising for a Democrat. Almost all of us would agree that higher standards and increased accountability are desirable goals and an important part of school reform. Putting aside such issues as how much teachers will wrench the curriculum in order to teach to the tests and the huge temptation to cheat on test outcomes, however, defining school reform almost entirely as higher standards, regular stan-dardized testing, exit examinations, and a system of rewards and pun-ishments—including the dissolution of poor performing schools—is truly simpleminded.

One of the most troubling aspects of the policies enacted by both Bush and Davis is the thinly veiled eagerness with which punishment is prom-ised to the lowest performing schools. Which schools will those will be? The same schools it always is. The same schools the Education Governor himself was suing. The same criticisms apply to President George W. Bush's No Child Left Behind law. Lots of rhetoric, lots of standardized testing, big punishments for low-performing schools, and inadequate funding for true school reform. A more accurate name for Bush's pro-gram is "Many Poor and Minority Children Left Way Behind."

The consequences of the first wave of simplistic school reform insti-tuted in the mid- to late-1990s, when school boards decreed the end of social promotion and instituted mandatory summer school attendance for students who did not pass, have already appeared. In October 2000, the San Francisco Unified School District Board of Education voted to rescind its new "tough love" graduation requirements because thirty percent of that year's seniors were not going to qualify for high school graduation in June. The Board acknowledged that it hadn't put in place the academic support program to accompany its new promotion and graduation requirements. Across the country, many cities and states have adopted this same combination: tougher standards (the easy part) but no money (the difficult part) for the additional academic support programs those standards require.

Like President Bush and the governors in many other states, California made no serious attempt to change the underlying social and economic conditions that, among other things, have led to the gross inequalities among California schools. Yet if the state had been truly serious about reforming the lowest-performing schools, it could have made a serious attempt to improve the quality of teachers in those schools. In a budget that contained $677 million for achievement awards, Governor Davis included only $55 million to increase starting teacher salaries. Even acknowledging the important difference between temporary funding for a rewards program and the permanent funding required to raise teacher salaries, we ought to be asking: how much would it cost California, with the fifth largest economy in the world, to raise teacher salaries by $15,000 a year in, let's say, the poorest forty percent of the school districts in the state?

Any parent who has worked in the elementary school classrooms of urban schools has seen poor kids, mostly African Americans and Latinos, who were already two years behind when they began kindergarten. But this isn't news. This is the reason why Headstart was begun thirty-five years ago—although there does seem to be a much greater need for such programs these days. State Superintendent of Public Instruction Delaine Easton in California under Governor Davis proposed universal pre-schooling for California. That seemed like a rea-

sonable, though modest, step toward narrowing the gaps between affluent and poor kids, but it was never enacted.

BLAME THE TEST

One of the most predictable things that will happen in a state that has
ended affirmative action in university admissions is that attacks on the
SAT I will increase to a fever pitch. While there has long been serious
opposition to the SAT I in California—mostly because it has been seen
as a hurdle to minority admissions—opposition to the test increased
sharply right after the passage of SP-1 in July 1995 when affirmative
action could no longer be used to at least partially offset what were perceived as the negative effects of the SAT I on the admission of African
American, Latino, and Native American students.

In September 1997, to take one example, the University of California
Latino Eligibility Task Force issued a report that called for the University
of California to drop the use of the SAT I. This recommendation was
the first formal statement by an official University of California entity
calling for eliminating the SAT I, and the first major step in a struggle
that rapidly gained momentum. Eugene Garcia, chair of the Latino Task
Force, was at that time Dean of the School of Education at UC Berkeley.
In particular, the Task Force report focused on the use of the SAT I in
the University of California Eligibility Index. Dropping the test, said
the report, would increase the percentage of Latino California high
school graduates achieving UC eligibility from 3.9 percent to 6.2 percent, a fifty-nine percent increase. In a public statement, then-UC
President Richard Atkinson said, "This is something we should move
on. I find this recommendation a very interesting one."

The public conversation quickly became muddled as various interested parties confused different issues. One issue was the use of the SAT
I (or the SAT IIs or any other standardized test, for that matter) in any
kind of numeric index or formula which was used with fixed cut-offs,
whether such an index/formula was used to determine minimum eligi-

bility for the UC system or to select applicants for admission by a campus that was unable to admit all eligible students who applied. A second issue was the use of the SAT I or SAT IIs in a selective admissions process where test scores were looked at individually and assessed against the applicant's circumstances and family background. Some critics of the SAT I wanted that test in particular eliminated completely from both eligibility and selectivity determinations, while others argued that the tests were unacceptable in any kind of index or numerical cut-off scheme but acceptable as one admission criterion among many when reviewed against each applicant's circumstances. Opponents of affirmative action raised an important related issue, arguing that dropping the SAT I for the sole purpose of increasing the enrollment of a particular racial or ethnic group would almost certainly be illegal and that they would certainly challenge such a policy in court. Part of this argument hinged upon whether the SAT I was an unfair barrier to Latino students or whether eliminating the SAT I would be tantamount to introducing surrogate criteria for race and ethnicity under Proposition 209.

OCR AND THE USES OF STANDARDIZED TESTS

While the public argument continued in California, the Office for Civil Rights in the U.S. Department of Education was moving to sharply curtail the role of admissions tests in selective college admissions on a national level. In 1996, OCR began to circulate an unofficial set of guidelines on the acceptable uses of standardized tests. John Hayes III, an attorney in the Kansas City office of OCR, and Theresa Fay-Bustillos, an attorney (now vice president) for the Mexican American Legal Defense and Education Fund, began appearing at national and regional admissions conferences and meetings to lay out what they claimed were acceptable uses of the SAT I and other standardized tests. Although these acceptable-usage criteria had never been circulated publicly by OCR and had not been formally approved by any government office, Hayes and Fay-Bustillos clearly gave the impression that colleges and universities would be held accountable to these standards. The core of their argument was called disparate impact and maintained that the use of any standardized test that had differential outcomes by race or ethnicity was inherently discriminatory.

For more than two years, admissions officers, attorneys, and representatives of testing companies engaged in an uncertain and contentious discussion of these guidelines until OCR finally issued them officially in draft form in May 1999. Many admission officers and, not surprisingly, the College Board and the Educational Testing Service reacted strongly against that draft. As Sara Hebel noted in the July 7, 2000, issue of *The Chronicle of Higher Education*, "many college officials viewed the document as an attempt to discourage them from using standardized tests." A much gentler version was issued as a second draft in December 1999 and a third draft in July 2000, quite similar to the second, titled, "The Use of Tests When Making High-Stakes Decisions for Students." Perhaps equally important, the document was subtitled, "A Resource Guide for Educators and Policy-makers." The public comment period ended in mid-August 2000, and the U.S. Department of Education issued the final version on December 15, 2000. The term "Resource Guide" was somewhat puzzling, and exactly what legal standing these guidelines had and how they would influence policy and legal decisions was highly uncertain.

Although many admissions officers around the country were particularly resentful of the heavy-handed way in which OCR went about pushing its ideas, beneficial things emerged from subsequent exchanges with attorneys and other interested parties. While the legal standing of the OCR criteria was uncertain, it certainly forced college and university admissions officials to reexamine not just their uses of tests but also the purposes of their admissions policies and the role that an individual student's circumstances and context should have in an evaluation of that student's accomplishments both in and outside school. OCR was accurate in its determination that some tests with relevant consequences for students were—and are—being used irresponsibly and with unfair consequences for some students, particularly where those tests have differential outcomes by race and family income and where those tests are used in rigid formulas with no regard for the individual circumstances of each student.

The high-water mark for the OCR effort to influence the use of standardized tests in high-stakes educational decisions probably came in April 2000 when Senator Paul Wellstone introduced in the U.S. Senate the Fairness and Accuracy in Student Testing Act, known as S460. MALDEF issued a press release in support of the bill with a testimonial from Fay-Bustillos. Wellstone's bill, however, was not taken up during the 2000 or 2001 sessions of Congress and never got out of committee.

RIGHT BETWEEN THE EYES

From mid-1999 until George W. Bush took office, it looked as if the OCR high-stakes testing guidelines, buttressing OCR's theory of disparate impact, were going to change the way K-12 and colleges and universities used standardized tests in important and major ways. In late April 2001, however, the U.S. Supreme Court, in deciding a case called *Alexander v. Sandoval*, put a bullet right between the eyes of the OCR campaign. In that decision, the Court ruled that private citizens must prove intent to discriminate on the part of public colleges and other state agencies in order to successfully challenge the use of instruments, such as standardized tests, that have a disparate impact by race or ethnicity. In a single stroke, the court obliterated OCR's carefully developed legal reasoning that disparate impact, even absent intent to discriminate, was sufficient grounds to challenge such instruments. *Sandoval* was a devastating setback for minority groups and women in the struggle toward a fairer and more equal society.

In deciding *Sandoval*, the court divided 5 to 4, along the exact lines of its decisions in the disputed Florida presidential vote that gave the November 2000 presidential election to George W. Bush, with Kennedy, Rehnquist, O'Connor, Scalia, and Thomas constituting the five. At the time, those two 5 to 4 votes made it most difficult to think of Justice Sandra Day O'Connor as a potential swing vote in any case focused on affirmative action in university admissions—and made O'Connor's opinion in *Grutter v. Bollinger* all that much more surprising.

RICHARD ATKINSON AND THE SAT I

In February 2001, Atkinson stunned the world of higher education when, in a speech to the American Council on Education (ACE), he announced that he was recommending that the University of California drop the use of the SAT I in its freshman admissions process. Atkinson's speech to ACE began a period of high tension between the university and the College Board, which owns the SAT I. At first, the university hoped to completely sever most of its ties to the Board. Atkinson, however, had been so eager to make his pronouncement at a national forum that he did so without having decided on a sound alternative to the SAT I. Challenged by UC faculty to name an alternative, he produced a sequence of two alternatives, each of which was dismissed by the faculty as poorly conceived or simply unsound. Atkinson then reluctantly entered into diplomatic negotiations with the College Board, which had been steadfast in its pursuit of the university; the Educational Testing Service; and, as a kind of tag-along, the American College Test. The College Board and ETS were determined not to lose their California market and agreed to make a number of changes to the SAT I.

A little more than two years after Atkinson's speech to ACE, having been outmaneuvered politically by the College Board, Atkinson and the university ended up embracing a revised form of the SAT I. That outcome, ironically, left the College Board in a stronger economic position than ever. The Board's market share in the competitive world of testing will remain intact, and its revenue stream from the SAT I will increase sharply because the revised test will carry a much higher price tag.

POGO, AGAIN

In addition to those barriers to meaningful school reform and greater social equality described earlier in this chapter, there is another powerful social force at work: the resistance of affluent parents to significant school reform. In the mid-1990s, Pedro Noguera conceived of and led The Diversity Project at Berkeley High School for four years. Noguera pointed out that Berkeley High had a powerful group of liberal white parents, most of whom lived in the Berkeley Hills, who gained for their children a private high school academic experience within the cultural richness of Berkeley High—and at a public price. In an interview that appeared in the October 13, 2000, issue of the *East Bay Express*, Noguera said:

> For example, we have been working at Berkeley High School to reduce tracking, especially in the ninth grade, because what we've seen is that kids relegated to the lower tracks really get the very worst education—very low expectations, very little rigor. . . .But very often the parents of privileged kids will oppose that, because they want a more elite education within public schools.

Meredith Maran, author of *Class Dismissed*, refers to some of these parents as "the hundred mothers who run Berkeley High."

In a similar vein, Jeannie Oakes, the UCLA faculty member who directs UC ACCORD and who studies social stratification and inequality in K-12 schools, wrote an essay called "Outreach: Struggling Against Power and Culture," which appeared in the November 1999 issue of *Outlook*, an online magazine produced by the Office of the President of the University of California. Long a supporter of university outreach programs, Oakes begins the essay by writing, "I can't help but see our outreach efforts as naïve. As spectacular as our work may be, student- and school-centered activities alone are unlikely to produce UC student bodies that reflect California's diversity." Oakes points out that we have lost sight of the fact that upper-middle and upper-income parents do not sit idly by as the university increases outreach efforts for disadvantaged students and schools: "As we extend our academic support programs to middle schoolers, advantaged families will begin even earlier. As we make popular SAT prep programs more widely available, advantaged families will seek more intense and longer-lasting preparation." Discussing school reform, Oakes writes that as "we help our school partners pursue effective college-going cultures and curricula, we can expect that wealthier and more powerful parents will push their schools to better position their children at the top of the new educational hierarchy." In a kind of mid-essay summary, she notes that "elites will outpace outreach in the race for educational advantage" and then adds, "While not a firm equation, hard work plus privilege will usually trump hard work alone."

To a significant degree, Oakes's observations parallel the work of Alfie Kohn, a prolific writer and speaker who opposes the tougher standards approach to school reform. In an article called "Only for My Kid: How Privileged Parents Undermine School Reform," which appeared in the April 1998 issue of *Phi Delta Kappan*, Kohn argues that the biggest impediment to school reform is often upper-middle class parents for whom the schools are working just fine, thank you. Kohn cites several examples across the country where affluent parents have overturned efforts at making schools work better for all students. That is what happened at University High School in Irvine, California, a few years ago. University High was enthusiastically taking part in something called The Transition Project, which had been funded by the California Legislature to help high schools move to a portfolio-based form of student assessment that would have eliminated letter grades, among other reforms. Reform-minded teachers and administrators within the high school were enthusiastic about restructuring University High, but they moved too quickly and didn't build political support among affluent parents—they may never have been able to build such support—and these parents, who were articulate, aggressive, politically connected, and politically sophisticated, killed the transformation (helped somewhat by a few teachers who just didn't want to change their ways and by the teachers union which opposed the longer school day that would have resulted). Kohn quotes Oakes's description of such parents as "Volvo vigilantes." For these parents in Irvine, the attitude was "Hey, it isn't broken for us. Butt out!" Kohn argues that these parents don't care about "all kids." They care about "my kid." For Kohn, those Volvos carry bumper stickers that read, "My child is an honor student at University High" with an unwritten addition to that sentence: "and yours isn't."

11 TROUBLE AHEAD

TIDAL WAVE II AND THE CONSEQUENCES OF
POOR PUBLIC POLICY-PLANNING

There is little question that the struggle over the consideration of race and ethnicity in university admissions will continue over the next several years. This struggle is likely to become even more heated than it has been because many states have not planned for the sharp increases in the number of college-going students that demographers have identified for at least the past ten years. This surge in demand will increase the competition for admission to both selective public and private colleges and universities and will have a powerful effect on the same institutions that have already been the focal point of the debate over affirmative action.

The July 2, 2004, issue of *The Chronicle of Higher Education* carried a story by Sara Hebel, titled "No Room in the Class." A table accompanied the article, using data from the Western Interstate Commission for Higher Education, which projects an increase in the country's high school graduates from 2,894,429 in 2002 to 3,195,259 in 2009, a gain of 300,830 students or 10.4 percent. At least fifteen states, including California, Florida, Georgia, New York, and Texas, are projected to have increases of more than ten percent, and two states—Nevada and Arizona—are projected to experience increases of more than twenty percent.

Citing Virginia where high school graduates are projected to increase by sixteen percent, Hebel describes how George Mason University in Virginia is no longer a safety school (that is, a school where a good-but-not-great student was nevertheless virtually certain of being admitted) for students denied admission to the University of Virginia and other selective state colleges such as the College of William and Mary, James Madison, and Virginia Tech. That same issue of *The Chronicle of Higher Education* carried a Point of View article by Gordon Davies, a senior advisor to the Education Commission of the States, titled "Today, Even B Students Are Getting Squeezed Out." Of the coming space crunch, Davies writes, "The financially poor and educationally disadvantaged probably will be the major victims. But the real political train wreck will occur as well-prepared, solid but unspectacular middle-income students increasingly discover that there's no room for them at selective public institutions."

And further complicating the debate over affirmative action is the fact that a significant portion of the increase in high school graduates will be Latino. Peter Schmidt, in the article "Academe's Hispanic Future" that appeared in the November 28, 2003, issue of *The Chronicle of Higher Education*, notes, "Hispanics have become the largest minority group in the United States and now represent about 13 percent of the country's population." Writing about a separate report released by the Western Interstate Commission for Higher Education in late January 2004, Jennifer Jacobson in *The Chronicle of Higher Education* issue of February 6, 2004, pointed out, "The report predicts that there will be 73 percent more Hispanic students graduating from public high schools by 2014 than in 2002. During the same period, there will be 11 percent fewer white graduates and 6 percent more black graduates."

In California, Clark Kerr called the increase in high school graduates "Tidal Wave II." In September 1999, the California Postsecondary Education Commission (CPEC) reported that by the year 2010, California's public institutions of higher education should expect enrollments to increase by more than 700,000 students. CPEC calculates that the University of California will need to accommodate 63,000 of these students by that year. This enrollment increase would mean that the university would need to hire 3,000 more faculty members.

Adding 63,000 new students to the University of California system is a Herculean challenge. Several of the campuses, including Berkeley and UC Santa Barbara, have growth restrictions imposed on them as a result of negotiations with their surrounding communities. Nevertheless, the UC Office of the President has allocated portions of the 63,000 to each of the campuses in the UC system.

Until just a few years ago, the state had invested nothing for at least thirty years in the development of new UC campuses to serve the predictable increase in demand for UC. Finally, the Legislature and the governor agreed to add a single UC campus—regrettably located near Merced, just seventy-five miles east of UC Santa Cruz and a hundred miles south of UC Davis, rather than close to Fresno or Bakersfield, the true centers of the San Joaquin Valley. By the year 2010, however, UC Merced will enroll just 5,000 students.

DAMAGE BY BUDGET CUTS

One of the reasons for the expected crush of students in so many states across the country is that most of those states have not invested in the expansion of public higher education, even during their relatively flush budget years. The collapse of the technology sector and the subsequent steep downturn in the U.S. economy that took place in 2001–02 subsequently created budget deficits in most states and, in the case of California and a few other states, a funding crisis. These factors, in turn, have resulted in budget cuts to higher education. The University of California system, to take the most egregious example, returned unread 1,600 freshman and transfer applications for the winter 2004 term because the campuses could not afford to take in any more new students. And for fall 2004, the UC system denied admission to 7,600 qualified freshman applicants, the first time the university was unable to admit every qualified student since the Master Plan for Higher Education was adopted by the state in 1960.

The budget damage has already shown up in other ways as well. For the spring 2004 semester at Berkeley, enrollment in upper-division philosophy courses was restricted to philosophy majors only because the Philosophy Department did not have the resources to provide classes, professors, and places for all of the undergraduates who wanted to enroll in a philosophy course. Imagine being a student at what has been called the finest public university in the world and being told that you could not take an upper-division philosophy course because the campus did not have adequate space.

Politicians in California and other states with severe budget problems seem to shrug their shoulders and say, "It's a shame, but there's nothing we can really do. The money just isn't there." That, of course, doesn't have to be the case. There is always the option of raising taxes to fund public schools and public higher education. Raising taxes, however, is just not something many politicians who wish to be re-elected are willing to do. Instead, they further exacerbate the funding crisis by trying to cut taxes for middle-income voters, including vehicle registration fee cuts (in California) and reductions in sales taxes. As we watch the deterioration of our public education systems, we truly are getting what we haven't paid for.

Part of what has happened over the past twenty-five years or so is that California legislators who were UC graduates, often UC Berkeley graduates, have been replaced to a significant extent by legislators who graduated from California State University campuses, who did not necessarily have a residential college experience, and who see college for most students as simply a bottom-line deal in which the only thing that matters is the piece of paper at the end that gets you into the job market. It will be difficult to offset the tendency of the bottom-liners to redefine the college experience for most students simply as two years at your local community college and then two years commuting to your local four-year university. This commuter model currently works for many students, but imposing it on a great many more students would be myopic and poor public policy. It will be a great loss for the people of California if the state allows what Ken Weiss of the *Los Angeles Times* calls "penny-pinchers in the Legislature" to turn an extraordinary public residential university system into just another factory-like commuter system.

Had it wished to do so, California could have solved its entire budget deficit problem and raise $26.4 billion over two years by instituting a temporary and modest tax increase on those Californians who have an adjusted gross income of $200,000 or more. Paul O'Lague and John Bachar, writing in the February 8, 2004, issue of the *San Francisco Chronicle*, outlined such a tax plan that would carry temporary tax increases ranging from 0.5 percent for incomes between $200,000 and $299,000 to seven percent for incomes of $5,000,000 and above. While it's remarkably easy to say, "Tax the rich," this proposal seemed to many Californians a reasonably fair way to solve California's budget deficit. The California Legislature, however, never seriously considered the possibility.

California no longer defines financial support for the University of California as an investment in the broad public welfare. Instead, it now defines a public university education as an individual benefit the cost of which should be borne to a large extent by those individuals who benefit directly from it. That meant instead of raising taxes, the state raised UC fees sharply for the 2004–05 academic year. Both California-resident students and non-California residents were affected, with sharper increases for non-California residents and for graduate students and even bigger fee increases for law, medical, and graduate business schools. The hardest blow fell on non-California–resident graduate students. Such graduate students in academic departments paid well over $40,000 in total costs for 2004–05, while nonresident law-school students at Boalt Hall paid $52,000 in total and daytime MBA non-California–resident students paid more than $53,000.

The fastest way to destroy the extraordinary quality of UC Berkeley is to seriously damage graduate education. That's because the heart of

Berkeley's international reputation is its faculty, and graduate education is what most faculty care most about. If the quality and scope of graduate education contract sharply, many faculty members will leave for competitor universities. The visa restrictions and delays in processing visas following the events of September 11, 2001, have already cut deeply into graduate enrollment at Berkeley and other research institutions. In fact, one staff member at UC Berkeley who works with international graduate-student instructors estimates that the enrollment of these students has dropped by one-third.

The high costs for nonresident graduate students described above will have dire consequences for Berkeley in two ways. First, Berkeley will cost as much or more than its most elite private university competitors, thus negating the comparative cost advantage Berkeley has enjoyed for years against the elite privates. Second, many academic departments, with fixed fellowship and graduate-assistant monies, will be unable to support financially as many graduate students as they have in the past. A reduction in international graduate-student enrollment at Berkeley, steep costs in relation to competitor institutions, and a greatly reduced ability to support graduate students financially could undo the quality of graduate education over a relatively short time. That, in turn, may cause the departure of many of the campus' most distinguished faculty and also make it more difficult for the campus to attract talented young faculty. Over the past decade, UC Berkeley also worked diligently to improve the quality of undergraduate student life, and the gains it made helped Berkeley compete with the other elite public and private institutions to which applicants to Berkeley have often also been admitted. Now the campus is headed in the opposite direction. It took decades for California to build what many observers agree is the finest public university in the world. It may take only a few years of short-sighted policies to sacrifice much of its outstanding quality and reputation.

On the other hand, in late October 2000, new Stanford President John Hennessy announced a five-year, $1 billion capital campaign to raise money for undergraduate education. Courtney Leatherman, reporting in the October 23, 2000, issue of *The Chronicle of Higher Education*, reported that Hennessy intends to use the money "to support a series of undergraduate programs known as Stanford Introductory Studies. They include freshman and sophomore seminars taught by tenured professors, sophomore college—an intensive two-week program in which groups of 12 students work closely with a professor—and independent student and research opportunities that provide support for students working on tutorial projects related to faculty research and summer-research fellowships." Stanford also plans to increase its endowment for financial aid, so that, in Hennessy's words, "we can continue to accept the most qualified students without considering their ability to pay."

THE RISE OF THE SUPER-ELITES

That recent announcement by Stanford that it will invest $1 billion in undergraduate education reflects a new phenomenon, the emergence of the so-called super-elites, which will also affect the future of affirmative action. The super-elites are those private universities with the strongest academic reputations and the largest endowments. At the same time that public and modestly endowed private colleges and universities face serious financial challenges, the super-elites are increasingly surging away from all other institutions. The wealth of the super-elites is staggering. As of June 30, 2003, nine universities had endowments valued at $4 billion or more. Twenty-two institutions had endowments valued at $2 billion or more.

Harvard's endowment has quadrupled since 1990 and, as of June 30, 2003, was valued at $18.8 billion. Yale's endowment was $11 billion as of that same date, with Princeton and Stanford close behind at $8.7 billion and $8.6 billion respectively. And these institutions manage their money extremely well. Harvard's endowment grew by $1.7 billion over the preceding year, a gain of more than 9.8 percent and an amount larger than the entire endowments of all but twenty-four colleges and universities in the country. That kind of astute management meant that the super-elites did not lose much ground during the stock market collapse in 2001–02 while many other institutions were headed for disaster and that the super-elites bounced back much faster than most other institutions.

One consequence of this immense wealth is that there is a large and growing gap in the faculty salaries offered by public universities compared to those offered by private universities. This faculty salary gap is likely to increase sharply between the super-elite private colleges and universities and everybody else. That, in turn, may mean that superstar faculty, a recent phenomenon, will increasingly be clustered at the super-elites and that, in turn, may further tilt the popular rankings even more heavily in their favor. Whether or not undergraduate students would actually have access to such faculty is an important question, but the public perception may simply be that these are the places to enroll because they are where the big names are.

Other than the super-elites, however, many private colleges suffered sharp drops in their endowments from the 2001–02 recession, and many of them face an added risk from the possibility of diminished enrollments. Ripon College, the College of Wooster, Oberlin, and Oklahoma City University are all recent, prominent examples. In March 2002, the College of Wooster cut thirty full and part-time jobs. The following month, both Oberlin and Oklahoma City University announced major budget crises. Oberlin, according to John Pulley in an April 16, 2002, article in the electronic version of *The Chronicle of Higher Education*, faced a $5 million shortfall for the coming year, most of it driven by an increase in health-care costs from $5 million to $9.4 million in just a couple of years. OCU faced a $2.5 million deficit because of declining enrollments over the past five years. According to Elizabeth Farrell in the April 11, 2002, issue of *The Chronicle of Higher Education*, OCU laid off twenty-seven employees and would leave thirteen positions unfilled. If an institution depends almost entirely on tuition for its operating budget and it falls fifteen percent short of its freshman enrollment goal, for example, it may be in serious financial trouble and it may have to divert more of its endowment income to operating expenses—or, much worse, be tempted to break a cardinal principle by cutting into the endowment itself. According to the Pulley and Farrell articles, Oberlin and OCU both considered this latter option in the face of their budget shortfalls.

Because of their wealth, the super-elites have also been able to create financial aid policies that other, less wealthy institutions simply cannot match. Princeton has been most aggressive in this thrust, adopting a policy of no loans in its need-based financial aid packages. Imagine coming from a family with a modest income, getting admitted to Princeton, and having the opportunity to earn a degree with a total cost over four years of at least $160,000 while incurring absolutely no loan debt. Yale has capped loans at $3,200 per year in its need-based aid packages, carefully figuring that a relatively small amount of borrowing in return for a Yale degree probably won't be perceived as enough of a burden to cause an admitted student to enroll at a competitor.

Harvard was initially much more coy—and shrewd—saying simply "Bring all offers from other institutions. We'll negotiate." In this way, Harvard saved money because it had to adjust only those financial aid packages where a student and his or her family were enterprising enough to pursue a better deal, sweetening the packages of those who asked rather than spending all of the money it would take to eliminate loans across the board for all enrolling aid recipients. In February 2004, however, Harvard President Lawrence Summers announced that Harvard would eliminate the family contribution required of financial-aid recipients for students coming from families with annual incomes below $40,000—on average, $2,300—and that it would reduce the expected family contribution for students coming from families with annual incomes between $40,000 and $60,000. Summers, quoted by Julianne Basinger and Scott Smallwood in the March 1, 2004, electronic issue of *The Chronicle of Higher Education*, said that the gap in opportunities for children from different economic backgrounds is the "most severe domestic problem in the United States." He continued, "Only by assuring access to everyone can we maximize the quality of our nation's college graduates." Summers then added a powerful zinger:

"We know that classes at Kaplan and Princeton Review may be the least diverse in America."

UC Berkeley, by contrast and despite a comprehensive financial-aid program, will include a combination of $8,000 in work and loans in all its fall 2004 aid packages. (The one exception is its elite Regents' and Chancellor's Scholarship program, which fully meets each student's demonstrated financial need entirely with grant and scholarship money.) In the fall 2003 Freshman Survey conducted by the Office of Student Research at UC Berkeley, 44.9 percent of the freshmen reported that they expected to amass at least $10,000 in loan debt by graduation. Losing common admits to the Ivy schools and Stanford drives most Berkeley faculty and senior administrators nuts, but, with such sharp increases in fees—especially for non-California residents—and lackluster competitive financial-aid packages, it's certainly not difficult to see why this happens.

In October 2003, the University of North Carolina at Chapel Hill announced that, beginning in fall 2004, it would eliminate loans in the financial-aid packages for needy students provided that those students work on campus ten to twelve hours per week. As Jeffrey Selingo noted in *The Chronicle of Higher Education* October 2, 2003, electronic edition, this change in policy will cost the university $1.38 million each year. That is a relatively small amount of money and is explained by the fact that UNC already uses grant and scholarship money to make up eighty-six percent of the aid packages of its neediest students—and by the fact that only 13.2 percent of UNC's undergraduates receive Pell Grants, one of the key markers of low-family income.

In February 2004, the University of Virginia announced a similar policy, in which the university will replace loans with grant money in financial-aid packages of students whose family income levels are at or below $27,600, which was one and a half times the federal poverty line in 2003. University of Virginia President John Casteen III noted that the changes in aid policy at the Ivy schools and at Chapel Hill had strongly influenced UVA's decision. As with UNC, the cost of such a policy will be relatively modest, because only 8.6 percent of UVA undergraduates qualify for Pell Grants. The UNC and UVA Pell Grant figures are low compared to the 32.4 percent figure for UC Berkeley. (All of these Pell Grant percentages are for the year 2001 and are taken from the study conducted by Tom Mortenson, published in the March 2004 issue of *Postsecondary Education Opportunity*, which is also discussed in Chapter 8.)

The rise of the super-elites means extraordinary opportunities for some African American, Latino, and Native American students, specifically those who have made an outstanding academic record and come from low-income families, and that will be a fortunate thing for those students. On the other hand, it means that increasingly other public and private colleges and universities will lose out on the most talented minority students, especially those from low-income families, even if they have also admitted them. Those losses will be particularly telling for the flagship public universities in California, Florida, and Washington where affirmative action remains banned. The fall 2004 freshman class at UC Berkeley enrolled 3,671 students. Among those 3,671, there were only 108 African American freshmen—and just thirty-nine males—who made up 2.9 percent of the class. Twenty-seven of those 108 African American students—24.8 percent—were recruited athletes. That figure of 108 fall 2004 African American freshmen is a 58 percent drop from the 257 African American freshmen enrolled in fall 1997, the last year of affirmative action, and the 2.9 percent figure represents the smallest proportion of African American freshmen at Berkeley in well over two decades.

THE POSSIBILITY OF MORE STATEWIDE INITIATIVE CAMPAIGNS TO END AFFIRMATIVE ACTION

Soon after California votes passed Proposition 209, Ward Connerly proposed that the race/ethnicity identification item on the UC application be removed, partly because he saw no need for it after 209 had been enacted but mostly because he believed that admissions officers would peek at this item and surreptitiously consider the race of an applicant in making admissions decisions. As a means to control cheating by admission officers, it was a poorly conceived idea because, even without that application item, a determined admissions officer could almost certainly identify the race or ethnicity of ninety-eight percent of the applicants he or she reads. Students, especially minority students, often disclose their race or ethnicity in many different ways throughout the UC application, in part because it is such an important part of their own identity and of defining who they are within American society. The most obvious place is in the required personal statement, but a careful reader can also find such information in course patterns (English as a Second Language classes, courses in African American Studies at a school such as Berkeley High), specific scholarship awards, specific types of community service, and in the honors and activities section of the application. And in many cases, of course, one can make fairly accurate guesses about race or ethnicity from names—both last and, in some cases, first—although this practice carries with it a significant danger of racial stereotyping.

Connerly anticipated this last possibility and, for a short time, proposed that, in addition to removing the race/ethnicity identification item from the application, the university also strip applicant names from the UC application. The proposal to eliminate the names of applicants died quickly, and his proposal to eliminate the gathering of racial and ethnic identification also faded from lack of widespread support. It resurfaced several years later, however, as the Racial Privacy Initiative, which qualified for the October 2003 ballot in California as Proposition 54. Connerly, Thomas Sowell, and others led a drive to gather signatures in order to qualify the initiative for the ballot.

The Racial Privacy Initiative would have prohibited the gathering of racial and ethnic identification data except in those few instances where such information is required by federal law. It would have meant that no racial and ethnic data would be gathered on employment, on California's K-12 enrollment and graduation outcomes, and on students who applied to (including those students who were admitted to) California community colleges, the California State University System, and the University of California system. At least in the case of the UC

System, racial and ethnic identification data on enrolled students would be gathered because enrollment data—as opposed to application and admission data—must be reported to the federal government.

On March 22, 2002, the *San Francisco Chronicle* published an opinion piece by Thomas Sowell in support of the Racial Privacy Initiative, called "A new push to end racial bean counting." Sowell blamed "racial bean counters" for the creation of racial quotas and, in what should become a standard negative example for logic and writing classes everywhere, he then argued that we can solve the problem of racial discrimination by eliminating the data that demonstrates there is a problem.

In a rebuttal carried a few days later in the same paper, Clifford Rechtschaffen noted that the initiative should more accurately have been called the "Racial Ignorance Initiative." In keeping with their recent behavior, UC Regents other than Connerly got into the act as well. In early April 2002, UC Regent John J. Moores, who owns the San Diego Padres baseball team, held what became a widely publicized fundraiser for the initiative. That prompted the deputy mayor of San Diego to call for a boycott of Padres games. Once again, much of the rest of the country could only shake its collective head in a kind of awed despair at the wacky politics of zany California.

On May 1, 2002, the *San Francisco Chronicle* published the results of a Field Poll that showed likely California voters favoring the Racial Privacy Initiative by a margin of forty-eight to thirty-four percent with only eighteen percent undecided. The Poll report noted that a high percentage of the people supporting the initiative had also supported Proposition 209. Opponents of the proposition, however, organized a strong campaign, aided in large part by a $3.8 million contribution from Lieutenant Governor Cruz Bustamente, and, surprisingly, the measure was soundly defeated sixty-four to thirty-six percent. Had Proposition 54 passed, Californians would have been plunged into an even deeper abyss than that created by Proposition 209, one in which it would have been almost impossible to document what we already know are enormous economic and education gaps based on race and ethnicity, and in which it would have been impossible not only to measure such gaps but to demonstrate any progress toward their elimination.

The *Grutter* decision in June 2003 and the defeat of Proposition 54 in October of that year were major setbacks for Connerly and his allies. Almost immediately following the *Grutter* opinion, however, Connerly announced that he was beginning a signature-gathering campaign in Michigan to place an initiative measure similar to Proposition 209, called the Michigan Civil Rights Initiative, on the November 2004 ballot. In March 2004, a Michigan court blocked the signature-gathering effort. When that decision was overturned in June, according to Brendon Fleming in the June 25, 2004, issue of *The Chronicle of Higher Education*, backers of the initiative announced that they would continue gathering signatures but would now aim for the 2006 ballot. On January 6, 2005, they submitted their petition accompanied by 508,202 signatures, needing about 317,000 valid signatures to qualify for the 2006 ballot. Both the political landscape and the demographics of Michigan are different than those of California, and if the measure does appear on the Michigan ballot, both supporters and opponents of affirmative action will watch it closely.

IT NEVER GOES AWAY

Because people in this country are so divided on issues of race and because so many parents and students are worried that someone else is getting some sort of unfair advantage, the controversy over the role of race and ethnicity in university admissions never goes away—even in the case of UC Berkeley, where the enrollment of African American, Latino, and Native American freshmen has been decimated since Proposition 209 took effect for fall 1998.

In October 2003, John J. Moores, then chair of the UC Board of Regents, released his own study in which, looking only at SAT I scores of admitted and denied freshman applicants for fall 1992, Moores found that Berkeley denied 641 applicants with SAT I scores of 1,500 and above and, at the same time, admitted 381 applicants with SAT I scores of 1,000 or below.

Moores' report, it should be noted, was given to the *Los Angeles Times*—by whom has never been made clear—just in time for an inflammatory article on race in admissions to appear on October 4, 2003, four days before California voters were scheduled to vote on Proposition 54—at a time when polls showed Proposition 54 was most likely to lose. Moores was a prominent supporter of Proposition 54, even, as noted just above, hosting a fund-raising party at his home for Connerly and Proposition 54.

Moores' study was deeply flawed; he ignored the fact that there are many separate freshman applicant pools and he counted as denied Berkeley applicants those students who did not complete their applications or who withdrew them after being admitted early by another institution. When Chancellor Berdahl and other campus staff pointed out these errors in a preliminary discussion, Moores agreed to correct them. Instead, he circulated the flawed study to his fellow Regents.

Moores then made harsh public comments about the Berkeley freshman admissions process and about the students with low test scores (who had made up 3.5 percent of all fall 2002 admitted students). In addition, Regent Ward Connerly suggested that the campus may have cheated to get around Proposition 209 because a significant portion of the 381 students are African American and Latino—the same Regent Connerly who publicly accused UC admissions officers of planning to cheat even before the first admission cycle was ever conducted under Proposition 209. Moores told the *Los Angeles Times,* "I just don't see any objective standards." Berkeley admission officers responded by pointing out that ninety-eight percent of fall 2002 freshman applicants—excluding those to the three highly competitive majors in Engineering—who were California residents and had SAT I scores of *1,400* and above had been admitted to Berkeley. More important, campus administrators noted that not a single one of the 381 students had been dismissed from the university for academic reasons.

Moores claimed to be befuddled by the Berkeley freshman-admissions process, but he was among the groups of UC Regents who visited UC Berkeley and other campuses during the preceding year to observe admissions practices firsthand. After going through a reader training session and then reading and discussing individual applications, Connerly, for example, praised the Berkeley process. Moores, however, was reportedly never engaged during his visit, talking on his cell phone and treating campus staff rudely. Had he paid attention during his visit to the campus, the process might not seem opaque at all. It is complex, but not opaque. These are not the same things.

Because nearly all 381 students came from severely disadvantaged backgrounds and overcame remarkable obstacles in achieving their academic records, the fact that so many of them were African American and Latino (and, as it happens, Asian American) should have surprised no one. Who does Moores think attends the most disadvantaged high schools in California? Most of us who live middle-class lives have precious little idea how many young people in California struggle against overwhelming hardship, adversity, and deprivation. Students who succeed academically despite having to work twenty or more hours a week, attend poor schools, endure extreme poverty, survive parents who are gang members, live in broken families or with no family at all, endure homelessness, overcome illness or disability, and/or survive in neighborhoods routinely rattled by gunfire deserve careful consideration by California's flagship university. That so many of them who gain admission to Berkeley then succeed there, as Chancellor Berdahl pointed out in a stinging letter to Moores, is testimony not only to their grit and tenacity but to their intelligence and academic abilities.

Moores then wrote an opinion piece that appeared in the March 2004 *Forbes*, in which he accused Berkeley of deliberately discriminating against Asian Americans in its freshman admissions process. Berkeley officials were stunned that the chair of the university's Board of Regents would make such an accusation publicly and in print.

There is no question that Moores, as a UC Regent, has every right to question closely every aspect of UC admissions policies and practices. It was difficult to understand, however, why he chose to do so through the media instead of within the structure of the university and the Board of Regents. It was also a struggle to understand why he seemed to be deliberately choosing such confrontational language. After the October 4, 2003, article appeared in the *Los Angeles Times*, Chancellor Berdahl provided a concise explanation of why some students with remarkably high SAT I scores were denied at Berkeley. According to Tanya Schevitz in the *San Francisco Chronicle*, Moores, who, after all, was one of Berdahl's bosses, replied, "This is under the blah, blah, blah category." The UC Berkeley website had posted student profiles of forty-one of the 381 students whose admission Moores had questioned. Moores described this posting as a "cheap public stunt."

Finally, in March 2004, Moores' colleagues on the Board of Regents voted 8 to 6 to censure him for his irresponsible and careless comments and accusations in the *Forbes* article. Nevertheless, as Chancellor Berdahl pointed out in a letter to him, Moores' carelessness and blatant disregard for the university's welfare damaged the integrity of the admissions process at Berkeley and disparaged students with low SAT I scores who are already at Berkeley and doing well. In addition, Moores' requests for data and documents added immensely to the workload of the admissions staff and put enormous political pressure both on the Admissions Office and on the chancellor and his senior staff. More than anything, however, Moores' behavior demonstrates that the issue of race and ethnicity in admissions never goes away.

THE NEW WAR ON POVERTY, SORT OF

The combination of severe budget cuts to K-12 and higher education occurring across the nation, the Bush administration's massive tax cut for the wealthy, and the iron resistance of legislators in many states to even consider the possibility of raising taxes to adequately support public schools and colleges has created a twisted version of Lyndon Johnson's War on Poverty. This war, however, is The War on the Poor. In 2002, 34.6 million people in the United States lived below the federal poverty line, which for a family of four was an annual income of $18,392. That was 12.1 percent of the population, and an increase from 31.6 million in 2000. In 2002, 14.1 million people lived in severe poverty, defined as half the poverty threshold of $18,392—an income of $9,196 for a family of four.

In an article titled "Cry California," which appeared in the September 14, 2003, *San Francisco Chronicle*, Mike Davis described the growing income gap among rich and poor: "In the Los Angeles areas, for example, the top 20 percent of the workforce earns 25 times more on average than the bottom 20 percent. Similarly, a third of Los Angeles residents lack medical insurance and must depend on a handful of overcrowded county hospitals whose doctors have recently given chilling testimony about the rising number of needless deaths from shortages of staff and beds." Stirring echoes of the world described by John Sayles in his short story "Old Spanish Days," Davis described the economic schism that divides the Coachella Valley with Palm Springs, Palm Desert, Rancho Mirage, Indian Wells, and La Quinta on the lush western side of the valley and a string of depressed, hardscrabble towns and cities from Mecca to Indio on the east side of the valley "where the resort maids, busboys, pool cleaners, and farmworkers live." He also writes, "On the gilded coast north of San Diego, an estimated 10,000 immigrant day laborers and service workers sleep rough in the wild canyons behind $800,000 tract homes." The east side of the Coachella Valley and the wilds of northern San Diego County make up part of what Davis calls "Third World California."

Jane Bryant Quinn in the February 2, 2004, issue of *Newsweek* itemizes the cuts to higher education in America and said, "The cost crisis is resegregating higher education, not by color but by class." Quinn should have said more: because there is such a close correlation between class and race in this country it is also a de facto war on African Americans, Latinos, and Native Americans. George W. Bush's No Child Left Behind law extends this war to K-12 through its heavy insistence on punishing the schools that have been deliberately most starved of money and other resources. Quinn quotes Tom Mortenson, a higher-education policy analyst, who describes what is happening to higher education as "creeping privatization." At some level, without a lot of people getting to vote on the matter, Congress, as the California Legislature has done, has decided that public higher education is no longer a public good but entirely a private benefit accruing solely to the individual—who therefore must pay for it.

One part of The War on the Poor includes the combination of no increases in taxes to support public K-12 and higher education, the subsequent steep increases in public college and university fees, a deliberate reduction in the amount of money set aside for need-based financial aid, and the reduction or elimination of outreach programs that have served low-income and minority students and their parents. These policies will mean that far fewer students from low-income families—particularly African American, Latino, and Native American students—will end up in college, especially in public colleges.

John Moores' attack on UC Berkeley students with low SAT I scores and his subsequent argument that SAT I scores should matter much more in the process seemed to many observers to be a form of class war. To argue that high SAT I scores should dominate in an admissions process is to argue that the process should tilt heavily toward affluent students whose parents are highly educated—the same people, as Professor Jeannie Oakes of UCLA points out in her article "Outreach: Struggling Against Power and Culture" that was cited in Chapter 10, who already have almost all of the advantages possible in selective college admissions.

12 WHAT ADMISSIONS POLICY-MAKERS CAN DO

The Supreme Court decisions in *Grutter* and *Gratz* are a firm reminder that colleges and universities need to pay careful attention to their admissions policies and practices, not just in the consideration of race and ethnicity but in all of the ways that they treat their applicants. Chapter 2 briefly discussed several of the key questions that admissions policy-makers must confront, whether they are boards of trustees, chancellors and presidents, faculty admissions committees, or deans and directors of admission. This chapter presents ten specific recommendations that follow from *Grutter* and *Gratz*, recommendations that should be of interest not only to admissions policy-makers but to anyone concerned with how our society allocates one of its most highly sought, scarce resources—admission to selective colleges and universities. Taken together, the recommendations yield a comprehensive, thorough, fair, and legal admission policy, including, as one element, affirmative action. They are intended to apply primarily to colleges and universities admitting freshman or undergraduate transfer students, but most of the recommendations also apply to graduate and professional schools.

Not all of the recommendations focus directly on the consideration of race and ethnicity. Those that do so will be of concern primarily to selective institutions that must choose among a group of qualified applicants or to institutions that have special admissions programs for applicants who do not meet formal admissions requirements but who have overcome difficult circumstances and who show great potential for college success. Because the legal issues regarding the consideration of race in the two University of Michigan decisions are complex, admissions policy-makers may wish to consult *Preserving Diversity in Higher Education: A Manual on Admissions Policies and Procedures After the University of Michigan Decisions*, an excellent analysis published in 2004 by three highly respected San Francisco law firms.

Some private and perhaps a few public colleges and universities—the University of Virginia, for example—may already be doing all of the things in the list that follows. A great many of the publics and some of the privates, however, take shortcuts in their processes in order to save time and money. Despite the effects of *Alexander v. Sandoval* on the disparate impact argument, discussed in Chapter 10, many of the other Office for Civil Rights principles in "The Use of Tests When Making High-Stakes Decisions for Students" remain quite sound and have been adapted in the criteria that follow.

1. An institution should have a clear statement of purpose for its admission policy. A college or university should have a clearly written, formal admission policy that describes the goals and objectives of that policy. This policy should be crafted by the senior policy-making body of the institution, whether a faculty committee, a committee of senior administrators, a combination of the two, or a committee of the board of trustees or regents, and the policy should be tied directly to the mission statement of the institution. If diversity is identified as one of the university's goals, the policy statement should include a broad definition of that term, making clear that diversity means a student body that encompasses students from a wide range of geographic origins, socio-economic backgrounds, races and ethnicities, special talents, and outstanding academic and personal achievements.

The O'Connor opinion in *Grutter* permits colleges and universities to determine enrollment goals that will achieve a critical mass of enrolled students from particular racial and ethnic groups. If enrolling a critical mass of African American, Latino, and Native American students is one of the university's goals, it must decide what critical mass means for racial and ethnic groups within that institution's student body and set admission/enrollment goals based on the determinations of critical mass. One way to do this is to use flexible target ranges that are reviewed and adjusted each admissions cycle.

Particular attention should be paid to the functions of standardized tests in such a statement. The purpose of the SAT I, for example, is to improve the prediction of first-year college grade-point average. If an institution's process uses the SAT I, but there is no reference to first-year college GPA in its policy, the institution has an obligation to explain in its statement of purpose exactly what function the test plays in its process beyond serving as a handy separator.

The admission policy statement should be tied directly to the university's mission statement, and the actual admission policy should flow directly from both the university's mission statement and the admission policy statement of purpose. In crafting its admission policy statement of purpose, there are probably a number of acceptable purposes or goals that an institution could select from or include in such a statement:

- To enroll a freshman class that will most benefit from the institution's curriculum and faculty
- To enroll a class with the most distinguished high school academic records
- To enroll a class that will encompass a wide range of experiences, viewpoints, and opinions that will contribute to the education of all of its students
- To enroll a class that will include critical masses of African American, Asian American, Latino, and Native American students
- To enroll a class that will reflect the racial and ethnic diversity of the state in which the institution is located

- To enroll a freshman class that will be the most engaging to teach in the classroom
- To enroll a freshman class that will go on to serve the community, the state, and the nation
- To enroll a freshman class that will bring the greatest distinction to the university after graduation
- To enroll a class that will earn the highest collective freshman grade-point average
- To enroll a freshman class that will have the highest four-year (or overall) graduation rate
- To enroll a freshman class that will support the institution financially after graduation
- To enroll a freshman class with the highest possible test score averages

Although it may seem obvious to an outside observer, the need for a clear statement of purpose or set of goals for a college or university's admission policy hasn't always been clear to admission directors, senior administrators, and faculty. Many universities have implied statements of purpose in their admissions policies yet have never formally crafted such a statement as an independent document.

To take one example, the Board of Regents of the University of California adopted the following statement:

> Mindful of its missions as a public institution, the University of California has an [sic] historic commitment to providing a place within the University for all eligible applicants who are residents of California, and to achieving, on each of its campuses, a student body that both meets the University's high academic standards and encompasses the cultural, racial, geographic, economic, and social diversity of California itself.

It is eminently reasonable to ask institutions to have such a statement. For one thing, how can a university know if its admission policy is successful unless it knows what that policy is supposed to achieve?

On the other hand, it can be intimidating to think that a federal court may pass judgment on such a statement and the methods for evaluating it. Universities need to be prepared for such a possibility, however, given the degree to which admissions policies are being challenged in court.

2. An institution should use appropriate criteria in its admissions process. A campus then needs to develop an admission plan or process that will enable the Admissions Office to carry out that admission policy. The admissions plan or process is the operational means by which the campus achieves its admissions goals. An institution should use a range of sound criteria in its selection process, and these criteria should be directly tied to its admission policy statement of purpose. Such criteria should certainly include high school (and college, if appropriate) courses completed, grades in those courses, and test scores—if a campus has a clear set of reasons for using them and does not use them in formulas or indexes. The criteria should also include intellectual curiosity and accomplishment, extraordinary talent, leadership, service to others, motivation, tenacity, and the ability to overcome hardship.

None of these criteria should be viewed as a static entity. That is, courses taken, for example, should be assessed against what was available in each applicant's high school, and this assessment should include any information provided by the applicant or the school regarding access to courses, particularly advanced-level courses. Such information could include restrictive tracking policies or cases where demand for a particular course clearly outstripped the number of spaces offered by the school or the cancellation of courses for such reasons as budget cuts, even though such courses might still be shown on a school's list of courses offered.

In every instance where it is legal to do so, these criteria should include race and ethnicity, but before deciding that race and ethnicity will be included in the admissions criteria, a college or university should carefully evaluate race-neutral alternatives. An institution should also seek balance among the criteria it uses in its admissions criteria. While academic criteria should probably dominate in such a process, a campus should guard against a single criterion, such as test scores, becoming an overwhelming determinant.

Institutions should avoid using criteria in ways that treat applicants as groups and that treat all members of such groups as exactly the same—not just on the basis of race and ethnicity, a practice which the Supreme Court struck down in *Gratz v. Bollinger,* but also on the basis of zip code or high school or leadership or achievement or hardship. Giving all students at a particular high school 300 points as "disadvantaged" without considering the wide variation in circumstances that are bound to exist from one student to another, even within a particularly disadvantaged high school, is careless and imprecise. So, too, are application reading processes that use *binary* review/scoring, a process in which an applicant gets, say, 150 points for "leadership" or "community service" or gets zero points, with no gradations between the absolutes. Student achievements and experiences are too complex to be adequately described by any particular index or to have any variable classified as totally present or totally absent. Ohio State and the University of Massachusetts at Amherst are the only two universities that publicly admitted to assigning points based on race/ethnicity following the Supreme Court's Michigan decisions, but there are most likely other institutions as well.

3. If an institution assigns formal weights or values to its admissions criteria, it should be sure that such weights or values are reasonable. As with the word "appropriate" in number 2 above, "reasonable" is an arguable term. Nevertheless, it's certainly possible to recognize unreasonable weights—a process, for example, in which test scores are the overwhelming determinant. Embedded in this issue is a rather thorny question: are there limits to the weights that should be given to individual criteria, specifically standardized test scores and honors or Advanced Placement courses? If so, who sets those limits and on what basis? Clearly, it should be the body that governs the admission policy within a particular institution, but it is conceivable that a federal court may ultimately answer these questions. Given the recent behavior of a number of federal judges around the country, it wouldn't be entirely surprising if a federal judge in the near future attempted to outline acceptable criteria in admissions policies and acceptable weights that may be assigned to individual variables in such policies.

4. An institution should regularly evaluate the individual criteria and the aggregate criteria to determine if they are achieving the goals attributed to them and to the admission policy in the statement of purpose. Although there are limits to the precision with which such validity studies can be performed, an institution should be obligated to do the best analysis it can on its selection criteria. In particular, it must regularly review the outcomes of admissions cycles to ascertain if race and ethnicity still need to be included among the selection criteria in order to achieve a critical mass of a particular racial or ethnic group within the student body.

5. An institution should consider the full range of applicants' achievements and qualities, rather than use formulas or rigid raw-numeric cut-offs in its process. Colleges and universities that have relied on formulas in their admissions decisions should reduce or eliminate such practices, especially if the formulas have been used as the primary academic measure—even if the formulas are used only for mass sorting.

A great deal of publicity has been given to the inappropriateness of using test scores as a single criterion or using sharp cut-offs on indexes combining multiple criteria in what the Office for Civil Rights in the U.S. Department of Education has called high-stakes decision making. Nevertheless, there are many selective institutions, both public and private, that use numeric formulas to separate applicants within their admissions process. Although Berkeley dropped its use of an index in 1998, other UC campuses still use the same index or one closely resembling it. Other large selective public universities use indexes of one kind or another to sort applicants and so do many selective private universities.

Admissions formulas most often combine grade-point average (GPA) and one or more test scores. The problem with such formulas is that they distort the qualifications and achievements of individual applicants in much the same way that assigning twenty points to every African American applicant to the University of Michigan did. Treating all GPAs as equal without examining what courses a student has taken in achieving that grade-point average or whether that GPA includes extra grade points for honors-level courses that may not have been nearly as available in many other applicants' high schools is clearly unfair. So too is assuming that all test scores mean the same thing for all applicants without consideration of an individual applicant's family income, parental education levels, race or ethnicity, language history, and access to expensive test-preparation courses. The use of formulas or indexes to make automatic admissions decisions is ethically questionable and is in direct opposition to the guidelines set forth in the O'Connor opinion. At the minimum, an institution that uses a formula or index to sort applicants should ensure that the application of any applicant dropped out of the admissions process by formula or index is reviewed by a senior admissions officer who has the authority to return that application, for a wide range of potential reasons, to the pool for further consideration.

There are at least two difficulties with an index like that formerly used by Berkeley (GPA capped at 4.0 × 1000 plus SAT I and three SAT II scores). The first of these is that changes in freshman applicant pools over time can distort the original values reflected in that index. Although OCR in Region IX in effect approved Berkeley's Index in its March 7, 1996, Letter of Findings in its full compliance review of Berkeley, and although the College Board had said that the Index was consistent with ETS guidelines on appropriate uses of the SAT because it combined more than one score with at least one other variable—in this case, GPA—Berkeley dropped the Academic Index Score because as the applicant pool became more and more competitive, huge numbers of applicants were bunched near or at the 4.0 GPA mark. That meant that they all got 4000 points—or quite close to that—on the

GPA side of the Index and that what then separated them from each other were their test scores.

The second difficulty with indexes or numerical cut-offs is the effect that measures with disparate impacts may have on different groups of applicants. Because test scores vary by race and by family income and parental education levels, the Berkeley Index worked against students with non-English first languages, students from low-income families, and students who were African American, Latino, or Native American. Berkeley could compensate for this disadvantage by giving preference in other parts of its process to economic disadvantage and, until fall 1998, race and ethnicity. Nevertheless, prior to 1998, Berkeley used the Index in part to determine placement of applicants in the cells of the admissions matrix, and a difference of just ten points in an applicant's Index score might have made a big difference in that applicant's chances for admission. The faculty admissions committee recognized that the Index was beginning to distort the freshman admissions process at Berkeley and rightfully eliminated it.

There is also the trap of being seduced by an elaborate formula that employs copious variables and gives the illusion of great precision. This temptation often occurs when the faculty chair of an admissions committee is a mathematician or statistician. There is also the related pitfall of believing that by adding to an index an explicit number of points for specific criteria further on in the review process, an institution has overcome the damage done by the original use of its index. In many cases, however, hundreds of students will already have been dropped out of the review because of their basic index scores.

It is easy to call for no formulas or raw numeric cut-offs in selective admissions, yet such a call may seem to ignore the harsh financial realities in the institutional funding of admissions operations. The use of formulas is almost always tied to the need to manage large volumes of applications with a small staff and limited financial support from the senior administration, usually in public universities—a sharp tension between ideal practices versus workload realities and individual institutional financial support. The *Grutter* and *Gratz* decisions mean that the appropriate use of numerics—individual standardized test scores, extra grade points for advanced-level courses, and formulas—is going to get a lot of attention in the next few years. It seems quite likely that formulas that do not account for differences in opportunity or applicant background are going to be—and deserve to be—increasingly under attack.

6. An institution should read as many individual applications as possible. Reading applications is labor-intensive and therefore expensive, but it's also the way to make the best-informed and fairest decisions possible. It is fundamentally important that, in such reading processes, there be careful training and norming of readers, that such training continue throughout the reading process, that individual reader outcomes be tracked and adjusted where necessary, and that the entire process be carefully evaluated when it is completed. (Norming is the process by which readers are guided to incorporate into their reading of applications the set of values and standards articulated by the faculty admissions committee.) Every application should be read by at least two different readers. The second reader must not know the evaluation(s) or score(s) assigned by the first reader, and there has to be a carefully thought-out process for resolving disparities in reader scores on the same application. There will almost certainly have to be formal tie-breaking procedures if, at the end of the process, an admissions office ends up with more applicants with the same evaluation or score than there are admissions spaces remaining.

Electronic technology means that an institution can provide much information to readers, have them enter evaluations or scores electronically, track both individual and reader-group evaluations and scores, and track both individual and reader-group volume every day of the cycle. Reader reliability and validity must be evaluated most carefully, and readers who cannot or will not embrace the normed values of the process must be dropped. Reading individual applications without formulas or even fixed weights does not mean wild and random subjectivity. A fair, effective comprehensive review process depends upon the careful professional judgment of experienced admissions readers.

7. An institution should consider an applicant's context in assessing his or her achievements. It should be obvious that, given the huge disparities in opportunities offered to American youngsters, it is crucial to assess a student's achievements against his or her circumstances. That doesn't mean just language history, family income, and parental education levels, although these three items are fundamentally important in the evaluation of standardized test scores. It also means learning and understanding as much as possible about the student's individual and family circumstances as well as those within his or her school and community.

Assessing an applicant's circumstances does not mean automatically rewarding applicants who have faced difficult circumstances. It means measuring their achievements against those circumstances. It means acknowledging the qualities of responsibility and dependability in a student who cares for younger siblings every day after school as much as for the student who is a leader in school activities. It means recognizing that an applicant who has taken only two Advanced Placement courses may have done all that he or she could have done if those were the only two AP courses offered in his or her high school and he or she did well in them.

8. An institution should learn all it can about the high schools that provide them applicants. Part of understanding the contexts of individual applicants is building accurate knowledge about individual high schools. Admissions officers are often quick to describe a high school as "outstanding" or "poor" or "a real disaster," but such easy judgments are often based on impressions from a two-hour school visit or from reading three or four applications from a school. A college or university, however, can build academic and socio-economic profiles of high schools using databases that are widely available, often combining data from the State Department of Education, the Enrollment Planning Service of the College Board, and its own admissions/student research database.

The UC Berkeley admissions staff, for example, has constructed sophisticated profiles of every high school in California. One section of UC Berkeley's high school profile focuses on a school's curriculum and includes the number of honors courses offered, the number of AP courses offered, the percentage of graduates completing the UC college-prep course pattern, and the state percentile rank for that completion rate. A second section includes graduation rates, the percentage of graduates taking AP exams, the percentage of AP exams taken on which students make scores of 3 or higher, the state percentile rank for that percentage, the average verbal, math, and composite scores on the SAT I, the average SAT I score for applicants to UC from this school, and the percentage of students taking the SAT I. A third section includes average parental income for the school, the percent of students who are Limited English Proficient, the percentage of students on Aid to Families with Dependent Children, and the percentage of students eligible for free federal meal programs. The profile also includes the number of applicants to Berkeley from the preceding year and the number and percentage of those applicants admitted.

On a second screen, Berkeley shows the individual applicant's academic and demographic information and calculates a percentile ranking on each of those variables for that applicant compared to all of the other current applicants from that high school and, in a separate column, compared to all applicants in that year's freshman applicant pool. In addition, the UC system has an advantage in that its arcane admissions regulations require each high school in California to submit a UC course list each year. That list shows all college-prep course accepted by UC from that school and also lists all of the honors courses (including AP courses) that the school offers. Readers can review these course lists electronically via a toggle switch if they are uncertain whether a course is accepted by UC or whether it deserves honors credit.

Berkeley, however, has only partial answers to four essential questions: 1) Does a particular high school track students and, if so, how? 2) How many seats are available in honors/AP courses compared to the demand for those seats? 3) Were all of the courses shown on a high school's course list actually offered that year? and 4) Were there conflicts in the high school's master schedule that in any way prevented a student from taking advanced-level courses? It is important to know the answers to these questions in order to understand why a particular student may not have taken honors/AP courses in a school that offers— or appears to offer—a significant number of them. Six years ago, the Admissions Office began sending an annual questionnaire to each California high school to gather this information. It's an imperfect process, but it adds important information.

If colleges and universities around the country agree on the value of such profiles, it ought to be possible to design and build those profiles for each state, perhaps by a state department of education working with a group of admissions directors, rather than have each campus compile a separate—and, therefore, expensive—set of profiles for its own use.

9. An institution should track the performance of the graduates of each high school who enroll at that institution and consider that information in evaluating applicants. An institution should track its entering students by high school and gather data on mean first-year GPA, one-year persistence rates, mean GPA at graduation, and six-year graduation rates. It should also calculate the mean GPA differential between high school GPA at entry and both mean first-year GPA and mean GPA at graduation. In calculating such data items, an institution has to pay careful attention to the number of students included in such calculations. Obviously, the fewer students from a particular high school, the more variation there may be from year to year. It is also important to note the distribution of students by major. There is some evidence that college and university grading practices in engineering and the sciences are significantly more stringent than in the humanities and social sciences. It is also important to remember that variables measured over six years focus on students who may have had vastly different opportunities and circumstances than applicants from the same high school six years later and that the longer the time span for a tracked item, the more likely it is that immeasurable intervening variables may have affected the statistical outcomes.

Some public and private colleges and universities are quite conscientious about such tracking, but others are not. For a number of years, the UC system produced performance reports that calculated mean first-year GPA for every California high school that sent at least five students to the UC system. These reports, which also had sub-sections with mean UC GPAs in English and math, were sent to principals and superintendents across the state. For whatever reasons—inertia, fear of potential political liabilities, sloth—nothing ever came from these reports, and about five years ago the Office of the President stopped producing them, pleading high cost. The reports were a missed opportunity. The university, for example, might have worked privately with the lowest-performing schools, using the performance reports as leverage to help strengthen their teaching and curriculum.

At Berkeley, admissions policy-makers argued about whether to use those reports and other tracking measures. Some staff members argued that Berkeley should not consider them because the results would somehow be used against applicants from disadvantaged high schools. Most people within the Admissions Office, however, believed that more information would be better and that this information would be crucial to understanding which schools were preparing students well despite truly difficult circumstances. Conversely, it's also hugely important to know which affluent schools are preparing their students well and which are not. Such information could certainly help admissions officers make better-informed judgments about which applicants have a good chance to succeed at Berkeley and which are simply not adequately prepared—and provide information on grade inflation both within specific high schools and across high schools in general. The importance of the likelihood of success as an admissions goal will vary widely from institution to institution, but no university should admit any student who does not have a reasonable chance to graduate.

Such tracking information may well complicate the consideration of admitting applicants from disadvantaged high schools, and policy-makers must be careful to balance the achievement of individual students in challenging circumstances against the overall achievement record of students from that particular school. There is also the danger that admissions policy-makers would be tempted to construct a super-formula, incorporating such information, particularly the mean first-year GPA differential. That is exactly the wrong direction to pursue. For the same reasons that the Supreme Court rejected the assignment of twenty points to every African American freshman applicant to the University of Michigan, this information should not be included in some algorithm nor used to reward or penalize groups of schools (the way that Boalt Hall did some years ago, as explained in Chapter 7). Rather, it is information that should be considered as part of the professional judgment that admissions officers make regarding the achievement of a particular applicant and the likelihood of success for that applicant at that university if he or she is admitted and enrolls.

It is also important to recognize that such comparative information is only part of the information that, in an ideal world, admissions officers would have. Parents, in particular, often believe that if their sons and daughters had just gone to Oakland Tech or Hayward High or some other so-called weak high school, they would have had much higher GPAs and therefore been admitted to Berkeley. Students, however, are often less worried about the differences between high schools and are often more affronted by students from their own high schools who deliberately took classes from the easiest teachers. Gathering information on the grading practices of individual teachers and knowing from which teachers in a particular school an applicant had taken courses would add a significant degree of fairness to selective admissions but, in almost every case, is just not possible.

10. An institution should develop, to the extent possible, verification procedures for information supplied by applicants. The verification of application information is important not just to prevent a small number of applicants from falsifying their race in order to gain advantage under affirmative action but to ensure as much as possible the fairness of admissions processes and to understand how students who have many advantages to begin with may magnify those advantages to the disadvantage of other applicants. In particular, admissions officers and policy-makers increasingly worry about the advantages affluent students have in their access to expensive test preparation and to private-college admissions counselors who advise and *package*—their word—applicants to colleges and universities.

Selective colleges and universities, for example, should think carefully about the possibility of adding a question to their application that asks if the applicant paid for a commercial test-preparation course and, if so, which one. They might also ask if an applicant had professional help on the application other than from his or her school counselor and, if so, the name of that person/service, much as the 1040 Form asks a taxpayer for the name of a professional tax-preparer if he or she used one. These items would provide important contextual information about an applicant and would further inform admissions readers.

Tanya Schevitz noted in the December 25, 2000, *San Francisco Chronicle* that Duke University took the first step in this direction by asking applicants on its fall 2001 application if they had help on their application essays. Duke did the same thing for its fall 2002 applicants as well. A follow-up article by Andrew Brownstein in *The Chronicle of Higher Education* of March 1, 2002, attempted to assess the two-year experiment. In it, Christoph Guttentag, the director of undergraduate admissions at Duke, candidly and realistically worried about the degree of honesty among applicants to Duke and among college applicants in general, but the rest of the article unfortunately failed to focus effectively on that problem—nor did it point out the failure of colleges and universities to address applicants directly on the issue of how much help is acceptable.

An even more serious problem is the issue of falsified information and plagiarized or purchased application essays. This is a difficult and vexing problem for admissions officers in selective colleges and universities even to begin to measure, and there is no simple solution to it. The Internet has made cheating on college-application essays much easier for students and much more difficult to identify with certainty by admissions officers. It used to be that an admissions director could have his staff read books like *Essays That Worked,* and everyone would recognize instantly the "In a way, I am like an uprooted tree" essay. It's also somewhat easy—at least in many instances—to identify an essay written by someone else—a overzealous parent, say, or a private-college admissions counselor—because the voice and tone of the essay often do not match those of a seventeen- or eighteen-year-old. The Internet, however, has made available thousands and thousands of impressive essays written by actual seventeen- and eighteen-year-old students and, in general, the broader or more open-ended a university's essay topic(s), the easier it will be to find an essay from another source that will serve.

It may be possible for an institution to build or buy the technical capacity to scan through websites offering application essays and then apply a keyword or phrase to screen all of the application essays the institution receives or to subscribe to one of the web-based plagiarism detection services such as *plagiarism.com*. Such a process, however, would require that all applications be submitted electronically or that the Admissions Office scan all handwritten essays into its computer system so that the essays could then be put through the screening program. Checking essays in this way would be cumbersome, time-consuming, and costly. And most such websites that offer student essays for sale do not permit unlimited viewing of the items they offer.

One potential control mechanism is the revised SAT I, which added a mandatory written essay in March 2005 (the ACT, another college-entrance exam, has also added an optional writing section). In January 2003, the University of Michigan and the University of Texas announced that beginning in spring 2005 they would require all of their undergraduate applicants to take a proctored writing test, almost certainly to be either the SAT I or ACT. Colleges and universities have worked out an arrangement with the Educational Testing Service whereby they may review a facsimile of the actual writing sample produced by a student in order to compare it with the more formal essays that the two institutions will require if they believe there is any reason to do so. Other colleges and universities that will require the revised SAT I can also do the same thing.

There are two other areas where cheating may benefit an applicant. The first is the section of the application usually called something like "Honors, Awards, and Activities." It is highly unlikely, for example, that a large public university would ever match up six applicants from the same high school each of whom claimed to have been student-body president, most—or all—of whom were lying. Some private colleges require that the college counselor in a high school sign-off on the list of honors, awards, and activities provided by each applicant. In California, where there are many very large high schools and many with no counselors, such a practice would probably be ineffective. Other colleges and universities require that an applicant submit documentation for such claims, but that is cumbersome and, in some cases, difficult or impossible for applicants to do. In addition, students who are exceptionally computer-savvy can produce their own documentation and make it look remarkably authentic. Employers, for example, are increasingly finding that it isn't enough just to physically see an applicant's master's degree complete with seals, embosses, and signatures; the company also has to verify the degree directly with the university in question. Recently, the UC system conducted a pilot verification process on a modest number of freshman applicants to UC San Diego. The results found a high degree of honesty among the students who were sampled. Such a procedure needs to be expanded and conducted on all of the UC campuses so that applicants know that such checks are routinely made.

The second area where cheating may benefit an applicant is in reporting personal and family circumstances. Lying about personal and family circumstances is a particular area of vulnerability for selective institutions, particularly in states that have ended affirmative action. In those states, there tends to be an even heavier emphasis on socio-economic disadvantage and other kinds of hardship than when affirmative action was permitted. A student may lie about family income, providing a much lower income than is in fact the case, and may lie by understating the level of education attained by his parents, if an application asks such a question. An admissions office can crosscheck income information with the financial aid office, assuming that low-income students will also have applied for aid. Although such a verification process can be cumbersome and imprecise, it may be necessary to add this step to an admissions review. The truth is, however, that students may be tempted to lie about other circumstances as well, including the death of a parent—or both parents or the entire family—the hardships of immigration to this country, or the presence of a debilitating condition or illness in oneself or one's parents. These kinds of claims are almost impossible to verify, particularly, as just noted, for applicants from large public high schools.

One possibility would be for public universities to require the same kind of letters of recommendation from freshman applicants that private colleges and universities require. One difficulty, however, is that the flagship public universities in many states may have two hundred or more applicants from some high schools. Teachers and counselors in those schools would object strenuously to the huge increase in their workloads if public universities were to require letters of recommendation. Equally important, there are many, many high schools in California and other states where there are no counselors at all. And, perhaps most important, such a requirement would greatly benefit students from private high schools, where counselors and teachers have far fewer students, more time, and already write remarkably polished and highly personal letters for their students.

In general, admissions officers give the public impression that they recognize falsification and plagiarism regularly and with ease. That is mostly a bluff, based on the relatively few essays that are obviously someone else's work—that is, the clumsy cheaters. It's likely that admissions readers get fooled at Berkeley, but it's impossible to say how often. The way that the Admissions Office would catch most of the perpetrators that it did catch is that they would brag to their fellow students about how slick they were and other students would turn them in. In such cases, an admissions officer would then write or call the applicant and politely ask questions and, in some cases, ask for documentation. The office did the same thing with cases of suspected falsification of race or ethnicity prior to Proposition 209. Staff would crosscheck applicants against another national database and write to students for whom there was a discrepancy. Often students would write back with a plausible explanation—for example, they were of mixed heritage and sometimes checked one box and sometimes another. About half the students to whom the Admissions Office would write would write back saying that they had made a mistake, or lied, or would not answer at all. These applications were then reviewed in light of that information.

Most admissions officers know that the word on the street is that hardship helps get a person into college. That notion is not true to the extent that many students and parents believe it to be, but that doesn't change the power of the perception. And it is certainly true that significant achievement in the face of hardship can be an important plus for many selective institutions. Most universities hang a lot on the section at the end of their application that applicants must sign: "I certify that all the information provided in my application is accurate and that I am the author of the attached personal statement. I understand that the university may deny me admission or enrollment if any information is found to be incomplete or inaccurate." It isn't much of a tool, and a student might well think, "If I told the truth, you'd deny me anyway. There's not much to lose here."

Probably the single most effective thing a university could do to limit cheating on its essay(s) is to offer applicants precise, focused essay topics and to change those topics every year. No more "favorite figure in history or literature" or "discuss some national or international issue of concern to you" kinds of topics. In addition, one important part of the problem is that just a few colleges and universities say in print what is or is not permissible when a student completes her application, other than the kind of vague statement just quoted from the last part of the University of California application. College and university application forms should include a carefully crafted statement from the faculty admissions committee or the dean/director of admission stating clearly what kinds of help and how much of it are within the boundaries of personal integrity, fairness, and ethical behavior.

The overwhelming majority of freshman applicants to selective colleges and universities are almost certainly honest and ethical in the completion of their applications—although part of the reason for believing this is because so many of the applications, specifically the essays, are thrown together carelessly. Cheating is not as much of a problem as are missed opportunities. That is, so many students don't take the application process seriously enough, or they wait until the last moment to write their essays, or they don't understand how to write about themselves. The result is that they often just try to be funny or they submit something that is shallow and that has been done carelessly, and they damage their chances for admission by failing to include information that might influence that decision. Still, because so many students do no more than an adequate job presenting themselves in their applications, students who cheat successfully have all that much more advantage in the admissions process—not to mention those whose parents hire private admissions consultants for their children.

Colleges and universities need to talk publicly and with each other about measures to control dishonesty and fraud in college and university admissions, particularly selective admissions. Could a university be found liable for damages if it denied a highly qualified applicant but admitted students who were later shown to have deliberately falsified honors and activities, lied egregiously about their backgrounds and experiences, or purchased their essays from websites? Such theoretical liability would be heightened by a university's failure to attempt to verify important application information in some way. It is conceivable that the emerging legal criterion called "due diligence," that is, the legal finding that an employer is liable for harm caused by an employee if the employer did not adequately verify the qualifications and education of that employee, could be applied to university admissions. If large public and private colleges and universities cannot control the falsification of information on college applications, they may be forced to retreat to strictly numeric measures, with all the inequity that some of those criteria carry.

Colleges and universities, of course, have contributed to this climate of dishonesty by falsifying test-score data submitted to college guides, employing self-serving Early Decision programs, doctoring photographs used in recruitment publications, and using cash awards to entice National Merit Scholars to enroll. Finally, we should also recognize that the problem of lying on college applications is part of a larger problem of fraudulent credentials and falsification of references and experience in American society. Dot-coms are springing up whose primary function is to verify academic credentials claimed by applicants for jobs. Newspaper stories seem to appear more and more often citing people in relatively high positions—school superintendents and college presidents, not to mention a rash of football coaches—who have lied on their résumés or, in the case of several historians, plagiarized heavily in their scholarly works.

A FINAL WORD

Depending on an institution's application volume and the kind of individual review process it adopts, moving to the kind of process described in this chapter may cost a significant amount of money. Yet the benefits to the entire society of a policy that ensures racial and ethnic diversity in our most selective colleges and universities are enormous compared to this cost.

Every American has a stake in the success of affirmative action in university admissions because this policy will go a long way toward determining whether the United States achieves the ideals set out in its founding documents and toward ensuring that every American has a full and equal opportunity to develop his or her gifts and talents, to pursue fairly and with genuine hope whatever form the American Dream takes for that person, to have the greatest possible chances for personal success however defined, and thus to contribute to the success of the entire country. It is worth recalling again Justice Sandra Day O'Connor's words from her majority opinion in *Grutter v. Bollinger*: "Effective participation by members of all racial and ethnic groups in the civic life of our Nation is essential if the dream of one Nation, indivisible, is to be realized."

And, finally, we should hold clearly in our mind's eye the image from those last three lines of W. H. Auden's "Musée des Beaux Arts":

> . . . and the expensive delicate ship that must have seen
> Something amazing, a boy falling out of the sky,
> Had somewhere to get to and sailed calmly on.

WHEREAS, Governor Pete Wilson, on June 1, 1995, issued Executive
Order W-124-95 to "End Preferential Treatment and to Promote Individual Opportunity Based on Merit";
  and
  WHEREAS, paragraph seven of that order requests the University
of California to "take all necessary action to comply with the intent
and the requirements of this executive order"; and
  WHEREAS, in January 1995, the University initiated a review of its
policies and practices, the results of which support many of the findings
and conclusions of Governor Wilson; and
  WHEREAS, the University of California Board of Regents believes
that it is in the best interest of the University to take relevant actions
to develop and support programs which will have the effect of increasing the eligibility rate of groups which are "underrepresented" in the
University's pool of applicants as compared to their percentages in
California's graduating high school classes and to which reference is
made in Section4;
  NOW, THEREFORE BE IT RESOLVED AS FOLLOWS:
  Section 1. The Chairman of the Board, with consultation of the President, shall appoint a task force representative of the business commu-

nity, students, the University, other segments of education, and organizations currently engaged in academic "outreach." The responsibility of this group shall be to develop proposals for new directions and increased funding for the Board of Regents to increase the eligibility rate of those currently identified in Section 4. The final report of this task force shall be presented to the Board of Regents within six months after its creation.

Section 2. Effective January 1, 1997, the University of California shall not use race, religion, sex, color, ethnicity, or national origin as criteria for admission to the University or to any program of study.

Section 3. Effective January 1, 1997, the University of California shall not use race, religion, sex, color, ethnicity, or national origin as criteria for "admissions by exception" to UC-eligibility requirements.

Section 4. The President shall confer with the Academic Senate of the University of California to develop supplemental criteria for consideration by the Board of Regents which shall be consistent with Section 2. In developing such criteria, which shall provide reasonable assurances that the applicant will successfully complete his or her course of study, consideration shall be given to individuals who, despite having suffered disadvantage economically or in terms of their social environment (such as an abusive or otherwise dysfunctional home or a neighborhood of unwholesome or antisocial influences), have nonetheless demonstrated sufficient character and determination in overcoming obstacles to warrant confidence that the applicant can pursue a course of study to successful completion, provided that any student admitted under this section must be academically eligible for admission.

Section 5. Effective January 1, 1997, not less than fifty (50) percent and not more than seventy-five (75) percent of any entering class on any campus shall be admitted solely on the basis of academic achievement.

Section 6. Nothing in Section 2 shall prohibit any action which is strictly necessary to establish or maintain eligibility for any federal or state program, where ineligibility would result in a loss of federal of state funds to the University.

Section 7. Nothing in Section 2 shall prohibit the University from taking appropriate action to remedy specific, documented cases of discrimination by the University, provided that such actions are expressly and specifically approved by the Board of Regents or taken pursuant to a final order of a court or administrative agency of competent jurisdiction. Nothing in this section shall interfere with the customary practices of the University with regard to settlement of claims against the University related to discrimination.

Section 8. The President of the University shall periodically report to the Board of Regents detailing progress to implement the provisions of this resolution.

Section 9. Believing California's diversity to be an asset, we adopt this statement: Because individual members of all of California's diverse races have the intelligence and capacity to succeed at the University of California, this policy will achieve a UC population that reflects this state's diversity through the preparation and empowerment of all students in this state to succeed rather than through a system of artificial preferences.

July 1996

GUIDELINES FOR IMPLEMENTATION OF UNIVERSITY
POLICY ON UNDERGRADUATE ADMISSIONS

On May 20, 1988, The Regents of the University of California adopted a University of California Policy on Undergraduate Admissions. The Policy states in part that:

"Mindful of its mission as a public institution, the University of California . . . seeks to enroll, on each of its campuses, a student body that, beyond meeting the university's eligibility requirements, demonstrates high academic achievement or exceptional personal talent, and that encompasses the broad diversity of cultural, racial, geographic, and socio-economic backgrounds characteristic of California."

On July 21, 1995, The Regents endorsed a resolution, SP-1, Policy Ensuring Equal Treatment—Admissions, which states in part that "the University of California shall not use race, religion, sex, color, ethnicity, or national origin as criteria for admission to the University or to any program of study." In adopting this resolution, The Regents also restated the goals of the 1988 Policy in Section 9 of SP-1 as follows:

"Believing California's diversity to be an asset, we adopt this statement: Because individual members of all of California's diverse races have the intelligence and capacity to succeed at the University of California, this policy will achieve a UC population that reflects this state's diversity through the preparation and empowerment of all students in this state to succeed rather than through a system of artificial preferences."

Effective with applicants seeking admission for the spring quarter of the 1997–1998 academic year, the following revised guidelines and procedures shall be followed for implementation of the University of California Policy on Undergraduate Admissions and of SP-1.

I. SELECTION GUIDELINES

These selection guidelines apply to campuses that have to select from a pool of eligible applicants and to students who have met the established UC eligibility requirements for admission.* These eligibility requirements are established by the university in conformance to the specifications outlined in the California Master Plan for Higher Education, which recommends that the top one-eighth of the State's public high school graduates, as well as those community college transfer students who have successfully completed specified college work, be eligible for admission to the University of California.

These guidelines provide the framework within which campuses shall establish specific criteria and procedures for the selection of undergraduate applicants to be admitted when the number of eligible applicants exceeds the places available.

Campuses receiving applications in excess of the number required to achieve their enrollment target for a specific term shall select students for admission as follows:

---

*These guidelines apply to those students eligible for admission. Up to six percent of new enrolled freshmen and six percent of new enrolled advanced standing students can be admitted by exception, as authorized by The Regents. *Refer also to the Policy on Undergraduate Admissions by Exception.*

A. Freshman Applicants

At least 50 percent but not more than 75 percent of freshmen admitted by each campus shall be selected on the basis of criteria as described in items 1 through 9, below. The remaining percentage of freshmen, exclusive of applicants admitted through admission by exception, shall be selected on the basis of criteria listed in items 1 through 9 plus criteria listed in items 10 through 13, below.

The following criteria provide a comprehensive list of factors campuses may use to select their admitted class. Based on campus-specific institutional goals and needs, individual campuses may choose all or some of the criteria listed below. It is strongly recommended, however, that admissions decisions be based on a broad variety of factors rather than on a restricted number of criteria to ensure attainment of the goals set forth in the University of California Policy on Undergraduate Admissions and in SP-1.

Criteria to Select 50 to 75 Percent of the Admitted Class

Criteria 1 through 9 below are designed to assess applicants' academic achievement and promise:

1. Academic Grade Point Average (GPA) calculated on all academic courses completed in the subject areas specified by the University's eligibility requirements (the a-f subjects), including additional points for completion of University certified honors courses (see 4, below). It is recommended that the maximum value allowed for the GPA shall be 4.0.

2. Scores on the following tests: the Scholastic Assessment Test I or the American College Test, and the College Board Scholastic Assessment Test II: Subject Tests.

3. The number, content of, and performance in courses completed in academic subjects beyond the minimum specified by the University eligibility requirements.

4. The number of and performance in University approved honors

courses, College Board Advanced Placement courses, International Baccalaureate courses, and transferable college courses completed. It is recommended that caution be exercised in order not to assign excessive weight to these courses, especially if considerable weight already has been given in the context of 1, above. Additionally, in recognition of existing differences in availability of these courses among high schools, it is recommended that reviewers assess completion of this coursework against the availability of these courses at the candidate's secondary school.

5. The quality of the senior year program, as measured by type and number of academic courses (see 3 and 4, above) in progress or planned.

6. The quality of academic performance relative to the educational opportunities available in the applicant's secondary school.

7. Outstanding performance in one or more specific academic subject areas.

8. Outstanding work in one or more special projects on any academic field of study.

9. Recent, marked improvement in academic performance, as demonstrated by academic grade point average and quality of coursework (see 3 and 4, above) completed and in progress, with particular attention being given to the last two years of high school.

Criteria to Select the Remaining 50 to 25 Percent of the Admitted Class
Criteria 1 through 9 listed above PLUS criteria 10 through 13 listed below shall be used to select this group of students. Criteria 10 through 13 are designed to further assess applicants' academic potential and promise as well as the potential to contribute to the educational environment and intellectual vitality of the campus. They provide evidence of personal traits, accomplishments, and experiences that show an applicant's promise to be a valuable contributor to the educational enterprise. These criteria, in combination with criteria 1 through 9, are devised to meet the goals of excellence and diversity outlined in the 1988 undergraduate admissions policy and in SP-1.

10. Special talents, achievements, and awards in a particular field, such as in the visual and performing arts, in communication, or in athletic endeavors; special skills, such as demonstrated written and oral proficiency in other languages; special interests, such as intensive study and exploration of other cultures; or experiences that demonstrate unusual promise for leadership, such as significant community service or significant participation in student government; or other significant experiences or achievements that demonstrate the applicant's promise for contributing to the intellectual vitality of a campus.

11. Completion of special projects undertaken either in the context of the high school curriculum or in conjunction with special school events, projects or programs co-sponsored by the school, community organizations, postsecondary educational institutions, other agencies, or private firms, that offer significant evidence of an applicant's special effort and determination or that may indicate special suitability to an academic program on a specific campus.

12. Academic accomplishments in light of the applicant's life experiences and special circumstances. These experiences and circumstances may include, but are not limited to, disabilities, low family income, first generation to attend college, need to work, disadvantaged social or educational environment, difficult personal and family situations or circumstances, refugee status, or veteran status.

13. Location of the applicant's secondary school and residence. These factors shall be considered in order to provide for geographic diversity in the student population and also to account for the wide variety of educational environments existing in California.

B. Advanced Standing Applicants

Advanced standing applicants shall be selected by each campus using the criteria listed below. Primary emphasis shall be given to criteria as described in items 1 through 4, below. However, in order to assess applicants' overall promise of success and to achieve strength and diversity in the campuses' advanced standing student body, consideration shall also be given to the criteria as described in items 10 through 13 in Section A above.

Primary consideration for admission of advanced standing applicants shall be given to upper division junior transfers from California Community Colleges.

Criteria to Select Advanced Standing Applicants

1. Completion of a specified pattern of number of courses that meet breadth or general education requirements.
2. Completion of a specified pattern or number of courses that provide continuity with upper division courses in the major.
3. Grade point average in all transferable courses, and, in particular, grade point average in lower division courses required for the applicant's intended major.
4. Participation in academically selective honors courses or programs.

(Refer to items 1 through 9 in Section A above for additional criteria to consider.)

II. APPLICATON PROCEDURES

A common filing period for submission of applications shall be established by the Office of the President in consultation with the campuses. These dates shall be observed by all campuses and may be extended only if a campus determines that additional applications are required to meet enrollment targets. All applications submitted during the prescribed dates shall receive equal consideration for admission.

Applicants shall file one application on which they shall indicate all the campuses where they wish to be considered for admission.

Campuses shall observe and publish a common notification period for notifying applicants of their admission status.

III. ACCOMMODATION OF UC ELIGIBLE APPLICANTS

UC eligible resident applicants who have not been admitted to any of the campuses of their choice shall be offered a space at other UC campuses where space is available. This process, called referral, reaffirms the long-standing University commitment to provide a place for every eligible California applicant who wishes to enroll.

In addition to the referral process, campuses may choose to offer other enrollment alternatives to UC eligible applicants. Examples of such alternatives may include:

1. Fall term admission to a different major;

2. Deferred admission to another term; or

3. Enrollment at a community college with provision for admission at a later time, if a stated level of academic achievement is maintained (for freshman applicants only).

Appendix 3 UNIVERSITY OF CALIFORNIA AT BERKELEY FRESHMAN ADMISSION POLICY

Fall 1998

BACKGROUND

The following selection criteria for freshman applicants to the Berkeley campus were developed by the Admissions, Enrollment, and Preparatory Education Committee of the Berkeley Division of the Academic Senate over the period September 1995–October 1996. During the process of their development they were discussed with and reviewed by the Divisional Council and the Committee on Educational Policy of the Berkeley Division, by the Undergraduate Admissions Coordination Board (chaired by the vice chancellor and provost and including senior leaders of the Berkeley Division as well as other faculty and administrative representatives), and by Chancellor Chang-Lin Tien. In May 1996, the AEPE Committee issued a progress report describing its key goals and concerns regarding the new criteria, the historical and educational context in which they were developed, and its recommendations for the criteria themselves; this report was also presented to and reviewed by Divisional Council, the Undergraduate Admissions Coordination Board, and the chancellor.

The final selection criteria were adopted by the Committee in October 1996 and by the Undergraduate Admissions Coordination Board in November 1996. Subsequent to their approval on the campus, they were also reviewed and accepted by the Office of the President and the Board of Admissions and Relations with Schools of the University-wide Academic Senate.

In developing these guidelines, the Committee strove to adhere to a philosophical approach that emphasized:

- Comprehensive, qualitative review and analysis of each individual's academic and personal achievements and likely contribution to the Berkeley community, based on careful review of the full applicant file;
- Continued refinement and expansion of academic criteria on which applicants should be judged;
- Continued movement away from categorical approaches to the evaluation of academic and personal accomplishments and characteristics;
- Avoidance of specified weights for particular criteria in favor of a comprehensive assessment of each individual's accomplishments and the context in which those accomplishments have been achieved (the exception to this is the assignment of the first fifty percent of Berkeley's admit spaces based on academic criteria alone, as specified by Regents policy); and
- Continued commitment to the goal of achieving academic excellence as well as diversity of personal experience and background in the members of the freshman class.

The new selection criteria will be used for the first time in the review of applicants for the Fall 1998 semester, which review will begin in mid-November 1997.

ACADEMIC CRITERIA

1. Uncapped UC grade-point average (taken from the UC application), including the pattern of achievement reflected in grades over time.

2. Scores on the SAT I (or ACT) and the three required SAT II tests.
3. College preparatory courses completed and the level of achievement in those courses, including:
   - college preparatory courses beyond the UC a-f minimums;
   - honors, Advanced Placement, and International Baccalaureate Higher Level (IBHL) courses;
   - college and university courses;
   - the senior year course load.
4. Scores on Advanced Placement tests and IBHL examinations.
5. Other evidence of intellectual or creative achievement.

    This criterion will recognize extraordinary, sustained achievement in any field of intellectual endeavor.
6. Achievement in academic enrichment programs.

    This criterion will be measured by time and depth of participation, by the academic progress made by the individual during that participation, and by the intellectual rigor of the program.

The heaviest weights will be assigned to the first three items, and they will make up at least seventy-five percent of the basis of the academic assessment. At the same time, no specific weight would be assigned to any of the variables.

PERSONAL CHARACTERISTICS AND ACHIEVEMENTS CRITERIA

1. Non-academic achievements, including accomplishments in the performing arts or athletics, employment, leadership in school or community organizations or activities, and community service.
2. Personal qualities of the applicant, including leadership ability, character, motivation, tenacity, initiative, and demonstrated concern for others and for the community.
3. Likely contributions to the intellectual and cultural vitality of the campus. In addition to a broad range of intellectual interests and

achievements, admissions officers will seek diversity in personal background and experience.

All achievements, both academic and non-academic, will be considered in the context of the opportunities an applicant has had, any hardships or unusual circumstances the applicant has faced, and the ways in which he or she has responded to them. In evaluating the context in which academic accomplishments have taken place, evaluators will consider the strength of the high school curriculum, including the availability of honors and advanced placement courses and the total number of college preparatory courses available, among other items. When appropriate and feasible, they would look comparatively at the achievements of applicants in the same pool who attended the same high school and therefore might be expected to have had similar opportunities and challenges.

November 4, 1997

BIBLIOGRAPHY

Admissions and Enrollment Committee. *Freshman Admissions at Berkeley: A Policy for the 1990s and Beyond (The Karabel Report)*. Berkeley: U.C. Berkeley Academic Senate, 1989.

Alexander v. Sandoval, S. Ct. 99-1908 (2001).

Argetsinger, Amy. "Nudging the Needy Into Nation's Top Colleges." *Washington Post*. April 13, 2004.

Arnone, Michael. "Texas A&M Will Not Consider Race in Admissions Decisions, Its President Says." *The Chronicle of Higher Education*. December 5, 2003. Online edition, www.chronicle.com.

———. "Texas Lawmakers Are Urged to Supplement 10-Percent Admissions Policy With Affirmative Action." *The Chronicle of Higher Education*. June 25, 2004. Online edition, www.chronicle.com.

Asimov, Nanette. "One in 7 California Teachers Unqualified." *San Francisco Chronicle*. December 7, 2000.

———. "Segregation by Income." *San Francisco Chronicle*. May 16, 2004.

Associated Press. "Recession Expanded Wealth Gap by Race." *San Francisco Chronicle*, October 18, 2004.

Atkinson, Richard. "Diversity: Not There Yet." *Washington Post*. April 20, 2003.

———. "Standardized Tests and Access to American Universities." The Robert H. Atwell Distinguished Lecture, delivered at the 83rd Annual Meeting of the American Council on Education, February 18, 2001. Washington DC. www.ucop.edu (accessed January 28, 2003).

Auden, W.H. "Musée des Beaux Arts." *Collected Poems*. Edward Mendelson, ed. New York: Vintage, 1991.

Barbieri, Karen, letter to the editor, *San Francisco Chronicle*. May 19, 2004.

Bartlett, Kellie. "A Glance at the Current Issue of *Social Psychology Quarterly*: How Race Affects Teaching Experiences." *The Chronicle of Higher Education*. February 27, 2004. Online edition, www.chronicle.com (accessed December 10, 2004).

Basinger, Julianne and Scott Smallwood. "Harvard to Stop Asking Parents Who Earn Below $40,000 to Aid Their Children's Education." *The Chronicle of Higher Education*. March 1, 2004. Online edition, www.chronicle.com.

Bell, Elizabeth. "Berkeley Schools Official to Head Orinda District." *San Francisco Chronicle*. July 25, 2000.

Benjaminson, Anne. "Affirmative Action: Five Years Later." *Daily Californian*. July 21, 2000.

Bensky, Larry. "Exit Interview." *East Bay Express*. October 13, 2000.

Berry, Mary Frances. "How Percentage Plans Keep Minority Students Out of College." Point of View. *The Chronicle of Higher Education*. August 4, 2000.

Bingham McCutchen LLP, Morrison and Foerster LLP, and Heller Ehrman White & McAuliffe LLP. *Preserving Diversity in Higher Education: A Manual on Admissions Policies and Procedures After the University of Michigan Decisions*. San Francisco, 2004.

Bled, Rory. "The College Advisor's Corner." Berkeley High School PTSA Newsletter. November/December 2000.

Bok, Derek and William Bowen. *The Shape of the River—Long-Term Consequences of Considering Race in College and University Admissions*. Princeton: Princeton University Press, 1998.

Bonetti, David. "Money Issues Drove Ross to Quit AFMOMA." *San Francisco Chronicle*. August 21, 2001.

Bowen, William and James L. Shulman. *The Game of Life: College Sports and Educational Values*. Princeton: Princeton University Press, 2001.

Branscomb, Leslie Wolf. "Moores' View on Prop. 54 Irks Latinos." *San Diego Union-Tribune*. September 29, 2003.

Brownstein, Andrew. "Are Male Students in Short Supply, or Is This 'Crisis' Exaggerated?" *The Chronicle of Higher Education*. November 3, 2000.

———. "Duke Asks Applicants If They Got Help on Essays, and Most Say They Did." *The Chronicle of Higher Education*. March 1, 2002.

Brush, Silla. "Activists File Papers to Put Measure Banning Affirmative Action on

Michigan's 2006 Ballot." *The Chronicle of Higher Education*. January 7, 2005. Online edition, www.chronicle.com.

Bunzel, John H. "Affirmative Action Admissions: How It 'Works' at UC Berkeley." *The Public Interest*. Fall 1988.

Burd, Stephen. "Top Civil-Rights Official Quits U.S. Education Department." *The Chronicle of Higher Education*. November 10, 2003. Online edition, www.chronicle.com.

Burdman, Pamela. "New Idea to Change UC Admissions." *San Francisco Chronicle*. November 13, 1997.

———. "Shut Out of the System." *Black Issues in Higher Education*. June 3, 2004.

Burr, Elizabeth, and Bruce Fuller. "Early Education and Family Poverty." Ch. 2 in *Crucial Issues in California, 2000: Are the Reform Pieces Fitting Together?* Policy Analysis for California Education (PACE). Berkeley: UC Berkeley School of Education, 2000.

Carmona, Ralph C. and Chang-Lin Tien. "Regents Should Reaffirm Affirmative Action." Commentary. *Los Angeles Times*. March 1, 1999.

Carroll, Lewis. *Alice's Adventures in Wonderland and Through the Looking Glass*. London: Macmillan, 1865. Reprinted by Barnes and Noble, New York: Barnes and Noble Classics, 2004.

Chávez, Lydia. *The Color Bind*. Berkeley: University of California Press, 1998.

Children Now. *Annual Report 2000*. Oakland, California. October 2000.

The Chronicle of Higher Education. Summary review of "Black-White Differences in Achievement: The Importance of Wealth," Amy J. Orr in *Sociology of Education*. Fall 2003. December 13, 2003.

The Chronicle of Higher Education. "Universities of Michigan and Texas Will Require Applicants to Take a Writing Exam." Notebook. January 31, 2003. Online edition, www.chronicle.com.

Coleman, Arthur L. and Scott R. Palmer. *Diversity in Higher Education: A Strategic Planning and Policy Manual Regarding Federal Law in Admissions, Financial Aid, and Outreach*. 2nd ed. New York: College Entrance Examination Board, 2004.

The College Board. *Guidelines on the Uses of College Board Test Scores and Related Data*. New York: College Entrance Examination Board, 2002.

Colvin, Richard Lee. "School Segregation Is Growing, Report Finds." *Los Angeles Times*. June 12, 1999.

Conley, Dalton. *Being Black, Living in the Red: Race, Wealth, and Social Policy in America*. Berkeley: University of California Press, 1999.

Connerly, Ward. *Creating Equal: My Fight Against Race Preferences*. San Francisco: Encounter Books, 2002.

Curry, B. and B. Kasbar, eds., *Essays That Worked: 50 Essays from Successful Applicants to the Nation's Top Colleges*. New York: Fawcett Book Group, 1990.

Dainow, Susannah. "University of Florida Expects a Decrease in Black Enrollment This Fall." *The Chronicle of Higher Education*. August 14, 2001. Online edition, www.chronicle.com.

Darity Jr., William. "Give Affirmative Action Time to Act." *The Chronicle of Higher Education*. December 1, 2000.

Davies, Gordon. "Today, Even B Students Are Getting Squeezed Out." *The Chronicle of Higher Education*. July 2, 2004.

Davis, Mike. "Cry California." *San Francisco Chronicle*. September 14, 2003.

DelVecchio, Rick. "Homeless Count: Alameda County Census Finds 6,000." *San Francisco Chronicle*. November 7, 2003.

D'Souza, Dinesh. *Illiberal Education*. New York: The Free Press, 1991.

———. "The Moral Conundrum of Success." *The Chronicle of Higher Education*. November 10, 2000.

Egelko, Bob. "School Districts Sued by Governor Over Problems." *San Francisco Chronicle*. December 13, 2000.

———. "Some Public Colleges Can Consider Applicants' Race." *San Francisco Chronicle*, December 5, 2000.

"Enhancing Student Transfer." A Memorandum of Understanding Between the California Community Colleges and the University of California. 1997.

The Fairness and Accuracy in Student Testing Act, S. 460, 107th Congress. (2000).

Farrell, Elizabeth. "Oklahoma City University Announces Layoffs." *The Chronicle of Higher Education*. April 11, 2002.

Fineman, Howard. "The Rollback Begins." *Newsweek*. July 31, 1995.

Finnie, Chuck and Julian Guthrie. "Signs of Trouble: S.F. School Officials Overlooked the Indications of Misspent Millions." *San Francisco Chronicle*. November 12, 2001.

Fleming, Brendon. "Mich. Petition Drive Delayed to 2006." *The Chronicle of Higher Education*. June 25, 2004.

Fogg, Piper. "U. of California Admits More Minority Students." *The Chronicle of Higher Education*. April 19, 2002.

Frank, Robert and Philip Cook. *The Winner-Take-All Society*. New York: Penguin Books, 1996.

Frankenberg, Erica, Chungmei Lee, and Gary Orfield. *A Multiracial Society with Segregated Schools: Are We Losing the Dream?* Cambridge: The Civil Rights Project at Harvard University, January 2003.

Friedman, Thomas. *The Lexus and the Olive Tree.* New York: Farrar, Straus and Giroux, 1999.

Gerassi, John. "A Long Way from Michigan." *The New York Review of Books*, February 23, 1967.

Gibney, James. "The Berkeley Squeeze." *The New Republic.* April 11, 1988.

Glater, Jonathan D. "Diversity Plan Shaped in Texas Is Under Attack." *New York Times.* June 13, 2004.

Gose, Ben. "Supreme Court Again Declines to Hear Appeal of Key Affirmative-Action Case." *The Chronicle of Higher Education.* July 6, 2001.

———. "Supreme Court Declines to Review Affirmative Action in Higher Education." *The Chronicle of Higher Education.* May 29, 2001. Online edition, www.chronicle.com.

Gratz v. Bollinger, 123 S. Ct. (2003).

Grutter v. Bollinger, 123 S. Ct. (2003).

Guernsey, Lisa. "Federal Judge Rules a Defunct Admissions Policy at U. of Georgia Unconstitutional." *The Chronicle of Higher Education.* January 11, 1999. Online edition, www.chronicle.com.

Hacker, Andrew. "Affirmative Action: The New Look." *The New York Review of Books.* October 12, 1989.

Healy, Patrick. "Civil-Rights Panel Readies Attack on Class-Rank Admissions Plans." *The Chronicle of Higher Education.* April 10, 2000. Online edition, www.chronicle.com.

Hebel, Sara. "Appeals Court Says Colleges May Consider Applicants' Race in Striving for Diversity." *The Chronicle of Higher Education.* December 6, 2000. Online edition, www.chronicle.com.

———. "Courting a Place in Legal History." *The Chronicle of Higher Education,* November 24, 2000.

———. "Little Is Changed in Latest Draft of Education Department Guidelines on Standardized Tests." *The Chronicle of Higher Education.* July 7, 2000. Online edition, www.chronicle.com (accessed February 25, 2003).

———. "No Room in the Class." *The Chronicle of Higher Education.* July 2, 2004.

———. "'Percent Plans' Don't Add Up." *The Chronicle of Higher Education.* March 21, 2003.

Hebel, Sara, Richard Morgan, Peter Schmidt, and Jeffrey Selingo. "Outlook for Higher Education in the 50 State Legislatures." *The Chronicle of Higher Education.* January 11, 2002.

Helfand, Duke, and Jessica Garrison. "Academic Performance Index: 80% of Affluent Schools Qualify for State Achievement Awards." *Los Angeles Times.* October 5, 2000.

Hi-Voltage Wire Works, Inc v. City of San Jose, 24 Cal. 4th 537 (2000).

Hopwood v. Texas, 78 F.3d 5th Cir. (1996).

Hu, Arthur. "Too Many Asians at UCLA?" Hu's On First. *Asian Week.* May 24, 1991.

Huerta, Luis. "Prop. 38 Makes Promises It Cannot Keep." Open Forum. *San Francisco Chronicle.* October 19, 2000.

Irving, Carl. "Texas Returns to Affirmative Action." *National CrossTalk.* Winter 2004.

Jacobson, Jennifer. "In Baby Boomlet, Number of New High-School Graduates Is Projected to Rise." *The Chronicle of Higher Education.* February 6, 2004.

Johnson, Jason B. "'A Dire Situation' for Working Poor." *San Francisco Chronicle.* July 23, 2004.

Johnson v. Board of Regents, 263 F. 3d 11th Cir. (2001).

Johnson, Wayne. Untitled speech to the California Teachers Association Action Day for Schools rally. Sacramento, California. May 8, 2000.

Kahlenberg, Richard D. *The Remedy: Class, Race, and Affirmative Action.* New York: Basic Books, 1996.

———. "Toward Affirmative Action for Economic Diversity." *The Chronicle of Higher Education.* March 19, 2004.

Klinkner, Philip and Rogers M. Smith. *The Unsteady March: The Rise and Decline of Racial Equality in America.* Chicago: The University of Chicago Press, 1999.

Kohn, Alfie. "Only for My Kid: How Privileged Parents Undermine School Reform." *Phi Delta Kappan.* April 1998.

Kozol, Jonathon. *Savage Inequalities.* New York: HarperCollins, 1992.

Latino Eligibility Task Force. *Latino Student Eligibility and Participation in the University of California: YA BASTA!* Report Number 5. Oakland: University of California, September 1997.

Leatherman, Courtney. "Stanford U. Announced $1 Billion Drive to Aid Undergraduate Education." *The Chronicle of Higher Education.* October 23, 2000. Online edition, www.chronicle.com.

Lemann, Nicholas. *The Big Test: The Secret History of the American Meritocracy.* New York: Farrar, Straus and Giroux, 1999.

Lively, Kit. "University of California Ends Race-Based Hirings, Admissons." *The Chronicle of Higher Education*. July 28, 1995.

Locke, Michelle. "UC Berkeley Puzzled by Drop in Black Admissions." Associated Press. June 1, 2003.

Lubman, Sarah. "Asian Equation Troubles UC." *San Jose Mercury News*. February 22, 1998.

Maran, Meredith. *Class Dismissed: A Year in the Life of an American High School, A Glimpse into the Heart of a Nation*. New York: St. Martin's Press, 2000.

Marcum, Diana, and Tom Gorman. "Rich City's Housing Funds Are Hot Potato." *Los Angeles Times*. October 27, 1999.

Martin, Glen. "Big Bucks in Big Sky Country." *San Francisco Chronicle*. October 18, 2000.

Mena, Jesus. "UC Berkeley Statement on Report Issued by the Center for Equal Opportunity, 'Racial Preferences at UC Berkeley,' Regarding Undergraduate Admissions." Press release. Office of Public Affairs, UC Berkeley. October 10, 1996.

The Merrow Report. "First to Worst." Public Broadcasting System. February 2004.

Metcalf, Stephen. "Reading Between the Lines." *The Nation*. January 28, 2002.

Miller, D.W. "The New Urban Studies." *The Chronicle of Higher Education*. August 18, 2000.

Monaghan, Peter. Interview with Philip Klinkner in Verbatim. *The Chronicle of Higher Education*. November 19, 1999.

Moores, John. "On My Mind: College Capers." *Forbes*. March 29, 2004.

Morrison, Gary. Memorandum to Provost and Senior Vice President C. Judson King. March 16, 1998. Office of the General Counsel, University of California. Oakland, California.

Mortenson, Tom. "Growing Income Inequality, Public Selfishness and Consequences for America's Children (and Our Future)." *Postsecondary Education Opportunity*. August 1998.

———. "Pell Grant Share of Undergraduates Enrollment at the 50 Best National Universities 1992–93 and 2001–02." *Postsecondary Education Opportunity*. March 2004.

Nakao, Annie. "California Home to Most Indians Among the States." *San Francisco Chronicle*. February 13, 2002.

National Task Force on Minority High Achievement. *Reaching the Top*. New York: The College Board, 1999.

Newsweek. "The Overclass." July 31, 1995.

The New York Times. "After Affirmative Action." Editorial. May 20, 2000.

Oakes, Jeannie. "Outreach: A Research Perspective." Testimony before the Senate Education Committee, the Assembly Higher Education Committee, and the Senate Select Committee on College and University Admissions and Outreach. Sacramento. January 7, 2004.

——. "Outreach: Struggling Against Power and Culture." *Outlook*, Office of the President of the University of California. November 1999. Online magazine, www.ucop.edu (accessed November 22, 1999).

Office for Civil Rights, U.S. Department of Education. *The Use of Tests When Making High-Stakes Decisions for Students: A Resource Guide for Educators and Policy-makers.* Washington, DC. 2000.

O'Lague, Paul, and John Bachar. "Playing Robin Hood with State Budget." *San Francisco Chronicle.* February 8, 2004.

Oliver, Melvin L., and Thomas M. Shapiro. *Black Wealth, White Wealth: A New Perspective on Racial Inequality.* New York: Routledge, 1995.

Olszewski, Lori. "Some Prop. 39 Backers Have Deep Pockets." *San Francisco Chronicle.* October 23, 2000.

Palomino, John. Letter of Findings from the Director of Region IX of the Office for Civil Rights, U.S. Department of Education, to Chancellor Chang-Lin Tien. San Francisco. March 7, 1996.

Pulley, John. "Oberlin College, Facing a $5-Million Deficit, See Years of Belt Tightening Ahead." *The Chronicle of Higher Education.* April 16, 2002. Online edition, www.chronicle.com.

Quinn, Jane Bryant. "Colleges' New Tuition Crisis." *Newsweek.* February 2, 2004.

Rechtschaffen, Clifford. "Why Race Still Matters." *San Francisco Chronicle.* March 28, 2002.

Regents of the University of California. University of California Policy on Undergraduate Admissions. Adopted May 20, 1988. http://www.universityofcalifornia.edu/regents/

Regents of the University of California v. Bakke, 438 U.S. 265 (1978).

Reich, Robert. "How Selective Colleges Heighten Inequality." The Chronicle Review. *The Chronicle of Higher Education.* September 15, 2000.

Sahagun, Louis, and Duke Helfand. "ACLU Sues State Over Conditions in Poor Schools." *Los Angeles Times.* May 18, 2000.

Sanders, Joshunda. "On Sorrow's Turf." *San Francisco Chronicle.* May 17, 2002,

San Francisco Chronicle. "Racial Privacy Measure Ahead in Field Poll." May 1, 2002.

Sarich, Vincent. Letter to University of California Regent William French Smith. April 4, 1990.

———. "Making Racism Official at Cal." *California Monthly.* September 1990.

Savage, David G. "Supreme Court Scales Back Part of '64 Civil Rights Act." *Los Angeles Times.* April 25, 2001. Online edition, www.latimes.com.

Schevitz, Tanya. "Report on UC after Prop. 209." *San Francisco Chronicle.* September 20, 2003.

———. "Teenage Overachievers Cram for Best Colleges." *San Francisco Chronicle.* December 25, 2000.

———. "UC Admissions Under Fire Again." *San Francisco Chronicle.* October 10, 2003.

———. "UC Regents Censure Colleague for Article on Admissions Policy." *San Francisco Chronicle.* March 19, 2004.

Schmidt, Peter. "Academe's Hispanic Future." *The Chronicle of Higher Education.* November 28, 2003.

———. "Affirmative Action Survives, and So Does the Debate." *The Chronicle of Higher Education.* July 4, 2003.

———. "Bill to Restore Affirmative Action in Washington State Appears Dead— for Now." *The Chronicle of Higher Education,* February 9, 2004. Online edition, www.chronicle.com.

———. "Friends and Foes of Affirmative Action Claim Victory in Rulings on Michigan Cases." *The Chronicle of Higher Education.* June 24, 2003. Online edition, www.chronicle.com.

———. "Head of Civil-Rights Panel Denounces Affirmative-Action Survey Sent Out on Panel's Letterhead." *The Chronicle of Higher Education.* February 13. Online edition, www.chronicle.com.

———. "Noted Higher-Education Researcher Urges Admissions Preferences for the Poor." *The Chronicle of Higher Education.* April 16, 2004.

———. "Oregon Colleges Brace for More Budget Cuts as Voters Defeat Tax Measure." *The Chronicle of Higher Education.* February 5, 2004. Online edition, www.chronicle.com.

———. "Texas A&M Ends Alumni-Based Preferences for Applicants, to Assure 'Consistency' in Admissions." *The Chronicle of Higher Education.* January 12, 2004. Online edition, www.chronicle.com.

———. "UMass and Ohio State U. Say They Will Stop Awarding Extra Points to

Minority Applicants." *The Chronicle of Higher Education*. October 10, 2003. Online edition, www.chronicle.com.

Schrag, Peter. "The Case for California's Festering School Inequities." Editorial. *Sacramento Bee*. August 4, 1999.

———. "Muckraking UC admissions: Race is still with us." Editorial. *Sacramento Bee*. November 19, 2003. Online edition, www.sacbee.com (accessed November 25, 2003).

Selingo, Jeffrey. "California Policy Most Helps Hispanic and Rural Applicants." *The Chronicle of Higher Education*. May 31, 2002. Online edition, www.chronicle .com (accessed July 13, 2004).

———. "Chapel Hill Says It Will Meet Financial-Aid Needs of Low-Income Students With Grants, Not Loans." *The Chronicle of Higher Education*. October 2, 2003. Online edition, www.chronicle.com.

———. "Critics Blast Plan to Expand Class-Rank Policy in Texas as Affirmative-Action Ploy." *The Chronicle of Higher Education*. January 11, 2002.

———. "Florida Gov. Bush Announces Rise in Minority Enrollments." *The Chronicle of Higher Education*. August 30, 2000. Online edition, www.chronicle.com.

———. "Pennsylvania Scraps Plan to Admit Top 15%." *The Chronicle of Higher Education*, November 3, 2000.

———. "Pennsylvania University System Weighs Admissions Plan Based on Class Rank." *The Chronicle of Higher Education*. April 7, 2000.

———. "What States Aren't Saying About the 'X-Percent Solution.'" *The Chronicle of Higher Education*. June 2, 2000. Online edition, www.chronicle.com.

Senate Special Committee on University of California Admissions. *A Public Hearing: Asian American Admissions into the University of California: The Report of the Special Committee on Asian-American Admissions (Shack Report)*. Berkeley. March 13, 1989.

Smith v. University of Washington Law School, 233 F.3d 1188 9th Cir. (2000).

Sowell, Thomas. "A New Push to End Racial Bean Counting." *San Francisco Chronicle*. March 22, 2002.

———. "Shallow People Playing God." Review of *A Is for Admissions* by Michele Hernandez. Conservative Currents. *Townhall.com*. October 22, 1997. Online magazine, http://www.townhall.com/thcc

Special Committee on Asian American Admissions. *Asian American Admission into the University of California: Report of the Special Committee on Asian American Admissions (The Shack Report)*. Berkeley: U.C Berkeley Academic Senate, February 1989.

Steele, Claude M. and Joshua Aronson. "Stereotype Threat and the Test Performance of Academically Successful African Americans." In *Black-White Test Score Gap*, Christopher Jencks and Meredith Phillips, eds. Washington DC: Brookings Institution Press, 1998.

Steele, Shelby. "X-Percent Plans: After Preferences, More Race Games—Guaranteed Percentages for Minority Students Are Latest Affirmative Action Strategy." *National Review*, February 7, 2000.

Sterngold, James. "Governor announces school suit settlement." *San Francisco Chronicle*. August 14, 2004.

Task Force on Black Student Persistence. "The Challenge Ahead: Improving Black Student Graduation." University of California: Berkeley, March 1987.

Thomson, Gregg. "Freshmen Persistence and Graduation Rates at UC Berkeley." Berkeley: UC Berkeley Office of Student Research, December 1986.

Tien, Chang-Lin. "A Tool for a Colorblind Society." *Los Angeles Times*. July 18, 1995.

—— and Charles E. Young. "Don't 'Fix' What Isn't Broken." *Los Angeles Times*. October 20, 1996.

Tienda, Marta and Sunny Niu. "Texas' 10-Percent Plan: the Truth Behind the Numbers." *The Chronicle of Higher Education*. January 23, 2004. Online edition, www.chronicle.com (accessed February 11, 2004).

Tinsley, Bruce. "Mallard Fillmore." *Denver Post*. October 29, 2001.

Title VI of the Civil Rights Act of 1964 (42 U.S.C.).

Traub, James. "What No School Can Do." *New York Times Magazine*. January 16, 2000.

Trounson, Rebecca. "UC Berkeley Admissions Dispute Becomes Heated. *Los Angeles Times*. October 17, 2003.

——, Tony Perry, and Stuart Silverstein. "UC Berkeley Admissions Scrutinized." *Los Angeles Times*. October 4, 2003.

——, Stuart Silverstein, and Doug Smith. "Against the Odds Is How They Have Prevailed." *Los Angeles Times*. October 24, 2003.

Trudeau, Garry. "Doonesbury." *San Francisco Chronicle*. July 2, 2000.

University of California. *Introducing the University 2002–2003*. Oakland: University of California, 2001.

University of California Office of the President. *2001–02 Regents' Budget*. Oakland: University of California, November 2000.

——. *Information Digest 2001*. Oakland: University of California, 1993.

University of California Outreach Task Force. *New Directions for Outreach*. Oakland: University of California, July 1997.

Van Der Werf, Martin. "Recession and Reality Set In at Private Colleges." *The Chronicle of Higher Education*. March 1, 2002.

Wallace, Amy. "UC Regents Panel OKs Minority Outreach Plan." *Los Angeles Times*. July 18, 1997.

———. "UC San Diego Medical School Takes No Blacks for Fall Class." *Los Angeles Times*. August 1, 1997. Online edition, www.latimes.com (accessed September 26, 2000).

——— and Dave Lesher. "UC Regents in Historic Vote, Wipe Out Affirmative Action." *Los Angeles Times*. July 21, 1995.

Walsh, Diana. "Auction fever hits schools." *San Francisco Examiner*. November 5, 2000.

Waters, Ethan. "The New Politics of Race." *San Francisco Focus*. April 1992.

Weiss, Kenneth R. "Davis Asks UC to Admit Top 4%." *Los Angeles Times*. February 19, 1999.Online edition, www.latimes.com (accessed October 3, 2000).

———. "One Last Chance to Be a Doctor." Column One. *Los Angeles Times*. August 5, 2000.

———. "Plans Seek More UC Pupils From Poorer Schools." *Los Angeles Times*. May 12, 1997.

———. "UC Law Schools' New Rules Cost Minorities Spots." *Los Angeles Times*. May 15, 1997.Online edition, www.latimes.com (accessed September 26, 2000).

Wells, Janet. "Racial Divide in Boom Time, Study Reports." *San Francisco Chronicle*. September 5, 2000.

Werner, Donald H. "College Admissions: Shaky Ethics." *New York Times*. June 4, 1988.

Wilgoren, Jodi. "Michigan Admissions Policy Upheld." *San Francisco Chronicle*. December 14, 2000.

Williams et al. v. State of California, filed in San Francisco Superior Court, May 17, 2000.

INDEX

Other Titles from Bay Tree Publishing

Further information is available at www.baytreepublish.com
Bay Tree Publishing, 721 Creston Road, Berkeley, CA 94708

$19.95 trade pbk,
ISBN: 0-9729921-3-8

Get Hired Now!™ A 28-Day Program for Landing the Job You Want
by C.J. Hayden and Frank Traditi

Built around the single most important factor in a successful job search, the power of personal relationships, this systematic, structured 28-day program leads job seekers through the key components of a successful job search: identifying the job search strategies that work for your goals; organizing and prioritizing job search activities; staying motivated in the face of frustration and rejection.

*Get Slightly Famous: Become a Celebrity in Your Field
and Attract More Business with Less Effort*
by Steven Van Yoder

Rooted in his experience as a public relations professional and freelance writer, Van Yoder shows how to tap the business secret everyone knows but few practice: it's easier to attract clients through your reputation than sell someone who has never heard of you.

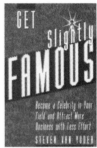

$16.95 trade pbk,
ISBN: 0-9720021-1-1

$15.95 trade pbk,
ISBN: 0-9720021-0-3

*Taking the War Out of Our Words: The Art of
Powerful Non-Defensive Communication*
by Sharon Ellison

Written by an award-winning speaker and internationally recognized consultant, this insightful and moving work provides practical techniques for breaking defensive habits, becoming more open, healing conflicts and building self-esteem.

Them and Us: Cult Thinking and the Terrorist Threat
by Arthur J. Deikman, M.D.
With a foreword by Doris Lessing

A clinical professor of psychiatry, Deikman makes the connection between classic cult manipulation and milder forms of group pressure that everyone has experienced. Deikman further shows how terrorist psychology represents an extreme along this familiar continuum. A foreword by novelist Doris Lessing discusses the implications of cult thinking for contemporary society.

$17.95 trade pbk,
ISBN: 0-9720021-2-X

APR 26 2005

CENTRAL ISLIP PUBLIC LIBRARY

3 1800 00216 4057

2164057

379.
26
LAI

Laird, Bob

The case for affirmative
action in university
admissions

$26.95

Central Islip Public Library
33 Hawthorne Avenue
Central Islip, NY 11722

GAYLORD M